"George Lakey is a national treasure, w... Dancing with George was a blast. His ... tagious approach to democratic action ... It's a story Americans need now more ... ."
—FRANCES MOORE LAPPÉ, author, *Diet for a Small Planet*, director, Small Planet Institute

"George Lakey's memoir is an epic of the personal in flow with the political—a dance with history indeed! As such, it is an outstanding example in the rich tradition of Quaker spiritual autobiography."
—DOUG GWYN, author of *A Sustainable Life: Quaker Faith & Practice in the Renewal of Creation*

"*Dancing with History* packs a powerful, honest, and deeply personal account of George Lakey's remarkable life and legacy of family building and movement building, honoring identity and liberation for all, 'raising the temperature' on what it means to live a life of social action and bearing witness. This book is a stunning testimonial, like walking through a historical landscape of a life of turning courageously to meet what's next."
—VALERIE BROWN, writer, Buddhist-Quaker Dharma teacher, leadership coach, and facilitator

"It is hard to express the depth of gratitude I have for the elders of social movements—people who have committed their lifetimes to cultivating the skills, frameworks, ideas, and ideologies that provide the foundation for activism today. George Lakey stands tall among these leaders. He will, I believe, go down as one of the great elders of the American radical democratic tradition. George is an expert in both building prefigurative community and planning strategic action. He is a master of pedagogy and a core resource for organizers thinking about how to train social movement participants. Countless grassroots leaders throughout the country are honored to claim him as a mentor. . . . His story is wonderfully presented in this autobiography."
—PAUL ENGLER, director, Center for the Working Poor in Los Angeles, co-founder, Momentum Training, co-author, *This Is An Uprising*.

"George Lakey shows us how to ignite positive change in the face of adversity. He weaves in passion, creativity, faith, and even humor. An inspiring read for our moment."
—DAVE BLEAKNEY, education director for the Canadian Union of Postal Workers

Dancing with History

a life for peace and justice

GEORGE LAKEY

new york • oakland • london

Seven Stories Press
140 Watts Street
New York, NY 10013
sevenstories.com

College professors and high school and middle school teachers may order free examination copies of Seven Stories Press titles. Visit https://www.sevenstories.com/pg/resources-academics or email academics@sevenstories.com.

Library of Congress Cataloging-in-Publication Data

Names: Lakey, George, author.
Title: Dancing with history : a life for peace and justice / by George Lakey.
Other titles: Life for peace and justice
Description: New York : Seven Stories Press, [2022] | Includes index.
Identifiers: LCCN 2022022539 | ISBN 9781644212356 (trade paperback) | ISBN 9781644212363 (ebook)
Subjects: LCSH: Lakey, George. | Pacifists--United States--Biography. | Nonviolence--United States--History. | Peace movements--United States--History. | Social reformers--United States--Biography. | Sociologists--United States--Biography. | Social change--Study and teaching (Higher)--United States. | Civil rights workers--United States--Biography. | Bisexual men--United States--Biography. | Quakers--United States--Biography.
Classification: LCC JZ5540.2.L35 A3 2022 | DDC 327.1/72092--dc23/eng/20220805
LC record available at https://lccn.loc.gov/2022022539

Printed in the USA.

9 8 7 6 5 4 3 2 1

contents

preface

As I write this memoir, I see around me widespread anxiety about the state of the world. It is based in reality, but in my experience, anxiety itself isn't very useful. Mahatma Gandhi once remarked that he didn't try to "conquer" his fear because he needed its energy to stand up to the greatest empire the world had ever known. Gandhi learned to transform fear's energy into the positive work of mobilizing for struggle. I've experienced that transformation many times in my own life, most dramatically in the civil rights movement, but also in struggles for peace, LGBTQ rights, labor rights, and the environment. I've included such stories in this book.

I find there's something deeply human about wanting to show up—to be, as Latin American activists might say, "presente!" One way I think of my life's mission for peace, justice, and equality is to make it right for everyone to be present.

Younger people often ask what keeps me going. I always point to the love I've found in friendship, family, teaching, faith, and community. Another part of my answer is that I've gained tremendous energy from investing in my learning curve: win, lose, or draw, I want to get better at this tough but bracing task of making a difference. I've wanted to learn from these seven decades of standing up for justice — from preaching racial equality at the pulpit of my church when I was twelve years old to being arrested for blocking the entrance of a Chase bank at age eighty-three, while participating in the 2021 Walk for Our Grandchildren in pursuit of climate justice.*

As we sat in rocking chairs, demanding that Chase stop funding the fossil fuel industry, I was reminded of the struggle against South African apartheid decades earlier, when advocating for divestment was one of the winning tactics. I vividly remember pushing the City of Philadelphia to divest from the apartheid regime—as well as the joy that comes from going beyond *awareness of* injustice and toward *acting for* justice. Inspired by the protesters in South Africa, we turned a large protest in front of City Hall one frigid evening into an all-night dance, fueled by the beat of South African movement songs. I found that hour after hour of dancing with friends and strangers alike did more than keep us warm physically. It reminded us that if we tune in to what's happening and act with others, we get to dance with history.

---

* My account of the arrest, plus a photo, are here: George Lakey, "Arrested in Rocking Chairs, Grandparents Protest Chase and Pressure Biden on Climate," Waging Nonviolence, July 3, 2021, https://wagingnonviolence.org/2021/07/grandparents-walk-biden-chase-climate/.

1

a working-class lad finds a place to stand

I was born in 1937, a year when Michigan autoworkers waged a major sit-down strike and broke through the resistance to unionization by auto giant General Motors.* That decade was a period of turbulence for workers, Black people, women, professionals, and young people. As the Great Depression lagged on, many were questioning a social order that had betrayed its potential for justice, equality, and peace—and they were acting out those questions.

I was the second child of three; my big sister, Shirley, was already four when I was born. My family lived in Bangor, Pennsylvania, a small slate-mining town surrounded by farms, midway between Scranton and Philadelphia. My dad, Russell, knew he had to hustle with an additional mouth to feed now, but there was nothing new about that. As a young teenager, his grandfather had come to Pennsylvania from Cornwall, in the United Kingdom, as an indentured worker for the slate mines. The Cornish were famous for their affinity for digging in the earth, be it for coal, copper, or slate. The family story was that this ancestor worked for years to pay off his passage to the United States, then more

---

* I include a brief account of that strike, including its antiracist organizing dimension, in my book *How We Win* (Brooklyn: Melville House, 2018), 64–68.

years to be able to send for his sweetheart to come and join him. Compared with that, my dad figured he had it pretty good. As a slate miner, he'd accepted that he'd worry about money all his life, and he did.

The street I grew up on was typical of my town: a block of duplex houses with front porches. Summer evenings usually found the older generation sitting on rocking chairs on the porch, telling stories—often funny, sometimes poignant—while we "young uns" listened and a neighbor or two leaned on the front banister. I can't remember a family occasion that wasn't full of stories. I got it: life is about stories, which have a beginning, middle, and end. The best ones were funny or dramatic, and some left me wondering: What is the meaning of all we go through?

My mother, Dora Shook, was from a Pennsylvania Dutch dairy farming family nearby and had felt more secure growing up— there was always enough food. As in Dad's family, she was one of six children. She loved to sing as much as her young husband did, and I grew up expecting that, if one person started a melody, the second was pretty much obligated to harmonize.

Harmonizing was also the expectation of the Welsh settlers who'd founded the town once slate was discovered, and there was a bit of Celtic rivalry between the Welsh and Cornish miners as to who could harmonize better. My mom's brothers decided as teenagers that the Pennsylvania Dutch were just as musical as the Celts, and proudly joined their dad in the Shook Family Quartet, singing at weddings, funerals, and family reunions.

My mother and her family were enthusiastic members of their church, but not my dad. He'd gotten turned off when area slate miners went on strike to gain a union and the local preachers had allied themselves with the owners of the quarries. However, Dad didn't discourage me, Shirley, or my little brother, Bob, from following my mother's path. With my mother, the four of us were active churchgoers, but I never got fully used to my dad's boycott, which he later abandoned after my siblings and I grew up and moved on.

My denomination, the Evangelical Congregational Church, was a split-off from a split-off from the Methodists, with each split yielding a more stubborn evangelical insistence on the wide distribution of spiritual gifts. I'd heard stories of child preachers touring the evangelistic revival circuit. In 1949, when I turned twelve, the church elders wondered if I had the makings of a preacher. Our minister told me I was to take the pulpit on a Sunday morning one month hence, to see what I could do.

I prayed earnestly for a theme, a message that God wanted me to bring to the congregation. Clarity came quickly, and I drafted and redrafted my first sermon.

My heart began to pound when I opened the tall doors to the sanctuary and walked to the front, the organ swelling on the early notes of the prelude. The minister and I sat in matching heavy oak chairs, as hard and uncomfortable as much of the theology that inspired them. I was so overwhelmed with the moment that I believed only Jesus could get me through the morning intact; even the stained glass didn't reassure me as it usually did. A glance to the choir loft settled me, finally: I saw my uncle Donald suppressing a smile at the latest choir-room joke; my uncle George standing with his chest out, as if posing for a Marlboro ad.

Finally, the moment for the sermon arrived, and I went for it, lacking the confidence to release my full passion but nevertheless speaking loudly and emphatically.

"God," I preached, "wants racial equality." I cited Biblical references and what I thought was common sense. I couldn't tell from looking at the faces of the grown-ups how they felt about what I was saying. As my nervousness lessened, I thought to myself that the sermon was coherent, persuasive—an airtight case!

After the final hymn, I went with the minister to the door of the church, to shake hands as people left the service. Had I passed my audition? Would I be encouraged to become a boy preacher? No one commented on the sermon, except in the most general and condescending ways.

I waited, still expecting the preacher and the elders who'd asked me to preach to circle up, congratulate me on the sermon, and discuss next steps in my formation as a preacher. Instead, when the last church member had left, they hastily dispersed.

The message was clear: "Don't call us; we'll call you."

ℵ ℵ ℵ

If racial equality was God's will, in 1949 it was not a wish my church wanted to hear. I was too hurt to ask my mother, who was there that morning, to explain what was going on. We both avoided the subject at the dinner table. Now, I think it might have helped if she'd reminded me of my dad's recent experience at the slate quarry where he worked.

Dad loved to argue, and he relished telling us a story about getting his coworkers upset. It was the summer before the 1948 presidential election. One of the famous Black people in public life at the time was Ralph Bunche, a political scientist and diplomat who performed important missions for the United Nations. As usual, the men at the quarry gathered at lunch break with their sandwiches and their talk of baseball. Dad interrupted, saying he thought it was a shame that Ralph Bunche was tied up at the UN, because that's who the Democrats should nominate for president. The men were furious and used the rest of lunch to heap scorn on Dad for the very idea of a Black president. It was obvious to me from the breadth of his smile while telling us the story that, according to the baseball box score in his head, it was Dad, 1, his coworkers, 0.

My big sister and I were proud of him sticking it to the other men, but I completely missed his other point. No one had explained to me that to be a worker is to struggle, and you score a point if you "get something started." Working-class culture encourages taking an initiative. Sure, the owning class usually wins—after all, the game is rigged—but we workers salvage our pride if we at least stand up for ourselves. Over time I began to realize that the struggle itself shows we're alive: we think, act, and take responsibility.

And, who knows—maybe next time we *will* win.

≈ ≈ ≈

I asked my dad's dad why there are strikes. "That," explained Grandpap George, "is because we workers don't own the mines and factories. When we own them, we won't need to strike."

In high school social studies I began to realize that accomplishing Grandpap's goals would require even wider collective struggle than the Michigan sit-down strikes represented—but still, even while a struggle gets bigger, there are some who are the early ones willing to speak our truth. Neither Dad's fellow workers nor the folks in Mom's church seemed ready to take on racism yet, but that didn't mean he and I were irrelevant. And we could keep at it, because Dad was Cornish, after all, and a hallmark of that nationality is said to be stubbornness.

I was willing to be early in speaking truth and found myself borrowing some self-esteem from it. But the tribe of Methodists left another mark on teenage me: I got curious about *method*. I began to ask the process question: *How* shall we act in a way that makes it more likely that we'll win? That question turned out to be central to my life's work. To answer it, though, required emerging from the internalized limitations of my class background.

As many women and people of color have learned, being brought up with cultural oppression means internalizing messages of inferiority. Young working-class people—white males as well as women and people of color—are subjected to a subtle but insistent drill about what it is we can and cannot do. We're brought up to be productive in the workplace; being managed is our destiny. Yes, many of us want to rebel in some way, even if it's against our interests—say, by refusing to wear masks or get vaccinated when a pandemic appears. The more the know-it-alls tell us to do something, the less we want to do it. This contradiction is built into class-stratified society, and one set of feelings we working-class people internalize—with resentment—is the worry that power figures above us really do know better than we do.

My mother's dad, a slate quarry worker, had a natural interest and skill in managing that was noticed by his "betters" but not reinforced. After years of faithful work in the church, he was allowed to be the assistant Sunday school superintendent, a post he occupied for decades while above him—in the role of superintendent—rotated people with professional middle-class or owning-class backgrounds.

Persuading so many workers to go along with an unjust hierarchical arrangement is the work of a classist culture, implemented through socialization as well as in schools, workplaces, movies and TV shows. We're told in subtle ways that we're not good enough to take leadership roles, and enough of us buy in sufficiently to this logic to keep the class system going. By my mid-teenage years, I'd gotten with the program. Sadly, despite my gifts for thinking, writing, and speaking, neither teachers nor textbooks gave me the lowdown on how class is structured. I drew the obvious conclusion: I simply "happened to be" among the inferiors who needed to focus on doing a good job and following the direction of my superiors.

≈ ≈ ≈

For me, a life-changing, liberating intervention started with an assignment in ninth-grade English. The assignment was to report oral history about our small town. We were to persuade elderly citizens to tell us stories, and dig into the files of the *Bangor Daily News* to check facts whenever possible.

Much of my schoolwork bored me, but this assignment seized my imagination. For one thing, it gave me an excuse to corner our neighborhood recluse, who as a child I believed to be a witch. As it turned out, Mrs. Grube had some interesting stories about Bangor's past fifty years, which led me to other elders and other stories. I found unexpected pleasure in going through the old, yellowed newsprint copies of the local paper. My copybook filled up rapidly.

Our teacher, Russell Baggot, had us reading the Thornton Wilder play *Our Town* at the same time, and it was no great leap for me to decide it would be fun to write a play about Bangor in *Our Town's* style. I shyly showed Mr. Baggott the play one day after school. He surprised me by suggesting that we actually cast the play and produce it. His friend, the equally new music teacher Robert Cathcart, could weave in some music, he suggested.

My play had the town mayor as its lead character, and Mr. Baggot suggested I take the role. I quickly said yes, but playing the role turned out to be much more difficult than I expected. In my play, the mayor is seen making a campaign speech, in which he gets to extol the virtues of small-town life. In the role, I needed to play a confident leader who manages an entire town. An invisible chorus of voices arose within me: "You can't do that!"

My ambivalence became visible when Mr. Baggot put me on a soapbox to make my speech. I was a robot, a tin man with no grease. I stood with my arms pinned to my sides as if by a straitjacket. I was in the throes of adolescent awkwardness, to be sure, but even worse was the fact that the script called for me to represent the most lofty position in my town.

When Mr. Baggot suggested an expansive gesture to me on the box, I simply turned red with embarrassment. I had no idea what to do with my arms. Poor Mr. Baggot had on his hands a hopeless case for a mayor.

During one evening rehearsal when Mr. Cathcart was on hand to help with the music, Mr. Baggot released the rest of the cast early in order to focus on the mayor's part. Mr. Cathcart stayed. Probably hoping to build my confidence, they ran me through a scene I found easy. We then turned to the dreaded stick-upon-a-box scene. I started blushing even as I pulled the soapbox from the wings.

Mr. Baggot explained, needlessly, the importance of my playing this scene as a stereotyped politician, exaggerating the inflection in my voice and my gestures as well. I stood on the box and launched into my portrayal of a heron with its mouth stuffed with peanut butter.

I could see past the footlights well enough to see Mr. Baggot, sitting beside Mr. Cathcart in the fourth row, give a sigh.

"George," Mr. Cathcart began, "you've often stood in chorus performance and really belted it out when we needed a crescendo. I wonder if you could try that now."

I tried, unsure that they could even hear me in the fourth row. My projection was turning into rejection.

Mr. Cathcart gave me a genuinely warm smile. "Try a deep breath, George," he said. "Now another. And another."

Mr. Baggot sat up a little straighter. "With your right arm, try pointing toward the wings."

I managed to do that. Pointing toward the wings I could do. That's where I wanted to be.

"Excellent!" beamed Mr. Cathcart. "Try the other arm!"

As the sweat soaked my armpits, I followed instructions to point in a variety of directions. I was miserably pessimistic. Could we convince the audience that the mayor could win an election based on his skill in doing semaphore signals?

Mr. Cathcart started to crack jokes between each of my tries at saying lines. He somehow avoided ridicule, simply managing to be funny. I found myself laughing big belly laughs standing there on the soapbox, eventually with tears running down my cheeks. Mr. Baggot then encouraged me to say my lines while laughing and gesticulating wildly, which made me laugh all the more. Sometime in there my shoulders stopped hurting, and the stomachache went away.

"Know what?" Mr. Cathcart said. "We need to knock it off for the night. If you want to, you can make your entrance again and just do the speech so we can go home."

I nodded, walked to the wings still giggling, turned, and strode back to the soapbox. I ran through my lines and gestures without thinking about either one, eyes focused on the last row of seats. I looked down at my teachers, who were smiling broadly at each other.

"Let's go home," they said.

≈ ≈ ≈

It wasn't until a decade later, in 1962, that I fully realized the impact of those teachers' work. President John F. Kennedy and Russian premier Nikita Khrushchev had begun their duel over the Soviet placement of missiles in Cuba, which were intended to defend Cuba against another attack that the United States was believed to be planning in its ongoing campaign to overthrow the Cuban government. Kennedy threatened nuclear war over the missiles, and both countries' armed forces were put on high alert.

With the world on the brink, time seemed to stand still. Public anxiety was extreme; my mother told me that in a beauty parlor in Bangor, a woman threw up and had to be helped home. I was then a graduate student at the University of Pennsylvania, and on campus I saw many anxious faces, haggard from lack of sleep. Students walked around with transistor radios on their shoulders, listening to the latest news of the crisis; they didn't know whether to bother to study, considering they might be dead before their next exam.

Although some peace-movement leaders were urging demonstrations and letters to the White House, I reasoned that such protests were pointless because the decisions were being made by two very small circles of insiders, leaving out even the US Congress and the Supreme Soviet. I thought it an ironic symmetry: when a decision mattered most, democracy was as irrelevant in the United States as it was on the other side of the Iron Curtain.

While I saw citizen action directed toward our government at that moment as a waste of time, the crisis still provided a teachable moment. After all, the two Ks might not destroy their countries just yet, and we citizens might as well learn something from this occasion when the word "defense" was being made a mockery.

I jumped up on a low wall across from the student union and began to speak. Waving my arms as if they were actually connected to my heart, I projected into the plaza my indignation that we were reduced to the role of spectators while our leaders played chicken with our lives. First dozens, then hundreds of students and faculty gathered, some of the students in the uniforms of the Reserve Officers' Training Corps.

"But you can't trust the Russians!" a student said. Relieved to get a response, I warmed even more to the occasion.

"You can't trust the Russians, this man said," I repeated loudly to the growing audience, "and I agree that leaders of armed nation-states can't be trusted. All the more reason why we shouldn't allow them to participate in a game where the stakes are civilization itself. We pay our taxes for a defense system, not a system where we are hostages put on the line to try to manipulate good behavior in our enemies!"

Immediately another listener in the crowd raised an objection, and slowly but surely the debate turned into a town meeting in which participants were expressing a variety of points of view, including my own, and I was the facilitator.

Three hours later, I was exhausted and badly needed the bathroom. When a particularly loud participant claimed the attention of the crowd, I quietly got off the wall and walked into the student union. I relaxed, ate a sandwich, and read the paper. Finally, I strolled outside to see if anything was happening. Hundreds of people were still crowded together, debating, while sub-conversations were happening at the edges. I listened in for a while, a smile on my face. We might be dead in a day or two, I thought, but at least we're looking more like classical democratic Athens than like a nation of panicked sheep.

As I walked home to supper I remembered ninth grade and my teachers, Mr. Baggot and Mr. Cathcart. For all I knew, they might now be appalled by my politics, but still I thought they would feel some pride in the loving attention they'd given me that night in the school auditorium. They helped me gain some relief from the internalized sense of inferiority that can keep me and other working-class people from speaking out in a confident way.

My sense of power came with grace: I had sufficient flexibility, so I didn't need to control the space. Real democracy values many voices speaking up. I wasn't reactive, overcoming the diffidence of some in my audience by leaping to the other pole, domination. I really value equality. I could be a facilitator, trusting that crowd to continue in the mode of speaking out and listening in turn.

On another occasion I might act as an organizer, using a crisis moment in a more strategic way to do movement building. But in October 1962, I was instead marking a life of learning, honoring my high school teachers' coaching in a historic moment on an Ivy League campus. When people support each other to get in touch with their inner power, even those of us who carry internalized oppression can put it aside to answer history's invitation to act.

Some activists hold in their heads the image of "*making* history," a metaphor encountered also in some media treatments of great leaders like Martin Luther King Jr. Others view history as the leader—something we might be able to engage with if we ready ourselves for an opportunity that history might provide. In that case, we'll hopefully move strategically at the right moment to make the most of that opportunity. I lean toward the second view, as it is in line with my sociological training, but I see more possibilities than either making, or following, history.

I like the metaphor of "dancing with history." It gives considerable weight to history's drive, but it leaves open the possibility that we, too, might at times move so strongly as to lead history. Further, dancing invites in other dimensions that matter to me—namely, music and spirit. As a young, highly impressionable activist in the civil rights movement, I experienced music mobilizing spirit in ways that spurred action more powerful than I previously imagined possible. Dancing supports skill, community, imagination, and daring. Not bad, as metaphors go!

2

lessons in leadership

Leadership is often a contentious issue in politics and social change. Two of my most influential learnings about leadership came through music.

When I reached my mid-teens, I couldn't imagine anything more enjoyable than making music with other people—except perhaps making love, and I hadn't experienced that yet. By the spring of tenth grade, I was doing everything musical it was possible to do in my town: high school chorus, barbershop quartet, musicals, band. There were a lot of options, since in that period—especially in working-class towns—listening to music took second place to the joy of making music ourselves. I proudly sang beside my mother's dad in the church choir, and I led my church's small instrumental group. With a saxophonist friend I started a dance band. I wasn't quite ready yet to go back to my piano teacher for more classical training, and yet the pieces I could play were beginning to bore me—a good sign.

Then the world beyond my town opened up. My trombonist friend James realized the dream of so many sixteen-year-olds: the passport to freedom called a driver's license. James heard about another playing opportunity with a New Jersey band that was looking for more brass players. Many places in those days had, in addition to a high school band, a town band composed of brass, clarinets, saxophones, and percussion.

By that time, I'd given up the baritone horn I'd first played in high school, replacing it with a tuba; James and I figured we'd be a welcome duo for the town band sponsored by the fire department in Hackettstown, New Jersey. James was a tall, dark, lanky boy of few words. He played John Philip Sousa marches with his trombone as if he was felling a tree with a trusty ax.

We had no idea what the big time would be like, but we were certain we were getting closer to it. I delighted in the repertoire for the concerts.

The band director looked to be about forty, with a lively spring in his step and piercing brown eyes. I observed his leadership style with fascination; I guess I knew, even at sixteen, that my life would bring me many opportunities for leadership. He struck that rare balance in amateur music groups: rigorous enough to challenge us and give us the satisfaction of a job well done, relaxed and funny enough to give us working-class guys the recreation we needed.

≈ ≈ ≈

That summer I saw a lot of men who weren't like the men in my family, church and neighborhood. I saw boys a few years older than me who wanted to pass as men—boys who, after a desperately hot day parading, drank beer as if it were soda, heaved it up all over the place, and later wished they could simply die. (That spectacle encouraged my lifelong practice of only occasional, and very moderate, drinking.) I also heard adult men's versions of leering contempt for women that made me feel even guiltier for the cruising expeditions James and I went on in his car, calling to girls through our open windows and insulting them if they didn't banter back.

Then, in Atlantic City on July 4, I encountered something that strongly influenced my concept of leadership and even experiential education in my teaching.

I could already feel the heat when I woke up early that day. Summers in eastern Pennsylvania and New Jersey were, even then, notorious for their combination of heat and humidity.

I dressed quickly in shorts and a T-shirt, carrying my red wool band uniform on a hanger to James's waiting car. The Hackettstown band was joining what was then the largest parade of my life, on the Atlantic City boardwalk in the days when the resort city was at its height.

The reality of the very long march brought me down. Ocean breezes hardly touched the heat and humidity. The size of the parade and density of the crowds created frequent delays. My sousaphone felt heavier when we stood than when we marched, so my shoulder and back began to ache halfway down the boardwalk.

The consistency of the crowd along the route encouraged us to play more often than we sometimes did, and we played our hearts out. Yes, we sounded *good*! I loved watching the children ogle us, and I made up a guessing game about which ones would decide that very day to join a band when they were old enough. As we reached the end of the boardwalk, we were playing with relief and joy. I anticipated sitting on the bus in a few short minutes, feeling the delicious combination of fatigue and satisfaction.

We circled up on the street and waited for our director to return from a brief errand. He joined us with as resolute a face as I've ever seen, dark hair wet with perspiration, posture as erect as ever. "Men," he said, "there's been a mistake. The bus driver apparently did not know he was to meet us here, and there's no way to contact him. We need to go back to where we started." (Today, the ubiquity of cell phones might make such a situation seem impossible, but the reality is that even today emergency situations still occur in which communication is blocked.) Our bandleader paused, waiting for the groans and curses to subside. "Now, there are two ways to get back there. One way is to straggle back in twos and threes on the sidewalk, feeling bad and mad every step of the way. The second way is to march back with the drummers keeping us in time, shoulders back, respecting ourselves for the bandsmen that we are.

"Men," he said, "we're taking the second way. Drummers, start the cadence while the men line up. One, two, three, four!"

The drummers hastily grabbed their drumsticks and started the beat. A few of us were caught in mid-groan, including me. James caught my eye and raised his eyebrows as if to say, "So *this* is how some people do it!"

For the first mile, it was all I could do to pay attention to "Left, right, left, right" and keep my eyes away from the array of stores offering cold drinks. Gradually I surrendered to what we were doing: noticed the beat was now inside my body, felt the closeness of the men on each side of me, watched James square his shoulders and hold his trombone as if he still loved it. I wasn't surprised that—as we began to play some favorite easy pieces—our steps got lighter. My back turned numb at some point, and I stopped worrying about whether I'd make it, because I could see that *we* would make it.

Listening to the men get into the bus with whoops and hollers, I realized what we'd done. Instead of July 4 becoming a story of stupid error and misery, it became a victory story we would tell friends and family over and over.

Most importantly, I had now seen a man give the tough-love leadership that ends in grace.*

ℵ ℵ ℵ

Decades later, I experienced another moment of group empowerment—this time while singing Handel's *Messiah*. Leadership, I

---

* See my book *Facilitating Group Learning* for examples of groups that learn their most important lessons by being deprived of "an easy fix"—such as through technology—and discover, experientially, strengths that they didn't know they had. George Lakey, *Facilitating Group Learning: Strategies for Success with Diverse Learners* (Oakland, CA: PM Press, 2020).

realized, is only partly about assertiveness; the other side is the acknowledgement of vulnerability. That lesson, too, began in my boyhood.

For listening to music, I found that the summer was best, because that's when the Methodist church on our block opened its stained-glass windows for its Sunday-evening service. The windows inhaled cool evening air and exhaled the sound of hymn singing.

As a small boy I'd stand outside the church, wondering if I would ever understand the Welsh words the congregation was singing. Not that it really mattered—the sound of those Methodists belting out their hymns in glorious four-part harmony was enough for me. I stood quietly under a tree, hoping in vain that this time they'd forget the sermon and just sing their way entirely through worship.

Inevitably, the preacher's tone would change, from announcing the next hymn to announcing the certain fate of anyone who did not repent. I didn't know the Welsh words, but the tone was unmistakable—I'd heard the same message in English, from my own Evangelical preacher. I'd shake my head in wonderment that a people blessed to make music like that would take a half hour off from doing so to listen to descriptions of hell. Even as a boy, I had an opinion about how God would prefer we use our time.

One of the mysteries surfacing in this memoir is where I got the idea I had a right to an opinion on such matters. Was it the attention my mom gave me while she listened to my thoughts and conjectures? She was the best listener I knew, and it wasn't because she had no opinions of her own—she had plenty, which went with her strength of character. It was more that she seemed to think the people she talked with were important, in her own eyes and in God's. She'd draw people out and also let them know where she stood. In contrast to my dad, who loved a good argument, she centered her curiosity. I so wish she'd been allowed to continue in high school and go on to college. She was pulled out in the beginning of tenth grade when the hardships of the Depression required it—the biggest heartbreak of her teenage years, she told me.

א א א

By age fourteen, I'd heard a rumor that George Frideric Handel's *Messiah* was an earth-shaking oratorio, challenging to perform but certain to inspire. I began agitating with our church choir director, Edison Treible, to prepare us to sing the Christmas portion of *Messiah,* which tells the story of Jesus's birth. I loved Edison because I thought he was a romantic like me, not only willing but even happy to be carried away by exalted emotion. He was a dark-haired, olive-skinned, middle-aged insurance salesman with eyes that seemed to take in everything. He wasn't really handsome, but he walked as though he was. He told me of times he'd been driving to see a client when a favorite classical piece of music would begin on the radio, and he'd simply pull over to the side of the road and listen until it was finished.

My efforts to persuade Edison to program *Messiah* instead of one more slightly boring Christmas cantata failed, until a dashing young couple came to serve the town's Presbyterian church. The Reverend Richard Rettew was a new graduate of the Princeton Theological Seminary; Anna Rettew played the flute and was ready to tackle the pathetic Presbyterian choir. I immediately started attending the Presbyterians' youth group, which, happily, met at a different time from my church's youth fellowship. This enabled me to spend a lot of time with the Rettews, who were definitely the most "with it" pastoral pair in town.

"What do you think of the oratorio *Messiah?*" I asked Anna Rettew one day as the youth group was gathering.

"It's wonderful. It's amazing; it's my favorite Christmas music," she said.

"My choir director is thinking about doing the Christmas part," I said, stretching the truth, "but he probably thinks we can't do it alone."

"Well, I'm sure we Presbyterians can't manage it by ourselves," she said. "Maybe I should give him a call."

And so it happened that I finally got to sing an oratorio I yearned for but had never heard. It was everything I hoped for. Even my soles tingled when we sang the "Hallelujah Chorus." Edison and Anna found some string and brass players to join the organ and piano, and we made a mighty sound. I don't know who I was happier for: Edison, with his radiant smile at the end; me, with a whole new kind of music to think about; or my grandfather, who looked as though he'd run a marathon.

"Jiminy hoss!" Grandpop said afterward, shaking his head and wiping his eyes. "Well, I never!" More head shaking.*

Uncle Donald chimed in, "I thought I'd have a stroke when we were doing those runs!"

Uncle George rumbled appreciatively from his bass place (he thought he could qualify as one of those low Russian basses). "Now everything we do in our Shook Family Quartet will be a piece of cake!"

I looked around the choir room and saw similar wonderment on the faces of all but the imported soloists. My hometown adult friends—the schoolteacher, the clerk at the pharmacy, the legal secretary, the sewing-machine operator, the electrician, the slate miners—were dazzled that they had made music that sublime. The boldness of their leaders, their own willingness to try something new, and their profound love for music made the birth of the Child a miracle again.

When I sang *Messiah* decades later, it was often with a pro-

---

* When I read this story to my mother decades after the event described, after her dad died, she laughed at this quotation. Then tears came. "Oh, George," she said, "your stories make our family sound just like they're right here!"

fessional group called Pennsylvania Pro Musica. I was included when the conductor wanted a few amateurs to add to the swell of the sound. Conductor Franklin Zimmerman was a scholar and professor of music at the University of Pennsylvania, and I loved his rehearsals for the musicological tidbits he would throw in. But some of the singers were cool to him and, for that matter, to performance itself; I learned why it is that the words "jaded" and "professional" are sometimes put in the same sentence.

It was time for another performance of the entire *Messiah*, in a beautiful church built in colonial days. We singers were robing up, and I thought I detected among the veterans even more than usual detachment. By contrast, I remembered my first *Messiah,* the shining eyes and nervous grins in the choir room as we adjusted ties and tried to hum a particularly challenging passage one more time.

Franklin came in, white hair awry, looking pale. He gathered us together. "I've just come from the hospital," he said, "where I took my wife. She's very sick." He looked around distractedly. "My concentration is shot," he said. "You'll have to help me."

This was new—he always acted in command. He went on: "If I motion to bring you in when you know you shouldn't sing, don't come in. Do it as we've done in rehearsal. I really need you."

Soberly, we filed into the church sanctuary and took our places. The historic, white-painted church was packed, today's Philadelphians sitting where George Washington and the Anglicans of his day had sat. Our conductor took the podium, paler than ever. He raised his baton, and the overture started.

The unity in the choir was obvious; we even stood closer to each other than usual. We ignored Franklin's occasional misdirections, and each time we did both he and we looked more confident. Our entrances became ever more accurate, and the soloists sang like angels. The audience was alive; in a long concert like the entire *Messiah* I expect listeners to go passive, but this audience seemed to become more attentive.

I prayed while we sang. Gratitude was growing within me. I noticed that Franklin looked more centered, and the orchestra responded with more clarity of sound.

When we came to the last piece—the "Amen Chorus"—I took a deep breath. In this chorus the choir sings only one word, but I find it the most challenging. Remarkably, Handel wrote the music for that word dozens and dozens of times without repeating himself once, the choir's voices chasing each other in an ever-rising note of triumph.

Only a few measures into the chorus I knew it was ours, and that we were held as certainly as I'd ever been held. I concentrated to avoid my tears getting in the way of voice production, then felt a bit irritated: surely I was the only one who was so sentimental as to be crying. I stole a quick look around me. I saw tears on every face among these professional singers. Franklin's eyes were glistening, his face full of color, his conducting sure and clear.

We sang the last amen. A hush fell, as though audience and singers alike were holding our breath. The people sprang to their feet cheering, and we exhaled, grins breaking out on our tear-streaked faces.

≈ ≈ ≈

I was brought up in a sexist and classist culture that, for men, rewarded emotional shutdown in place of vulnerability; and for working-class people, holding back in cross-class situations instead of assertiveness. For years I've turned to these two stories about musical directors to help me practice—as an organizer or workshop facilitator—the kind of responsive leadership that empowers others. Movements need empowered people, which for many of us means accepting and practicing qualities that contrast with ones we're conditioned to hold. Whether or not I'm having a good day on that front, I'm grateful for exemplars, in history and in my life, that inspire me to stay in the game.

3

college offers breathing room
and fresh challenges

My best friend, Gary, whose family was poorer than mine, pointed out that a state teachers' college was affordable if we worked summers and then, during the school year, got part-time jobs. Maybe we could go to college together!

I'd need all the emotional support I could get, since my dad was opposed to college and my mom was staying out of the fight. Dad had been taken out of tenth grade to get a job in a slate mine, to help the family survive the Depression. His dream for me was to finish high school, stay in Bangor, get a job, and have a family. That's a life appropriate for a solid working-class lad.

However, I'd been inspired by my piano teacher to go to college—she'd even sent for college catalogues to show me after our lessons. She convinced me I was meant for a wider world than my hometown. Now Gary had the college bug, too.

Since he attended a different elementary school from mine, I never noticed Gary until the summer before fifth grade. At the time, my lack of athletic ability had me feeling insufficiently masculine, so I was trying to "man up" in my self-presentation. By contrast, even from a distance, I noticed that Gary seemed comfortable with being effeminate. I did my part to enforce the Boy Code: I yelled at him from across the street, "There goes that silly Gary Jones."

He didn't take offense. Maybe he heard a note of fascination in my voice.

At the beginning of fifth grade, Gary transferred to my school, and suddenly we couldn't find enough recess time to talk with one another. His blue eyes twinkled when signaling the wicked comment he was about to make about someone, and I was charmed that he trusted me enough to be that sinful in my company. In my church, children were taught not to speak ill of others, but apparently the Lutherans were looser. I tried not to let on how shocked I was, but I laughed louder than he did after his zingers, so maybe he knew.

My church was looser than his, though, in monitoring the use of the Sunday school piano. After I delivered the afternoon newspapers and Gary did his chores at home, we would let ourselves into my church basement to play. I knew better than to bring him to the piano at my home—what parent could stand endless repetitions of "Chopsticks" and "Heart and Soul?" In the empty church basement, our uproarious piano sessions did more than anything to bring us into harmony.

"Of course, we *could* be playing a Steinway," Gary announced one day, in that tone he reserved for something that might be borderline forbidden.

"Where . . . how?" I stammered. As working-class boys, we had dreamed of Steinway pianos but never been close to one.

"My aunt just got one." Gary's eyes were bright. His aunt had married a doctor, and some relief might be in store for his family's poverty; it was too early to know.

"Can we really play it?" I asked.

"Let's go see."

Gary's aunt let us into the house, noting we were heading toward the living room. "Go ahead, play something," Gary said.

"No, let's play together," I said, wondering as I did how we could possibly defile this instrument with "Chopsticks."

We compromised, sitting tight together on the piano bench while I played a classical piece I'd just learned. We quieted, breathing together—then just that fast, the spell was broken.

"Heart and Soul!" Gary yelled, and four hands hit the keys in a round of resonance, arms touching, fingers glancing: two boys in love.

≈ ≈ ≈

Reassured by the idea of going to college together, Gary and I sent for catalogues from a few of the state teachers' colleges. Pennsylvania had fourteen of them; the deal in those days was that the state would provide an almost free college education to bright working-class youngsters in return for our willingness to teach in public schools that paid poorly. (I knew teachers who had part-time jobs on the side in order to be able to feed their families.)

By this time, I was getting used to taking heat from peers for being so close to Gary. "Are you guys 'going down' tonight?" I'd be asked in a semi-public setting, which would induce snickering; clearly they assumed we were having sex. The classic stereotyped narrative of butch-femme relationships was in operation, even though I barely qualified as butch. My gym teacher had a strong opinion about decidedly non-athletic me, and constantly gave me grief for talking and laughing much more than was appropriate for a "real man."

My friendship with Gary was an intense introduction to 1950s sexual politics, and neither of us then had the words to describe what I've just written. In our small, rural town, we'd heard references to "smutty" sexual acts, but we didn't know two men could be lovers. In today's world, it's hard to believe how naïve we were.

But there was so much else to think about. We quickly zeroed in on West Chester State Teachers College: it was a strong music school and close to Philadelphia, with its fabulous orchestra. Gary wanted to focus on elementary ed, and my choice was secondary ed: English and social studies. We both wanted to be close to music, and the many free performances at the college sounded like paradise.

In those first months at West Chester, I was swept off my feet. Just outside the large auditorium, I stood in the shadows one evening while a small group of music majors practiced a cappella pieces; they liked the resonance in the gothic stone archway. English lit had a treasure trove for a reading list. American civ had articles that might get me beyond the pieties of conventional politics. Modern dance could work for my phys ed requirement, even if it was a stretch for clumsy me.

Gary and I quickly found our way to the drama club. I was relieved to find that non-music majors like me were allowed to join the college choir after an audition. My campus job was shelving books in a library that made the Bangor Public Library look tiny.

The one thing I wanted to change was that I was in a different dorm from Gary, so as soon as college rules allowed, we found a chance to be together, in an intense community of peers. Eleven of us male students moved into the top two floors of a three-story house in a residential area a block from campus. It was owned by Art and Elaine Klinger, who lived with their baby on the first floor. We affectionately called the house Klinger Hall—although the affection was suspended each morning, when up to five men at a time crowded the one small bathroom trying simultaneously to shave, brush teeth, comb hair, take a bath in the showerless tub, and get out in time for breakfast. And that was only the first shift. If you've seen circus clowns tumbling out of a tiny car, you can imagine a horde of naked men squeezing past each other to run to their rooms and dress for their eight o'clock classes.

One evening, as was usual, my roommate Burt had us in thrall. Burt had straight, light brown hair cut short, and often wore horn-rimmed glasses of matching color. His high cheek bones and prominent lips and forehead gave him an intense look. When he told us stories, though, the animation of his body and the dancing of his brown eyes turned him into an unlikely elf. "So, this man stops his car in front of my house after going around the block three times. I was mowing the lawn, and I watched him go around—maybe it was four times. Each time, he stared at me, and each time he drove slower."

The three of us leaned in: my other roommate, Bill, plus Gary and me. It was late, and we were tired of studying but somehow full of energy. Burt always had a story, usually funny in its improbability. Most people thought Burt was a nerd, but if you listened to his stories it sounded like Burt had the zaniest life of all of us.

"So, what did the guy do when he stopped?" Gary voiced the question on all of our minds.

"He called me over to his car, so I went over, but not too close. And . . ." Burt started to laugh. "He asked me if he could have a pair of my dirty underpants!"

Our laughs were mingled with shrieks. Tears came to Gary's eyes, he was laughing so hard.

"What did you do?" Bill asked.

"What do you think?" Burt said. "I got him a pair of my dirty underwear and told him to fuck off!"

This time the shrieks predominated. Then we heard thumps on the floor under our feet — the guys in the room beneath us wanted to get to sleep. It was late. Tom appeared from next door. As a veteran studying on the GI Bill and ten years our senior, Tom often seemed to feel he should play the uncle and give us some guidance. But this time he was grinning from ear to ear. "I've heard that one, Burt," he said. "I don't believe it."

Burt rolled his eyes. "You never believe my best stories, Tom. I think you're just jealous because you've lived such a protected life—never got off that army base in Germany." Tom dove at Burt, and soon they were mock-wrestling on the floor.

Bill, our resident Goody Two-shoes, separated the wrestling Burt and Tom and shushed us all. Burt didn't even try another story. Maybe he thought we were too giddy for it.

Tom and Gary went back to their room next door, Gary suppressing lingering giggles at the thought of the stranger driving off with Burt's underpants. (Gary and I had decided that our rooming together in Klinger Hall was overdoing it. We were fond of Lebanese philosopher Kahlil Gibran, and we took his advice: "Let there be spaces in your togetherness.") As I drifted off to sleep, I noted that our shrieking response to Burt's story left out the disgust and homophobic harsh judgment I would have expected at home. My roomies seemed, well . . . *excited* by the story.

ℵ ℵ ℵ

"George, I finally got the Brahms intermezzo the way I want it. Want to hear it?" Burt was walking me to breakfast. He'd just changed his major to music so he could lavish attention on the piano and start learning to play the pipe organ.

"Of course," I said.

Burt winked. "How about four o'clock this afternoon? Come to my practice room."

I grinned to myself. Even though I'd decided against trying to make a career in music, I wanted a college with a strong music department so I could have music around me all the time. Making friends with Burt was excellent. He had perfect pitch and knew the great composers like the back of his hand. He'd even gotten me into his solfeggio class as an auditor, and I was spending the semester singing Bach chorales. It doesn't get better than that.

Today, Burt wanted to play for me. I might be the first to listen to him let a Brahms piece show his soul.

After I closed the door of the small practice room and watched Burt take his seat, I continued to stand. I felt formal, perhaps a bit in awe. The warmth of Brahms's internal harmonies had me smiling soon enough. Then I found myself gazing at Burt's hands. I'd never really seen how beautiful his strong fingers were, how flexibly they moved, lining out the melody, cascading the sixteenth notes, decisively striking low notes, reminding me that the piano is a percussive instrument after all.

The Brahms was suddenly over, leaving me in a trance. I applauded, embarrassed; I didn't know what to say, and neither did he. I clapped him on the shoulders, only intensifying the awkwardness, and backed out of the room.

Maybe we weren't ready yet to feel this much together. Later, we would be.

ℵ ℵ ℵ

With the change of semesters a new student moved in to Klinger Hall, Jack from Philadelphia. While trying not to show it, we were all interested in our first Big City boy, since the rest of us were from small towns. Jack took to hanging out on the third floor, sharing our late-night pizza and Burt's stories.

One of the ways Jack was more sophisticated than the rest of us was his acute sense of who around him might be open to sex with other men—what I was later to learn is called "gaydar." One night, five of us happened to be in Tom and Gary's room, including Jack. Burt was rehearsing late, but the other four of us from our floor were there. We were slumping on bunks or sitting on the floor, tired and winding down. "My back is itching so bad," Jack said to no one in particular. "Would somebody be willing to scratch it?"

Gary reached over and started to scratch, then pulled up Jack's sweater to get to the skin. "That looks great," yawned Tom, who was sitting on the floor next to me. "Who wants to do me?"

I turned to oblige, and Bill reached down from the bed he was lying on to dig into my shoulder blades.

I sank into the delicious difficulty of enjoying both scratching and being scratched. One by one, sweaters and then shirts and then undershirts were pulled off. Someone turned off the lamp—I thought it was Jack, so maybe it was a Philadelphia thing. I heard slight moans of pleasure from here and there, and felt my pants being gently tugged off. I helped by raising my hips. It was too dark to be sure whose bare leg was slowly stroking mine, but I knew it was Tom's chest my head was rubbing against. The moans continued, mostly sweet and almost lazy, but sometimes urgent. I suddenly disentangled myself and went out of the room into the pitch-black hallway.

So, I asked myself as I stood there naked, *is this me?*

The response took at most two seconds. *Yes.*

And, is that okay? I asked, probing whoever it is inside that answers my endless questions.

The response took a little longer. We both knew the answer would be provisional.

Yes.

I went back to rejoin the puppy pile on the floor.

The next two weeks felt dreamlike, not only because a part of me was shocked and disoriented but also because we never talked about what had happened. Even Gary and I, used to talking about everything, took a bit of time before we could debrief something so momentous.

I did my usual thing of searching the library for books, but I found little. Fortunately, psychotherapist Robert M. Lindner had just put out his groundbreaking book *Must You Conform?*, in which he rejects the pathologizing of same-sex relationships.*
That helped.

As I reached for a way to ground myself in this broadening of my identity, I kept coming back to what I'd always come back

---

* Robert Lindner, *Must You Conform?* (New York: Rinehart, 1956).

to: a belief in me and the validity of my experience, even when it was sharply different from "the world's" idea of what ought to be. That belief was shaped by my close identification with Jesus. He'd expected the conventional wisdom of his time to be seriously lacking, and so did I. "You have heard it said . . . but I say unto you. . . ." It's not that I believed myself to be godlike; it's just that Jesus and Emerson and Thoreau and others I respected were simply not that impressed by conformity.

It wasn't until I wrote this memoir, though, that I realized how lucky I was to be given this free-spirited introduction to sex with other men—and how lacking it was in the tropes of selfishness and domination that some of my female classmates were subjected to in their first sexual experiences with men.* And also, how fortuitous that Jack showed up to engineer the whole thing!

Burt must have sensed something different in the atmosphere, but he didn't ask questions, and I didn't know how or whether to tell him. The violence of homophobia haunted not only the schools and streets "out there" but even the rooms of Klinger Hall; Gary and I once found ourselves consoling a bloodied second-floor student who got a fist in his face when his glance at a housemate in the bathtub lingered too long. I still remember the blood dripping off his face, for merely *looking too long at someone in the bath*. Without knowing it, in that moment I put up more walls. The lesson was to hide any shred of you that wasn't a "real man."

And what about Burt? Would witty and Brahms-loving Burt put a fist in my face if I told him what had happened when he was away? Who knew for sure?

My brother Bob came to visit me and hang out for a couple of days, to experience a college campus for the first time. Bob had

---

* Later I found British author Aldous Huxley, who started to dazzle me in high school, projecting a similar introduction to sex as normative—light, aware, considerate, affectionate—in his utopian book *Island*. Aldous Huxley, *Island* (New York: Harper and Row, 1962).

switched in high school to college prep at my urging, and was considering being the second one in our entire extended family to go to college. I invited him to see our fine basketball team, knowing that Bob's love for sports would ensure a good time.

All the beds in Klinger Hall were taken, so Burt suggested that if I shared his bed, Bob could sleep in my bunk. The invitation didn't surprise me; I knew that Burt was a generous guy. Besides, Klinger Hall closeness was increasing at such a rate that I wouldn't have been surprised if we next shared collective toothbrushes.

The basketball game was exciting. West Chester won, and I introduced Bob to the players in the locker room after the game. He was thrilled by the experiences of his day and also exhausted, falling asleep before I could say goodnight. I crawled into Burt's bed in a proper back-to-back position, whispered goodnight, and relaxed.

As I was about to drift off, I felt a gentle rubbing along my leg. Rather than wait to find out if it was accidental, I decided to rub back, just the slightest bit. The rubbing came again. Burt wanted to play, after all. We turned simultaneously to face each other, grinning in the streetlamp's light through the windows. His beautiful fingers touched my cheek, smoothed my eyebrows. I saw the confidence in his face—it wasn't his first time. Well, it wasn't my first time, either. Tonight, I wouldn't be retreating into the hall to find out whether this tenderness was right for me.

א א א

Gary and I still checked in with each other each day. Now we had additional territory to explore. Gary asked Jack where to go in Philly, which led us to Allegro, a gay piano bar in what is still Philadelphia's Gayborhood, Washington Square West.

We loved the camaraderie we found there, standing around the piano singing songs by Cole Porter, often with our arms on the shoulders of strangers while eyeing someone across the room. We learned to handle the risk that the police might raid the place, since a gay bar was illegal. We even relaxed about missing the last bus back to West Chester—someone would most likely take each of us home for the night. If not, there was always the YMCA.

When we left the bar separately, we'd meet up in Center City by noon to compare notes on our adventures while traveling back to West Chester. For me, some nights were more enjoyable than others, but I always looked forward to breakfast, when I would grill the guy with questions about the norms and folkways of the gay world. (Who could predict I'd one day study sociology?) One of the norms I learned was, never have sex with your best friend. Lovers come and go, but a best friend is forever.

Despite my adventures in the Gayborhood, I didn't lose my romantic interest in women. But I was satisfied with living my life and being open to new experience. At that moment, the exotic—and transgressive—character of the gay underground appealed to the rebel in me.

And besides, in the 1950s, women my age were usually looking for life companions. I decidedly was not. Trying to negotiate a light romance with a woman seeking husband material seemed much more complicated than singing Cole Porter at a piano bar and having a fling with a man who caught my eye. I preferred simplicity in my dating life, so I could attend to whatever it was that was moving profoundly within me—a sense of life mission that was newly starting to take shape.

I did notice, though, that as important as Jesus was to me still, I'd moved some distance from my evangelical upbringing

4

finding Quakers and a loving partner

There was no church of my denomination in West Chester. I decided to make that fact an opportunity to explore how various people worshipped. I didn't know any other students who were doing this, but to me, leaving my hometown was about exploring, and what could be more basic to exploration than different approaches to the meaning of life?

At first, I chose where to go almost at random. Over time, I began to see that different churches had different strengths.

I finally arrived at a Friends Meeting. West Chester had an old Quaker tradition—the sign at the edge of town said "West Chester welcomes thee." The Quakers' formal name was Religious Society of Friends, and in West Chester they were so quiet that for a long time they remained below my radar.

I walked in not knowing what to expect. There were many people on plain benches—no pews. There was no altar or cross to focus the room. Instead, in front there were a few risers with some people sitting on benches facing the rest of us, like a choir but silent. No one was standing or seeming to preside.

Quiet reigned. I slipped into an empty place and realized that the quiet didn't quite reign; it pervaded. As the minutes went by, noted by the ticking of an old wooden clock mounted on the wall, I shifted the metaphor again. Now it seemed like the quiet was simply there, waiting to be joined.

I tried joining.

An older woman on the facing bench got up and told us about a spiritual experience she'd had a few days before. I looked around but saw no sign that this had stimulated anyone to follow up, to make a comment on what she'd said, or to give thanks. Instead, the quiet continued.

Just as I started to wonder if I liked this strangeness, someone two rows from me rose and prayed. He was an older man, somewhat frail, and spoke with an undercurrent of emotion. Suddenly I was a boy again at my home church, attending Wednesday night prayer meeting with my grandfather. We'd entered what the pastor called "a season of prayer." My grandfather, this strongly built slate worker, was on his knees along with the other men in the room, who were keeping an expectant silence and then testifying, or praying out loud, or singing with tearful eyes. I loved the spontaneity, the pauses, the way that the very limbs of these men conveyed their earnest reverence.

Those juicy Wednesday nights had dried up when I was, what—fourteen? Fifteen? Prayer meeting became simply a mini Sunday-morning service held on Wednesday nights—supportive, perhaps, but with the numinous gone missing. I stopped going, pleading homework as an excuse to my grandfather.

Now, a young man rose from the front row across the room from me, wearing a plaid flannel shirt, no tie, no jacket. He talked of conflict inside himself, the challenge of his privilege when he came back from doing a weekend of volunteer work in a Philadelphia slum. He sounded real, perplexed, wanting help. Yet no one rose to give him advice.

The stillness got stronger, as though it had a texture, something that could support weight.

An outstretched hand appeared in front of my chest. Surprised, I turned to find the owner of the hand smiling and realized that, all around me, people were now shaking hands. I raised my hand to meet his and again met his eyes, which this time were twinkling. "Welcome," he said.

On my way out I paused to look at the bulletin board on which notices were posted. A Quaker committee of some kind was urging people to write to Congress protesting the military draft. It suddenly hit me: I'd heard somewhere that Quakers were pacifists! I continued out the door, shaking my head as I descended the broad front steps. *Well,* I thought tolerantly, *even the best people must be forgiven their eccentricities. I guess I'll go back and worship with them again.*

ॠ ॠ ॠ

In the late 1940s and '50s, the United States went through a period of anti-Communist hysteria. One outcome was to require people serving the public, like teachers, to sign a loyalty oath, in which they stated that they were not presently—nor had they ever been—members of the Communist Party, or conspired to overthrow the US government.

When I encountered the loyalty oath, just after graduating high school, I realized that even many adults simply conformed with what was expected rather than asking themselves what was right and wrong. I refused to sign it, when it was put in front of me as a teen, because civil liberties are more important. I remembered Ralph Waldo Emerson's statement, "To thine own self be true; every heart vibrates to that iron string." It was an adage I could quote at the drop of a hat. I wanted to become *that* kind of adult.

By making integrity so important in my college years, I was about to upset part of my own worldview. When I went home for a weekend, I enjoyed singing in my church choir again, standing next to my mother's dad, who still struck me with awe. On one of those Sunday mornings, I paged through the back of the hymnal looking for meditation material during the long period it took for everyone to take communion. I almost kept turning the pages when I saw the Sermon on the Mount, thinking that I already knew it well, then decided to read it again. For the first time, it spoke to me.

What does a Christian adult do with the Biblical record of Jesus's clear statements against killing? "You have heard that it was said, 'An eye for an eye and a tooth for a tooth.' But I say to you, Do not resist one who is evil. But if anyone strikes you on the right cheek, turn to him the other also."*

I was eighteen. That moment opened a major conflict within me that continued for a year. My dad had been in the military during World War II, and his brother was killed on the Pacific front. My other uncles had been in the army and navy. They were men I looked up to, and they took their Christianity seriously. That should have been enough. Still, for me, adulthood required taking personal responsibility for ethical decisions, and here was Jesus seeming to contradict the prevailing assumption in my family that killing other humans might be justifiable.

I read everything for and against pacifism I could get my hands on and was relieved when most of what I found was against it, offering reasons why killing is acceptable under some circumstances. I didn't want another difference to come between my parents and me—I was aware of ways in which I was already changing from how my parents had brought me up. A college education will do that for a working-class lad.

Still, I heard the Sermon on the Mount echoing inside me.

I had discussions, both thoughtful and passionate, with my college friends that went late into the night. I read and read and discovered a major flaw in the non-pacifist writings: those writers would assert that they were pragmatic, but on closer reading, it turned out they were boxed in by assumptions that hampered

---

* Matt. 5: 38–39 RSV.

their creativity. For me, creativity was central, and this was a grave deficiency. After all, if the Wright brothers had been as limited in their creativity as these "realists" seemed to be, Wilbur and Orville would never have gotten an airplane off the ground. As in the history of technological invention, so also in the history of break-throughs for more human and successful ways of waging conflict: the trophies go to those who aren't willing to be tied to assump-tions about what cannot work.

Early Quakers, for example, put the Sermon on the Mount into practice. Flying in the face of prevailing assumptions, they accepted no guns when they settled in Pennsylvania but instead reached out to the Lenni-Lenape people they found there and sought to make agreements that would keep the peace. Looking back from today's viewpoint, we can see a lot wrong about the entire project of Europeans settling in the United States. The point that grabbed me about those early Quakers, however, was they defied the assumption of the Christians to the north and south of them that guns for protection were essential, and main-tained their pacifism. As it turned out—let the pragmatists take note—Quakers were the *safest* people on the American frontier!

It's widely assumed that our ethical obligation to protect usu-ally requires violence—and that assumption is what allows many Christians to break with Jesus. The more history I looked at, the more dubious I found that belief. I saw it as hindering our ability to deal creatively with the real problems of protection when we encounter them.

In terms both of logic and history, war—as an ethical option— was looking more and more raggedy to me. But I still didn't want to become a pacifist. In desperation, I turned to a book by one of America's leading Marxists called *The Case Against Pacifism.** It didn't convince me, either.

---

* John Lewis, *The Case Against Pacifism* (London: G. Allen & Unwin, 1940).

The debates I was most drawn to were framed in pragmatic terms: Is a violent or nonviolent strategy more likely to succeed in this or that situation? That's because what stimulates me is the opportunity for creativity: facing a problem, drawing on research from nonviolent struggle in many contexts, then devising something that might work in this conflict we're facing. I met many non-pacifists who believed they were pragmatic but who *assumed* that violence is more powerful and effective than a nonviolent alternative could possibly be. This assumption is hardwired into our culture, even though it's often been found to be untrue. In 1848, to cite just one case, the Hungarians tried violence to get out from under Austrian domination. It failed. When they later turned to a nonviolent strategy, it worked.*

In debates about what to do in this or that situation, my debating opponent has often demanded a 100 percent guarantee that my nonviolent alternative will work, otherwise "of course" we should resort to violence. That's not pragmatic. Pragmatic people develop cases for each alternative and then compare the risks of success and failure for each alternative. Because of the unconscious power of the violence paradigm, my debating partners often omit our existential reality: even after a rigorous risk assessment, we cannot know for sure what will happen. By studying national-level mass struggles between 1900 and 2006, political scientists Erica Chenoweth and Maria Stephan found that movements choosing nonviolent means doubled their chances of winning compared with movements that chose violence.** Doubling the chance of winning by choosing nonviolent means is not the same as a guarantee, but it sounds pretty good to a rational person.

---

* Gavin Musynske, "Hungarians Campaign for Independence from Austrian Empire, 1859–1867," Global Nonviolent Action Database, last updated May 18, 2011, https://nvdatabase. swarthmore.edu/content/hungarians-campaign-independence-austrian-empire-1859-1867.
** Erica Chenoweth and Maria J. Stephan, *Why Civil Resistance Works: The Strategic Logic of Nonviolent Conflict*, (New York: Columbia University Press, 2011), 7.

We are most responsible for that over which we have some control: our own actions. We know the quality of the act of killing, and we know the quality of the act of nonviolent struggle. This frame has given me a clear basis on which to choose.

By the end of that intense year of searching, I took a very deep breath and wrote to my draft board that I was a conscientious objector. In those days young men were required to register with the draft board and expected to keep the board current on their status or else be assumed to be eligible to be called up for military service.

To my surprise, I found that committing to a pacifist stand gave me additional motivation and freedom. Instead of torturing myself over the ethics of each war as it came along—I expected, as time has shown, that the US empire would be embroiled in war after war—I could save myself the time and energy and instead devote my life to *alternatives* to war. It was the path of peace and change, I discovered, that was the creative one.

I was now heading toward age twenty, wanting to move toward maturity. Wouldn't a truly mature person rather nurture and create nonviolent ways to defend freedom and advance justice, rather than hurt and destroy?

א א א

The summer between my first and second years at West Chester was spent working in a factory while living at home. I felt at home doing factory work, but I also was bored by the repetition and the utter lack of interest on the part of the boss in any suggestions I offered about how to improve the work process. I was repeatedly receiving the message that seemed to be built into the consciousness of managers: they know best, and the worker's job is simply to obey, even though we often know the immediate work process better.

I enjoyed my family time, catching up with my big sister, Shirley, who was in love with "the boy next door," and my younger brother, Bob, who was still intrigued by the idea of college. Dad wanted him to remain in Bangor, restarting our older debate. Dad had lost none of his amazing appetite for argument. (Bob did go to college after all.) Meanwhile, for dessert, what could be better than my long, vulnerable talks with my mom?

In September 1956, after once again hitching a ride with Gary to West Chester, I noticed on the college registration form a chance to indicate a religious preference. Remembering positively my occasional drop-ins at Quaker Meeting, I wrote "Quakers," to see what would happen. I soon received in the mail a postcard from one Cynthia Arvio, saying she was having a coffee at her house for Quaker students.

I showed up, curious about her and about what actual Quaker students might look like. It turned out that only one other student showed, and neither of us was a Quaker. We were both motivated by curiosity. He, a Black student, was curious because he'd heard about the role Quakers had played in the Underground Railroad, including in the vicinity of West Chester.

We had a delightful conversation in a room with one wall entirely filled with books, relaxing on easy chairs that I learned were rescued from used furniture stores. The Arvios' three little girls wandered in to check us out. Cynthia told us that at college she'd majored in writing. Caring for her family didn't give her much time, but she liked to use some of it to write poetry. Her husband, Ray, was away a lot, because he worked for a Quaker agency that had him traveling among colleges to stimulate student discussions about peace and justice.

When my fellow student said he needed to leave, I asked if I could stay a bit, to examine their library. Cynthia disappeared to put her children to bed, and I found myself entranced by the collection of edgy authors and titles on the shelves, arranged in no particular order.

"My job at the college is in the library," I said when she returned. "Would you like me to put your books in some kind of order?" Her laugh was hearty, and I enjoyed the light in her eyes. I hoped very much she'd say yes.

"I'd have to check with Ray about whether he wants them ordered," she said and smiled. "I want him to meet you, anyway. He'll be back Friday—how about then?"

Cynthia and Ray became long-lasting mentors, comrades, and intimate friends. I soon began organizing other students to walk over to the Arvios' for evenings of discussion about racial equality, pacifism, economic justice, and the tension between the individual and the collective. Cynthia alerted me to Rev. Ralph Abernathy's coming to town; he was a key colleague of Rev. Martin Luther King's in leading the bus boycott in Montgomery, Alabama. At the meeting, I was deeply impressed by the Montgomery story— amazed that Black people could stand up to the Ku Klux Klan in hard-core Alabama and win a victory. I began to read *Liberation*, a magazine containing articles by King and other pioneers in developing the practice of nonviolent struggle.

I took the train into Philly and spent a day sorting clothes at the warehouse of the American Friends Service Committee, helping its project to aid refugees fleeing wars with only the clothes on their backs. That was my start in many years of volunteering with the AFSC, a Quaker organization committed to extensive anti-racist and peace education along with service projects. In 1947, AFSC had received the Nobel Peace Prize, alongside British Quakers, for heroic work assisting war refugees.

Ray Arvio suggested I spend my summer vacation in an AFSC youth project. He gave me a list of options, from which "Interns in Industry" caught my eye. Project members found assembly-line jobs and then, in the evenings, had seminars with academics, union organizers, and other activists. The intention of the project was to offer college students from non–working-class backgrounds a gritty experience of blue-collar working life and explore the implications.

In Bangor, I'd already been a part-time janitor in two appliance stores after school and held seasonal full-time factory jobs. I certainly didn't think I needed more working-class experience, but this was the only AFSC project where I could earn money for tuition, so I signed up to spend my summer in Lynn, Massachusetts.

As it turned out, I deepened my working-class identification in Lynn, both through the evening educational seminars and through close association with students from other social classes. College for me had so far meant hanging out with other working-class students; that's pretty much all we had at West Chester. In Lynn, I got a chance to practice communication with my roommate, Alex, and others who'd been born into higher economic classes, and in that way I began to get clues about how different from them my class background had made me. For some reason, I didn't raise those differences in conversation with others; much later I'd realize that subject was just as verboten as was our talking with the only Black student in the summer project about what it was like for her. I was surprised to learn that the other students weren't Quakers, either; I guess we'd be called Quaker-curious.

א א א

I noticed Berit Mathiesen immediately: vivid blue eyes, curly brown hair, erect posture, and a clipped accent from who knew where. (I later learned that Norwegians in those days learned Oxford-accented English.) Berit had a way of leaning forward when she talked, her musical voice expressing her strength and determination, smarts and curiosity. I wanted to know her. I was nineteen and decided to go for it.

On the way to the beach on our first real break, a large group of us walked together. I walked on one side of Berit, while an intern named Jerry walked on the other. He asked her about her town in Norway. I was flummoxed. How dare he know the regional geography of Norway when I didn't even know the location of the country itself? Jerry not only had the longest, darkest eyelashes I'd seen on a man but wit and knowledge, too. The road to the beach began to seem endless as the heat rose to the back of my neck.

I knew only one thing for sure: Jerry couldn't possibly be as good for Berit as I could be. Why was he still oozing charm in her direction, and why wasn't she turning to me?

By this time, my misery had me looking around the indifferent scene of houses and occasional stores. I saw an ice cream shop and decided to go for sweetness. On impulse, as I started to leave the group, I said, "Berit, would you like an ice cream? I'm getting one for myself."

"Sure," she said in that musical way of hers, and shot me a dazzling smile.

It was possibly the shortest time a young man ever took to buy two ice cream cones. We licked them together and laughed about nothing at all, while Jerry retired from the field. Two years later, almost to the day, Berit and I were married in Norway. I'd found out, in the meantime, where her country was.

But that's leaping ahead. When I arrived at the project, I was cynical about romantic love; it was fun, exciting, and at the same time not to be taken seriously. I was a serious guy, and this ten-week summer project looked to me like a good place to develop my Life Plan. And, on the side, why not fall in love with one of the project members, either a boy or girl?

The first challenge was to find a job. The first day of job-hunting in the industrial part of Lynn was a wretched experience for me; I was turned down more than fifty times. That evening, back in the project house, we compared notes, and I was not alone. Solidarity—and youthful resilience—are useful qualities. The next day I got a job in a laundry. Berit, on her first job-hunting day, got a job in a shoe factory. She claimed, with a smile, that her job was quite spiritual: molding inner soles.

The summer expanded my universe in multiple ways. Geographically, I'd never been so far from my corner of Pennsylvania. Politically, I'd never met so many organizers, activists, or Quakers, who took turns coming by in the evenings to lead educational seminars for us. All this plus, night after night, canoodling with Berit in the dark garden behind the project house, enjoying the smoothness of her cheeks, the light in her eyes, the invitation to explore.

I learned from the evening seminars that it is not a strange idea to have a mission, a Life Purpose. That reassured me, because I was eager to know mine. The routine, boring work each day at the laundry was in its way a relief, because it left my mind free to wonder what my life was to be centrally about.

My mission had to be important, I felt, in order to justify my radical departure from parental expectations: teaching or working a blue-collar job in Bangor, raising a family, taking my part in church work, and relaxing with my fishing buddies. I was a romantic; dreaming came easily to me. I felt an alternative rising within me but at first didn't know quite what it was.

One night, instead of canoodling with Berit, I spent the night walking on the town beach beside the ocean. I worked hard and loved to sleep, but on this night, I felt too full of expectation to be sleepy. The night sky was dazzlingly clear and the ocean, still a rare wonder to this rural boy, reinforced my sense of limitless possibility. As the hours rolled by, I became clear on what my own life mission was: to help social movements to bring more justice and peace to this world.

I felt lucky to learn so young that I had a calling, although how to put it into practice was unclear. I was still learning about my strengths and talents; what did they add up to in the world of service and social movements? I was already enthusiastic about vision—I liked to imagine how unjust systems could be reorganized to support justice—but would social movements be interested in that? I liked teaching, and that might be how I'd make my living: probably high school social studies, so the subject matter would be consistent with my mission.

I realized with regret that this would mean giving up serious involvement in music, like directing a church choir or leading a band, or for that matter directing plays and musicals in community theater; that kind of thing is way too time-consuming. High school teachers had summers off and, in some towns, an occasional sabbatical year, which would give me more time for my mission. I might develop organizing skills that the AFSC would hire me to use.

The AFSC staff people I was getting to know were anything but narrow drudges; they listened to jazz or folk music while they supported developing leaders and movements. Charlie Walker was recently back from Montgomery, Alabama, where he met Martin Luther King and helped out with training for the bus boycott. Charlie would later supervise part-time work I did for the AFSC, tell me action stories that helped me understand nonviolence, and delight me with his enthusiastic piano playing.* I was beginning to see that behind the scenes in the world of social movements was a community of activists who were in it for the long haul, paid or unpaid, looking out for one another's well-being. I could be one of them, I thought, even though at age nineteen I didn't rightly know what my most useful gifts would be and whether I'd be good enough to be hired to use them.

---

* Charlie was among the first Americans to write practical manuals on nonviolent action, lead trainings, and urge a global view by being a founding member of World Peace Brigades; in some ways my peacemaking career followed and built on his. As a student, I also became close with his wife, Marion, and their family, giving piano lessons to several of the children. See Brenda Walker Beadenkopf's biography *A Quaker Behind the Dream: Charlie Walker and the Civil Rights Movement* (Oviedo, Living Parables of Central Florida, Inc., 2019).

I had no idea whether movements could achieve big goals or small ones; make a nonviolent revolution or settle for poverty reduction and shortening a war. But the difficulty of knowing ahead of time seemed like anything else in life: As a teacher, could I inspire students or just keep them on track? Could I help build a new community park or just add more basketball courts? The mission that I accepted that night inspired me with its positivity, its direction, and its reassurance that I would put my verve and smarts into something much bigger than myself. As in any enterprise, how successful I would become depended on much that was beyond my control. What I could be sure of was the worthiness of the work.

≈ ≈ ≈

Toward the end of summer, when my feelings for Berit reached the point that I wanted to see her again at Christmas vacation, I told her I was strongly attracted to men. I figured that if she wanted to split for that reason, better sooner than later. Our relationship would then turn out to be what I'd been expecting at the start: a summer romance.

I assumed that a simple summer romance was her expectation, too. She knew her next step was a final college year halfway across the country, at Midland College in Fremont, Nebraska. Her move after graduation was to return home to Norway, a requirement built into the Fulbright travel grant she was on.

There was a good chance she would react negatively to my attraction to men. Even though we'd been spending the summer in a bubble that supported progressive attitudes, the larger world was hugely anti-gay, and no one in our project was out as LGBTQ, so who knew what anybody in the project really thought?

I was happy being passionate with Berit, and I'd been happy with my nights with Burt. In my explorations of the Philadelphia gay world with Gary, I'd met bisexuals who told me that's how it was for them. I'd also read enough of the work of anthropologist Margaret Mead to suspect that everyone is somewhere on a spectrum that has, at each end, exclusive attraction to one gender. I figured, back then as today, that our culture was messed up with its homophobia, just as it was with its racism and sexism and militarism. (At that point I didn't have a name for classism.) So what else was new? And, just as being Black or a woman or a pacifist made you more vulnerable in this society, I knew you could be beaten up or killed for being gay, too. Prudence, not shame, called for the closet.

In that light, whatever Berit's reaction would be, I didn't fear the possibility that she would shame me about my gayness; I'd write off her scorn as being unenlightened. Still, I was nervous about telling her, because even though this was a summer romance, I wanted more time with her. And I didn't want to wait to tell her until I'd fallen farther down this slippery slope called love, for fear of my heart being broken.

So one night, behind the project house, I told her about my sexuality, and to my relief Berit said it wasn't a problem. I figured that was one more way that Norwegians were more advanced than Americans. Much later she told me more about her thoughts at the time; having already experienced my passion, she assumed my attraction to men was something I "would grow out of."

And so, as our summer AFSC project in Lynn was winding down, Berit agreed to join me in West Chester for Christmas vacation. Back at school, in September, I checked with the Arvios, who readily agreed to let her stay at their house at Christmastime.

Then Ray got a new job as youth work director at the Norristown YMCA and hired me as his assistant. That was a relief, since I'd been earning money as a dishwasher in West Chester's leading restaurant and was ready for a change. A big feature of the YMCA work was to plan and implement a summer camp. I easily persuaded Ray to hire Berit as a counselor for the 1958 camp season, assuring we'd be together until she returned to Norway at the end of the summer.

≈ ≈ ≈

It was Cynthia Arvio who suggested that I go to what would be my first protest: a demonstration against the testing of nuclear bombs in the atmosphere. I was still more excited about discussions about philosophy, and stories from the actions of others, than doing an action myself. How would I behave if we were physically attacked? I was scared of being hurt, and also of not knowing how to respond—nonviolently, sure, but what were the specifics of that?

"Go back to Russia!" someone yelled, among the other catcalls and boos from passing drivers as two dozen of us walked in our circular picket line. It was 1958. Senator Joseph McCarthy was dead, but anti-Communist crusaders continued their effort to take back reforms of the 1930s and '40s. We were picketing in front of the federal building in Philadelphia to support four remarkably brave men who were in jail in Honolulu.

They'd been arrested while sailing the Pacific Ocean on their way to the nuclear testing zone over the Marshall Islands. Their ship was called the *Golden Rule*, and they were protesting the nuclear arms race—specifically atmospheric nuclear testing, which was spreading cancer-producing strontium 90.*

I held a sign and walked behind a woman named Lillian Wil-

---

* Nicole Vanchieri, "The Golden Rule and Phoenix voyages in Protest of U.S. Nuclear Testing in the Marshall Islands, 1958," Global Nonviolent Action Database, February 19, 2011, https://nvdatabase.swarthmore.edu/content/golden-rule-and-phoenix-voyages-protest-us-nuclear-testing-marshall-islands-1958. This remarkable adventure was also described by the crew's captain, Albert Bigelow, in *The Voyage of the Golden Rule* (Garden City, NJ: Doubleday and Company, 1959), made an e-book by Pickle Partners Publishing in 2018, https://www.pp-publishing.com.

loughby, who said her husband, George, was on the sailing ship's crew. I was alarmed by the angry shouts coming from the passing cars. I didn't see any police there to protect us. The others in the picket line didn't look worried, but I wanted reassurance—so I asked if we should be worried.

To my surprise, she chuckled. "Well, you wouldn't want them to ignore us, would you?"

That was the first of many mind-expanding remarks I would hear from Lillian in the decades to follow. When George Willoughby came back from the *Golden Rule* protest, I quickly latched onto him as well; he became my longest-running mentor, paying all-around attention to my development as a leader, family man, and thinker. A decade later, George Willoughby and I would become coleaders for many projects and campaigns.

Meanwhile, Lillian's salty wisdom frequently ran ahead of me. It would take me years of social-movement research to fully grasp the value of strategic polarization in nonviolent campaigns, but Lillian knew it intuitively. It matched her vocation as a culinary expert: If we're unwilling to make the water boil, we'll have trouble cooking the food! On that day in spring 1958, I was grateful she was there, and also proud of myself for going to my first demonstration and gaining the feel of it. I soon realized that the first time for anything might include the jitters, which came along with stretching myself. And how would I find life interesting if it didn't include stretching?

That demonstration in solidarity with George and his crewmates on the *Golden Rule* was my introduction to the third successful large-scale direct action campaign that I knew of in that period, after the steelworkers' strike in 1952 and the Montgomery bus boycott in 1955. All three campaigns used nonviolent tactics of disruption and noncooperation in order to achieve their victories. I counted myself lucky, when barely twenty years old, to participate in the campaign for an atmospheric nuclear test ban treaty, a momentous victory that was won in 1963.

Over a decade later, the voyage of the *Golden Rule* inspired a group of Canadians to launch, after consultation with AFSC activist Larry Scott, a voyage from British Columbia to Amchitka Island in Alaska to protest US nuclear testing there. They called their ship *Greenpeace*, and went on to grow their initiative into the organization famous for global direct action campaigning on behalf of environmental justice.*

Few people knew at the time—or know even now—the architect of the strategic thinking that won the atmospheric nuclear test ban treaty. Lawrence C. Scott was a southern preacher who became a pacifist, discovered Quakers, and became peace education secretary for the American Friends Service Committee in Chicago; I'd been reading articles of his in pacifist magazines. But the Willoughbys just called him Larry Scott, and so did I once I met him.

Built powerfully, Larry had, I noticed, the stance of a leader who was always ready to take concepts and put them into action that added up to something. As it turned out, I would be fortunate to hear him think out loud about strategy for decades to come, including while organizing high-risk actions against the Vietnam War. He viewed the existing effort to stop the nuclear arms race—the "Ban the Bomb" campaign—as an exercise in futility, because nuclear deterrence had become the cornerstone of the Great Power national security system. However, if *part* of that system was vulnerable and could successfully be attacked, the win might start to build a platform for taming the arms race and more. Larry had learned that the radiation unleashed by nuclear testing in the atmosphere, strontium 90, fell to the earth and was carried by grass into the stomachs of cows, turned up in milk, and

---

* Max Rennebohm, "Canadians Campaign Against Nuclear Testing on Amchitka Island (Don't Make a Wave), 1969–1971," Global Nonviolent Action Database, December 6, 2009, https://nvdatabase.swarthmore.edu/index.php/content/canadians-campaign-against-nucle-ar-testing-amchitka-island-don-t-make-wave-1969-1971.

from there increased the risk of cancer in babies. What government could justify inducing cancer in babies?

Larry argued the case for this achievable-goal campaign in national liberal and peace-inclined circles and was able to generate a national meeting of leaders to consider it. They agreed to a campaign and in that meeting, pushed by Larry, agreed to setting up two different campaigning groups: one for liberals and one for radicals. The liberals would do educational work and lobby. The radicals would use nonviolent direct action—like that of Lillian Willoughby, who committed civil disobedience at a Nevada nuclear testing center and later was again arrested for sitting in at the United States Atomic Energy Commission headquarters in Washington, DC.

In another brilliant move at the national strategy meeting, Larry won agreement that groups with different approaches wouldn't attack each other. Instead, each would focus on their own outreach to maximize the numbers of people working in the national "division of labor." This 1956 meeting was key to the rapid winning of the campaign in 1963 and, through that victory, placed the question of arms control and disarmament squarely on the table.

Larry, I later came to understand, believed that each social movement has its own ecology, composed of different segments of the population. The different parts might be based on social groupings (women, youths, seniors) or economic classes (businesspeople, workers, farmers) or shared experience (veterans, medical workers), or activity preference (lobbying, education, direct action), or something else. Thoughtful organizers can research an emerging movement's ecology, notice what's missing, and add the missing parts to build and strengthen the movement's power.

That first experience for this young activist—participating in a campaign with a carefully thought through strategy—led me to expect, and later ask for, carefully thought through strategies behind actions. I was disappointed to find an alarming number of leaders willing to skip the strategy part of leadership.

5

I'm more activist than my college can handle

Thanks to reading Emerson and Thoreau—as well as the practice I gained by defying my father's wishes— by the time I came to college, I had already developed a strongly individualist stance. A decade and a half later, I'd shift to a deeper appreciation of community, but I remember vividly that moment at age eighteen when, sitting in an easy chair in the college library's reading room, I was thrilled to read Henrik Ibsen's final words in his play *An Enemy of the People*: "The strongest man in the world is he who stands most alone."

As a columnist in West Chester University's student newspaper, *The Quadrangle*, I was the only one who wrote about contemporary social and political issues. My individualism was anarchistic rather than conservative, since my class background gave me every reason to be on the left. A classmate and I, in our last year in high school, had coauthored a major paper that challenged the conventional view of history we were being taught. We did our own research and described the story of the United States as a long succession of progressive and radical social movements, with Blacks, abolitionists, women, farmers, and workers struggling for justice. This was two decades before the publication of Howard Zinn's *A People's History of the United States*, but my friend and I didn't find it all that hard to dig out the truth.

Now, in our college student newspaper, I voiced views that of course were out of step with mainstream thinking. The newspaper's faculty advisor, who was my favorite English professor, began to warn me to watch my step. When I failed to flavor all my columns plain vanilla, the faculty advisor added more pressure: I would now have to run each draft by him. I refused, and resigned from the staff.

Then Dottie and Art Klinger, our "house parents," told me that after protests in Philadelphia made the newspapers, they started to receive visits from the office of the dean of men at West Chester, asking if I had gone to the city to participate. Eventually, the college president, Charles S. Swope, called me into his office. He ran such a dictatorial shop at West Chester that the American Association of University Professors had put West Chester on its list of institutions where its members should not teach as long as he was president.

Dr. Swope, given his reputation, tried an unexpected move. "George," he said with a smile, "I suggest you transfer to Swarthmore College. It's nearby, and a place where students have all this freedom you seem to want."

I allowed my anger to show. "I love this college," I said. "I'm learning a lot, and my friends are here. I don't want to go to Swarthmore." I got up and left his office.

I omitted an additional consideration: there was no way I'd be able to afford Swarthmore.

My life continued to be busy and fulfilling. I directed a play in the round, my first time with that format. Although I didn't see it at the time, the choice of material was significant: *Hello Out There!*, William Saroyan's one-act play, centered on a man in jail.

One day, as I passed the office of the dean of men, Associate Dean Jim Bonder stepped out and pulled me aside. He was as tall as I was and even more muscled than the football players he coached. Putting his nose about an inch from mine, he said, "Lakey, do you know I disagree with everything you believe in?"

The nerd within me responded. "Well, Dean Bonder, I don't see how that could possibly be true."

With a sneer, he wheeled around and went back into the office.

≈ ≈ ≈

My graduating class voted that I should take the paid position of editor in chief of our yearbook. I steeled myself for what might come next. The faculty advisor for the yearbook asked to see me. "I expect you realize that all your work will need to be reviewed for my approval."

In defiance, I wrote an open letter of resignation to the college administration, copying to student-body presidents of colleges up and down the eastern seaboard.

In those days, I resisted strategic thinking, despite the examples of the civil rights movement and Larry Scott. Each of my moves was an act of integrity born of my rebel spirit, influenced by the transcendentalists and the Quaker history of nonconformity. Opened by my subversive sexuality (although I remained in the closet), I also welcomed the pulse of the Beat generation. One night I read Allen Ginsberg's "Howl" out loud to Cynthia Arvio; Ginsberg's rhythms and transgressive content left both of us transported.*

Although my activism was supported by the off-campus activists who were befriending me, my own consciousness remained highly individualistic. I didn't see fully how even rebels are influenced by larger forces moving in society. And as the summer of 1958 arrived, I definitely didn't want to obsess about "big picture" questions, because Berit was on her way to spend her summer with me.

In my explorations of Philadelphia, I'd gotten to know a number of gay men whose loneliness was only partially stemmed

---

* Allen Ginsberg, *Howl and Other Poems* (San Francisco: City Lights, 1956).

by their participation in the gay world. My positive experience of family—first as I grew up and then when I "adopted" the Arvios—anchored the idea of family within my vision of my future life. I didn't find its equivalent in my explorations of the Philly gay world, even though I loved the excitement, the acceptance of sexual expression, and the freedom from hypocrisy I found there. Family mattered to me, and given the pervasiveness of homophobia, I also had trouble visualizing my life mission being carried out from a base in the gay community. And my mission was central to my identity.

I was grateful to be young, figuring I had a lot of time to work all this out. Berit was coming to be a counselor at the Norristown YMCA camp, delighted to have her BA in sociology and ready to do something besides study. We intended to have a great time extending our "summer romance" until she returned to her home across the Atlantic. Then maybe, in my last year at West Chester, I'd find some creative solution for how to make my complicated sexuality line up with my complicated mission in a society that at that time gave scant support either to sex *or* a mission for justice and peace.

There was no way I could imagine at the time that the 1960s would bring sufficient change so that my comrades and I could begin to taste sexual liberation and equality—nor that we could, in the seventies, create an intentional community that provided a container for both family and mission.

א א א

Ray Arvio loved innovation as much as I did, and that year he planned a radically different program for the YMCA campers than the institution was used to. Before Berit arrived, I'd moved with the Arvios to the camp's location, next to the Perkiomen Creek in the beautiful Pennsylvania Dutch countryside near Schwenksville. Cynthia would be head cook, and I would work with Ray on the program. We unpacked the camp, assisted by some student friends from my previous summer in Lynn, who would work alongside veteran local YMCA counselors when the camp opened.

Once Berit showed up, it took some effort for Ray to pry us apart, but we got into the swing of things. The first part of the summer would be devoted to a day camp, then the overnight camping would start. I was fine with the day camp part because Berit and I, after hanging out with friends for a bit in the evening, would have time for ourselves. The overnight camping didn't sound so attractive.

The hours with Berit deepened as we shared more and more fully in quiet walks along the stream. By midsummer I was sure I wanted us to join our lives together. This cosmopolitan Norwegian who'd traveled to France by herself when she was twelve, then won an international essay contest in high school that took her to Britain and then the United States, was fundamentally as down-to-earth as I was. She could sweat through a second summer of American heat, in a camp with American children prone to misbehavior, and still have leftover energy to play with me at night.

By midsummer I asked her if she would like us to live together in the future.

"My parents couldn't handle our living together without marrying," she said.

In those days, the next move was mine to make. I was leery of marriage; Margaret Mead was again influential here, linking monogamy with a power institution called the patriarchy. I was not at peace with that. Still, I wanted to be with Berit.

I asked her to marry, and she agreed. Our memories diverge at this point: she remembers a shared understanding of marriage as monogamous, while I remember agreeing to marry as being the price of our living together but leaving the question of monogamy open. As it turned out, I was monogamous in practice for a dozen years, because I found that building a strong relationship between two people with plenty of differences was enough of a stretch for me. The question of polyamory didn't arise strongly for us until the 1970s, when we lived in an intentional community where that was a live issue, both philosophically and practically. It was only then that we agreed to open our marriage.

Back in 1958, however, we had more urgent matters to think about. At the end of that summer, Berit was scheduled to return to Norway; the terms of her Fulbright scholarship required that she remain in her country for two years before applying for a new US visa. I still had the 1958–59 year of college to complete at West Chester. We agreed that I would come to Norway in the summer of 1959, after I graduated, and we would marry in her hometown, Skien.

After camp, we still had time to go to Bangor and hang out with my family. They were delighted about our getting married, although sad the cost of travel meant they couldn't be present for the ceremony. My parents appeared confident that Berit and I would settle in the United States, even if not in Bangor; they saw Berit as more grounded than me and therefore good for me. I was, after all, their "wild one"—many families had one—and, having fled the coop, I might now roost somewhere safe.

Gary offered to drive Berit and me to New York, where she would depart on the Norwegian ship *Bergensfjord*; he and his partner, Ben, would treat us to a good time in the Big Apple before departure. The fun included our riding in the back seat of Ben's convertible on a balmy night amid the bright lights of Manhattan. We needed all the bright lights we could get, considering it would be ten and a half months until we saw each other again.

After our last hug, Berit disappeared up the gangplank, then reappeared on deck. She and the other passengers were given rolls of ribbon crepe; holding one end, they threw their ribbon to whoever they were saying goodbye to. I held my end tight as the

Bergensfjørd pulled slowly away from the pier. While Berit and I looked at each other our ribbon tightened, then broke. Gary held me tight as the ship disappeared from view.

6

the only white student in the dorms of a Black college

My standing up for student power at West Chester by defying censorship at the newspaper and yearbook was in tune with an openly rebellious trend emerging among Black people in the late fifties. Without knowing it, I was beginning to dance with history. In 1957, Black citizens in Tallahassee, Florida, organized and repeated the success of the 1955 Montgomery bus boycott. In 1958, young Black people in Durham, North Carolina, held sit-ins to integrate an ice cream parlor, and in Kansas City, Missouri, the target was a restaurant in a department store.*

Started by pacifists in the 1940s to experiment with nonviolent direct action, the Congress of Racial Equality (CORE) had successfully integrated some of the segregated restaurants and lunch counters in the northern United States. Now, CORE was increasing its reach into the South, leading nonviolence-training workshops and introducing the sit-in technique to southern students in historically Black colleges. The culmination of each nonviolent workshop was usually to do a sit-in at a local lunch counter.**

---

* Information on these campaigns and more can be found on Swarthmore College's Global Nonviolent Action Database, https://nvdatabase.swarthmore.edu/.
** Short descriptions of these civil rights campaigns, and more than a hundred others, are in the Global Nonviolent Action Database, https://nvdatabase.swarthmore.edu.

Cynthia and Ray knew and hugely admired one of the founders of CORE, Bayard Rustin, who they'd met through their membership in the War Resisters League. Rustin actually got his start in West Chester, where he grew up and shocked everyone when, as a high school student, he sat on the main floor of the local movie theater, where "only white people may sit." In 1955, Rustin helped the young Martin Luther King Jr. strategize during the Montgomery bus boycott, and he remained a key advisor for the rest of King's life. The Arvios urged me to meet the charismatic Rustin.* As movement insiders, they knew that Rustin was gay, but they didn't know about my gay experience so assumed I was straight and probably naive. Protectively, Ray took me aside and explained that, if at some point Bayard invited me to have sex with him, I could say no without jeopardizing the chance of our working together.

As it happened, I didn't get to work with Bayard until the sixties, though in spring 1959, I did join twenty-six thousand other young people in the youth protest Bayard organized in Washington, DC. After standing out as a rebel at West Chester, it was a relief to me simply to act with so many other students. The demonstration was part of a series of 1950s youth marches in DC that Bayard organized, which he made use of as test runs for the historic 1963 March on Washington.

After saying goodbye to Berit, I thought everything seemed set for my senior year at West Chester. I couldn't have been more wrong. While Berit and I were at the YMCA camp, Gary had become romantically partnered with Ben, a Philly physician who was moving into a small townhouse in the Gayborhood and had furniture he needed to store. They cooked up an idea: Gary, Bill, and I could move out of Klinger Hall in August and share a nice apartment in the College Arms, the large private apartment house

---

* An outstanding biography of Bayard Rustin is John D'Emilio, *Lost Prophet: The Life and Times of Bayard Rustin* (Chicago: University of Chicago Press, 2004).

across from campus. Ben would subsidize our rent, and we could use his furniture, including his baby grand piano: a win-win.

Bill and I agreed, enabling Gary to show off his skills as an interior decorator, which would later become his career. After moving in over Labor Day weekend, and still smiling with satisfaction, we arrived in line for registration for our senior year.

The deans, who'd clearly decided we were troublemakers and feared our gaining a more independent living situation, pulled each of us out of line, "You have a choice," they said. "Either move into the men's dorm where the dean of men has his apartment and can keep his eye on you, or you can't register."

Bill decided to knuckle under, but to Gary and me, it was an intolerable demand. We said no, but now had to figure out how we would finish school.

Six miles away from West Chester, on the commuter railroad line to Philly, was Cheyney State Teachers College. Now called Cheyney University of Pennsylvania, it is the oldest historically Black college in the United States, founded by Quakers with the aim of training Black people in the North to go South and teach formerly enslaved Black people. Cheyney later joined the fourteen-college system to which West Chester belonged.

"Let's check it out," Gary said. "Cheyney might accept our credits, so we could live in our beautiful apartment, commute on the train from West Chester, and graduate."

I didn't see my transferring to Cheyney as itself an action against racism; we were simply trying to finish school. But I did realize that Cheyney was another chance to experience the larger world. I knew I was ignorant, and was filled with curiosity. I was somewhat nervous that I might be held at a distance by the other students. Because I was used to being a contributor wherever I went, I hoped I'd find a way to be active in campus life. Yes, I would be different from others at Cheyney, but in my life it felt like I was always different, and I accepted that.

As we strolled through the campus, we saw only Black people, which is what we expected. We found the dean's office, and Dr. McKinley Mencken was soon free to see us. He was a short, stocky Black man with round horn-rimmed glasses. Gary and I felt awkward and embarrassed about our abrupt departure from West Chester, but Dr. Mencken set us at ease. His broad smile reassured us. He saw no problem: we should register today and start classes tomorrow. (One reason for Dr. Mencken's friendliness, I realized later, might have been that the state was starting to pressure all of its colleges to integrate. West Chester had only a handful of Black students. Cheyney had a few white day students.)

The downside for me was that Cheyney didn't yet offer a major in secondary education, which had been my major at West Chester. Gary was already majoring in elementary education, but I'd need to switch to elementary ed, which would add a semester's work.

I didn't hesitate. I'd just made a plan to move to Norway, and with my sense of possibility expanding like crazy, I was no longer so sure I wanted to teach high school anyway. Get a degree, I told myself—that could be useful no matter what I'd end up doing.

A few weeks later, I had even more reason to be glad for Dr. Mencken's openness. At dinner in our apartment, Gary told me that he wanted to make another change. His face was even more animated than usual. Gary's growing dream was to become an interior decorator, and Ben had just offered to finance his education at Parsons School of Design in New York City, starting immediately.

"I'm sorry it means giving up the apartment, George," Gary said with feeling. "I know you can't maintain it by yourself, and Ben can't support me and you both! But I'll bet the dean would be glad to have you on campus."

Sad as I was about the abrupt change in plans, I knew Gary was probably right. Dr. Mencken agreed to a scholarship—there were no campus jobs left to subsidize my boarding costs—and Gary helped me move into Burleigh Hall, the men's dorm on the quadrangle, where I'd be the only white student living on campus.

I'd been brought up in a town where no Black people lived inside the borough limits; the few Black families lived outside town on a dirt road. Turf was then and is now such a big deal in our racist system, and now I'd be on Black people's turf. Might the other students resent this white guy invading their comfort zone? I noticed that I felt uneasy, even though I didn't understand then that the freedom of my own movement was partly a product of my white privilege; the rules of white supremacy are such that that whites can take ourselves wherever we choose, and Blacks cannot.

I said goodbye to Gary and left my bags in the Burleigh Hall lounge while I went to the office that gave out room keys. When I returned, my bags were lying open on the floor; they'd been gone through. A few students sat in the lounge openly waiting for my reaction. Startled, I blushed with embarrassment and humiliation and stared back at them.

"Who did this?" I demanded.

They shrugged their shoulders.

I couldn't think of anything to say that would do any good, so I gathered my things and retreated to my room. Was trying to live in the dorm going too far?

≈ ≈ ≈

Things gradually got easier. When I checked out the student coffee shop, two students quickly introduced themselves. At first sight, Earl Wilkie and Marybelle Moore were a pair of opposites: Marybelle was short and young, while Wilkie was tall and older, a veteran coming back to school on the GI Bill. They were both fun-loving and artistic, Marybelle a poet and Wilkie a sculptor. They introduced me to their friends, and I began to relax.

The next several weeks sped by as I caught up with my home-work, signed up for activities, and hung out with my new friends. The college choir lost its accompanist, who needed to take a full-time job to stay in school (a lot of students at Cheyney had full-time jobs, I learned), and so I took on the role. Our director, D. Jack Moses, was inspiring; he taught us to perform from our hearts, whether we interpreted the classics, jazz, or spirituals.

As much as I loved the music making, the chance for me to contribute also helped me to accept the dynamics around me as the college's only dorm-based white student. I realized some students would probably always resent my presence because I was an everyday reminder of white privilege in their midst. And who knows what unconscious behaviors of mine were what we today call microaggressions? Yet some students seemed genuinely glad I was there. And in the middle were those who reserved judgment—and I could see the sense in that. In fact, feeling the weight of that middle group kept me more cautious, less provocative than I had been at West Chester. I was all the more grateful to Marybelle and Earl and their circle that took me in.

Decades later, I occasionally asked myself why I didn't stay in touch with my Cheyney friends. Then it occurred to me that I didn't stay in touch with the friends I made at West Chester, either, even though those relationships had been longer and more intense. And then I asked why I didn't stay in touch with my grad school buddies, and colleagues at schools where I'd taught, and the organizers I'd worked with most closely in the intensity of various campaigns. In each set of relationships there was plenty of comradeship—and, yes, love. So what happened?

When I contrast myself with my daughter Ingrid — who amazes me with the continuity she maintains with friends and comrades she's been close to in different phases of her life—I realize that this might be one of the differences between introverts and extroverts. Ingrid is highly extroverted. By contrast, I went to the fifty-year reunion of my Cheyney graduating class, where of course the con-versations were frequently trips down memory lane, and at dinner one of my classmates looked across the table at me and said, "And then there was George, who somehow seemed very present, but at the same time very self-contained." That, plus how I stimulate myself by continually embarking on "my next new thing," seems to leave scant energy for reconnecting with companions who were important to me in the new things of yesterday.

≈ ≈ ≈

As I settled in, I found myself loving how integrated Cheyney was—not racially, but in the easy flow between heart and head, experiment and tradition, the cosmopolitan and the rowhouse world of Black Philadelphia. Despite majoring in education, Earl Wilkie was frequently seen carrying a sketch pad and could simultaneously draw a vase and speculate about what Freud might think of his drawing. In the circle that included him and Mary-belle, I would be drawn into a discussion of French existentialism one minute and then, in the next, I'd find myself laughing at an uproarious send-up of a Black preacher. Cheyney was all that.

My off-campus life was as full as ever: I was writing a daily letter to Berit, preparing to leave for Norway in June to get married, convincing my mother's dad to loan me the money for passage, attending Quaker Meeting in West Chester, and going to nuclear disarmament demonstrations with the United Pacifists of West Chester and Vicinity. At Cheyney I shared information about the protests I attended, and while the campus wasn't full of activists, the environment supported taking a public stand for justice and peace.

The culture of Cheyney was spacious compared with what I was used to at West Chester. Two of the men on my floor in the dorm were openly romantic partners and could be seen cuddling affectionately in the student coffee shop with no eyebrows raised around them. After three years of fighting at West Chester to broaden its culture, I loved being able to relax into a setting where people defined community more broadly.

One day, the waitress in the student coffee shop asked what flavor milkshake I wanted.

"Vanilla," I said.

"Of course," said Marybelle in her best teasing drawl.

Several students standing close enough to overhear giggled good-naturedly. *Wow!* I thought. *Now we're making friendly jokes about our difference.*

Marybelle, first in her class in Philadelphia's elite Girls High School, had turned down an Ivy League scholarship to come to Cheyney. She told me she was tired of tokenism.

"Maybe I'm a token now," I said, smiling.

"Maybe so," she said. "If so, you're the privileged kind."

I nodded. I was beginning to get a clue.

****

Over the sound of the rhythm and blues playing in the shop, I heard my name called. It was Vivian, my friend and fellow student at Cheyney. "Hey George, next Tuesday is when I come to your music club, right?"

I nodded in agreement. Vivian was a soloist in the college choir; she had a delicious soprano voice and a generous disposition. She had readily agreed to sing for the weekly music club I led at a boarding school for African American orphans across the road from the campus.

"Let's practice tomorrow before supper," Vivian said. "I've decided what I want to sing: "One Fine Day," from *Madama Butterfly*."

"But Vivian, it's so tragic!" I said. "Why bring such a sad song?"

"Tragedy is something they know a lot about," Vivian explained. "I'll sing it in Italian, but they'll get it."

The children sat mostly on the floor, in circles around the piano and Vivian. Some were leaning back on each other. A few were ready with paper and crayons, because earlier I had told them to listen to music with their fingers when they wanted to. In a few brief strokes, Vivian sketched the storyline of the opera for the children, and let the music do the rest.

I watched as her voice reached their hearts. By the end, all the faces in the room were wet with tears, including Vivian's eyes. A holy silence followed briefly, then a chorus of voices asking questions about love, and death, and leaving family to live with others. I've never seen Puccini mean more.

7

starting a new family in a social democracy

Berit and her dad, Johannes, met my ship at the dock in Oslo in June 1959. Sixty years later, my body still remembers our hug on the pier—ten and a half months was a long time to wait! Johannes's smile was genuine, and I was immediately grateful that Esther wasn't there; one thing at a time, I thought.

Before leaving Oslo, we drove to the palace where Berit's oldest brother, Einar, worked as part of the military guard. He was also cordial, and funny. I began to relax. *Maybe I do have a chance with this family.*

The winding drive to Berit's hometown of Skien took three hours, past farms and forest. Her dad wisely suggested that I might enjoy sitting in the back seat with Berit, so we cuddled while she caught me up on the wedding arrangements and pointed out some of the sights. "See that rock formation over there?" she pointed. "Look at the top, on the left. Could it be a big ugly face?"

I allowed that it could.

"It's a troll," she said.

"What?"

"You see," she said, smiling and speaking more quickly, "trolls like to wander around at night, but if they are caught above ground when the first rays of sunshine hit them, they are frozen into rock." She assumed a solemn tone. "In Norway, this is a well-known fact."

She turned to the front seat and, in Norwegian, told her dad what she'd said.

I heard a chuckle from the front seat. "First day off the boat and you're already filling him with our superstitious silliness," her dad said.

After Berit translated, I laughed with appreciation. "I want to hear it all," I said. "In my country, we have plenty of myths; it's refreshing to hear some new ones."

We entered Skien by the road that ran along the fjord, and so I saw the older part of town first: docks, fishing wharves, factories, stores, and then the open-air market. At the head of the market stood a large brick church with two tall towers: the Lutheran church where we were to be married in five days.

My stomach lurched. *Is it really a good idea to get married so far from my home?*

We were already pulling up to the Mathiesens' house; the family lived only a few blocks from the church. There, in the doorway, stood a serious-looking Norwegian mother. Taking a deep breath, I eased myself from the car and walked across the gravel driveway toward her. Berit said, unnecessarily, "Mamma, dette er George."

Suddenly, Fru Mathiesen smiled and threw open her arms. She hugged me hard, as if she really meant it. I asked Berit later about that, and her eyes misted—the stakes were high for her, too. "Mamma told me," she said, "that when she saw you get out of the car, her first thought was how far you were away from your mother, and her heart melted." As I got to know Esther Mathiesen, though, it would turn out we had much more in common than that. If the Enneagram personality chart had a consciousness, it would surely have been smiling, mother-in-law the same type as son-in-law: living in the heart, fond of drama, drawn toward the sad and tragic sides of life, and also cherishing celebration and exaltation. In short, two romantics.

The next five days sped by: introductions to key relatives, a visit to the priest to be inspected and briefed, a fitting for the rental of white tie and tails, and endless cups of strong coffee with pastries I'd never seen before and a strange kind of goat cheese that was brown and sweet. I soon realized that learning Norwegian was my big priority; Berit's family members knew almost no English, and her patience for translation was ebbing fast. My first attempts at words got uproarious responses, because my accent was wretched. It took me weeks to realize that Norwegian was half sung as it was spoken—the intonation was that important.

On my Morning of the Big Day, the classic feelings washed through me: unreadiness, uncertainty, homesickness, a sense of entrapment, and generalized, nameless terror. Einar led me to the church, where I saw two empty chairs sitting in front of the altar, waiting for me and my proxy best man, Soren. Already some townspeople had arrived, a half hour before the service. Soren spoke English and assured me that I shouldn't take it personally that I would be displayed for the entire time before Berit and her dad arrived; yes, the townspeople were full of curiosity about the man she'd picked up while studying in the United States. Berit's singing and poetry reading were favorites in her hometown, so naturally they would turn out. Moreover, he said, the display of the bridegroom was an old custom.

We took our places, and I stilled my trembling knees, realizing I was being scrutinized carefully. Fortunately, I'd asked the organist to play Bach for the entire half hour, and it grounded me quite a bit.

Berit took my breath away, my gorgeous bride in her long white gown coming into the church with her dad. My doubts and fears fell away as she walked down the aisle with measured stride; I expanded in the pageantry of love. The service was in Norwegian, but the priest asked the big question in English so there could be no mistake. I'd read a translation of his sermon ahead of time and sat there listening with a happy buzz, stealing little glances at this woman I would now be family with.

The wedding party afterward was notable for the number of people I didn't know, the variety of foods I tasted for the first time, the number of conversations I didn't understand, the warmth and openness the guests directed toward this stranger who'd married into their land, the countless times I got to touch Berit in one way or another, and the chair that collapsed under the weight of a relative who ate too much.

In life, the great moments of commitment invite some wonderment at all that we didn't—and couldn't—know at the time. I knew my parents were delighted with Berit and sorry they couldn't afford to come and share the joy of the day, but I didn't know whether Gary and I would stay close given that my marriage to a woman made it much less likely I'd be involved in the gay community he'd become part of. I knew Berit's family welcomed me, but I didn't know if they would like me once I could speak Norwegian and argue with them. I knew I was ready for the adventure of a new culture, but I didn't know if I'd want to become a Norwegian. I knew I loved Berit profoundly but, since I didn't believe that love is eternal, I didn't know if I would love her forever.

I suppose that's the point of commitment: it creates the container for risk when there's so much we *don't* know. If we waited until we knew everything, we'd miss life entirely; without risk, life is going through the motions.

And so, at age twenty-one, I risked, starting a journey that fundamentally shaped the rest of my life. Sixty years later, I'm a bit surprised that I acted so decisively. Who *was* that young man?

Before coming to Norway, I'd heard tantalizing bits from Berit about how they did things in her country. Some of it reminded me of my eleventh-grade social studies teacher, who was enthusiastic about early US socialist and populist movements. "That's where President Franklin Roosevelt got some of his best ideas," he told us. "Norman Thomas kept running for president for the Socialist Party—he ran six times! When Roosevelt got elected, he implemented some of Norman Thomas's programs."

When I was a sophomore at West Chester, I heard about a public meeting on democratic socialism in Philly and took the train in to satisfy my curiosity. Founded in 1885 to nurture religious humanism and contribute to progressive causes, the Philadelphia Ethical Society, on Rittenhouse Square, was famous for its openness to the margins; like my social studies teacher, its leadership seemed to think, that good ideas often originate outside the mainstream.

The audience for the meeting was scanty; I was the only young person there. A panel of four sober-looking white men in their forties sat behind a table on the stage. They each took a turn making some points, most of which were highly abstract. I noticed frequent references to European history and European "theoreticians." After the prepared mini-lectures, the four jumped into a competitive round in which each tried to sound smarter than the others; I could tell that was what they were doing even though I had no idea which, if any, was winning. Finally, the moderator asked for questions from the floor, but apparently the rest of the audience was as bored as I was.

I left that day convinced that socialism was a doctrine for professional middle-class intellectuals but not for a working-class boy like me. Later I realized that's a little like concluding feminism is a philosophy for men, not women.

It wasn't the panelists' arguing that put me off; I was brought up in a family of passionate arguers. The difference in my family was that we'd been taught to listen to others' arguments to see if we could learn something and find common ground. It would be many years before I went to another meeting on socialism in the United States.

But now I was in Norway, where Prime Minister Einar Gerhardsen had, as a young man, been a manual worker in the streets department in Oslo. His democratic socialists were in leadership, rebuilding their society from the capitalist land of poverty from which farmers and working-class Norwegians had fled to America. Berit's stories of the devastation left by Nazi German occupation were also vivid and educational; she gave me a tour of Skien as I had given her one of Bangor. Norwegian socialists had had to recover not only from the predations of the owning class but also from the impact of the war.

The car that met me at the dock in Oslo was Johannes's pride and joy. He'd just gotten it after years of seeking permission from the government to buy a replacement for his old jalopy—in 1959, the country still had rationing! He was able to get a new station wagon because he needed it for his gardening and flower shop business.

I asked him once why the rationing went on such a long time. He told me that the national priority was lifting people out of the worst poverty; recently the Oslo slums had finally been cleared and replaced by good, affordable housing. He and Mama were both from working-class backgrounds and agreed with the government's priorities. At same time, they were also proud that they'd been able to work and save their way into middle-class ownership of a thriving flower business. Berit filled me in on what that had meant for them, and how the degree of risk was lessened by the assurance of health care, quality education for their children, and a secure pension waiting for their old age.

I thought about my wealthy country, able to end quickly the rationing I remembered from my boyhood during World War II. Despite being the richest country in the world, my country still had horrendous slums and did little to lessen anyone's risks except those taken by the wealthy.

Just that one comparison—tackling poverty in universal terms—spoke volumes about the priorities of democratic socialists and capitalists. Still, I wanted to test what I was told. One weekend, while we were visiting Berit's family in Skien, I borrowed a bike and cycled around that industrial town, looking at the housing. It took nearly all day, but I finally found it: *one house* that looked to be substandard!

After the wedding, Berit and I moved to Oslo, to an apartment house near the University of Oslo's summer school, which was for foreigners planning to study in Norway. I quickly enrolled, which meant I received intensive Norwegian language learning, as well as background on the country's history and major features. Minister of Health Karl Evang gave a lecture that described the universal health care system paid for by taxes so there would be no financial barrier to anyone receiving care. During a question-and-answer period, one of the students asked how Norway's high degree of economic equality came about. Evang said a variety of policies can combine to bring that result, but the art is doing it in a way that increases democracy and individual freedom. This, he said, they had done.

I was impressed, but still it would be many years before I could call myself a socialist. My political comfort zone was "liberal," and I, with working-class practicality, was worried in those days about being labelled pejoratively as a visionary. Yet the more I learned about Norway's "combination of policies," and variations on them among the Scandinavian countries, the more I realized that it was possible to be both a visionary and practical.

For example, in September, on matriculation day at the university, I stood in line, chatting with a Norwegian student next to me. I put down my fee of a hundred Norwegian kroner (about fourteen American dollars, then) and double-checked to see if I had really paid in full. "How," I asked, "can free university make sense in this modern world?"

"Look," the Norwegian student replied, "wouldn't you say that brains are an economic resource to a country?"

"Well, yes, of course," I responded.

"Then," he continued, "why wouldn't you want to develop your resources fully instead of letting a barrier like money get in the way?"

My excitement about this and similar revelations led me to my choose in my own mind an identity as a "practical visionary." Philosophical and moral conceptual development without practice left me cold, but practice without theory invited muddling along without larger impact. The academic field that seemed to center most of my preoccupations, including conflict, culture, race, and class, was sociology; that field even shared with psychology the task of researching the dynamics of organizations and small groups. If I were to become a college teacher instead of teaching high school, sociology struck me as a good subject match. As it turned out, studying sociology at the University of Oslo gave me valuable tools and led eventually to my 2016 book on how the Nordic economic model benefits the people there—and could benefit my people, too.*

Because I wanted to gain a good grasp on the field before returning to the United States to finish my degree at Cheyney, I realized I'd better get cracking. With any luck, I'd be able to pass the foundational exams in sociology within the year I had. Attendance at lectures and seminars was optional, and since my Norwegian was not yet fluent, I decided to skip most of those and focus on reading the dozens of books in English on the required list. That turned into a great pleasure, because whenever I was particularly taken with an author, like George Caspar Homans, I could pursue other books and articles by that person. People were as important to me as ideas, so following the thought of an admired scholar was, to me, more satisfying than skipping from one large idea to another.

---

* George Lakey, *Viking Economics: How the Scandinavians Got It Right and How We Can, Too* (Brooklyn: Melville House Publishing, 2016).

University students in Norway had a remarkable degree of freedom. Some did a periodic study blitz interrupted by ski vacations, and some got lost in the lack of structure. I followed the norm, which was a routine of studying from nine to five, Monday through Friday. That left evenings and weekends for Berit, including visiting her relatives, with whom I drank untold amounts of coffee.

We also made friends with some American Fulbrighters, who shared our worry that Norwegians believed all Americans were scared into idiocy by "the Communist menace." Yes, many were, we told the Norwegians we knew, but not *all*. US embassy staff were also picking up on the Norwegian scorn, so when we Americans asked the embassy to host a public reading of Arthur Miller's brilliant satire, *The Crucible*, we got a quick yes. I played John Proctor, a defiant man in colonial Salem refusing to go along with a witch hunt, and Berit played one of the young women accused of witchcraft. That was about the only political thing we did that year, except for marching against Norwegian participation in NATO.

I grew curious about what was happening at the university outside my circle. I heard there was a young mathematician attracted to sociology who was interested in peace research, so I looked him up. Johan Galtung, later to be acclaimed as the European founder of peace research, told me he needed volunteer researchers to help him do his first project. He wanted to do content analysis of statements made to the public by policymakers advocating foreign aid: Did they balance national interest with altruism? If they leaned one way or the other, what were the consequences in terms of results and public support? Galtung had already written a book describing his experience as a Norwegian pacifist imprisoned for refusing to accept alternative service for conscientious objectors.

I also heard about a young American who was based at the university's Institute of Philosophy, Gene Sharp. Meeting him turned out to be life-changing.* I found him dressed in American jeans in a cubbyhole of an office, speaking British-accented English. He'd gotten his sociology master's degree in his home state of Ohio, he told me, before refusing cooperation with Selective Service and serving time at a federal prison in Danbury, Connecticut. Gene served as secretary to a man described by *Time* magazine as "America's number one pacifist," A. J. Muste, then went to London to help edit the pacifist newspaper *Peace News*, which has been in print since 1936.

As a result of these activities, Gene had developed a growing sense of discontent with pacifists, which he attributed to insufficient attention to nonviolent alternatives that challenge what violence was expected to achieve. His emphasis on practical alternatives rang a bell with me, but what was new was his belief that research was a necessary condition for developing those alternatives.

I'd been so wowed by examples like the Quakers staying safe when they stuck with their peace testimony while living on the colonial frontier that I was prepared to rely on new victories coming out of edgy moral commitment. I'd read—and was thrilled by—a quote in one of A. J. Muste's essays: "Our political task is precisely, in Martin Buber's magnificent formulation, 'to drive the ploughshare of normative principle into the hard soil of political reality.'"**

Until I met Gene, I simply wanted to add a generous dose of creativity to Buber's advice, borrowing from the example of

---

* See my perspective on Gene's relation to politics, "Will the Real Gene Sharp Please Step Forward?" *Waging Nonviolence,* July 16, 2019, https://wagingnonviolence.org/2019/07/gene-sharp-cold-war-intellectual-marcie-smith/; see also my personal perspective on him as my mentor, "Gene Sharp—the Lonely Scholar Who Became a Nonviolent Warrior," *Waging Nonviolence,* February 1, 2018, https://wagingnonviolence.org/2018/02/gene-sharp-scholar-nonviolent-warrior/.

** Mike Davis cites this quote in his essay "The Year 1960," *New Left Review* 108 (Nov/Dec 2017), https://newleftreview.org/issues/ii108/articles/mike-davis-the-year-1960. I've been unable to find the original source.

technological invention. Without dismissing creativity, Gene said we urgently need to understand *how* nonviolent action delivers results. Someone wanting to invent a new kind of transportation has science on their side. When we create strategy for a nonviolent campaign, do we understand what we are actually working with?

Conventional thinking urges us to write off certain opponents as beyond the leverage of nonviolent struggle. Gene said he left his journalism job in London to research the Norwegian teachers' battle with the Nazi occupation of Norway during World War II. The teachers' nonviolent resistance prevented Nazification of Norwegian schools, despite Nazi dictator Vidkun Quisling having the backing of a German army as large as one soldier per ten Norwegians.* I was stunned; that's not supposed to be possible.

Gene got me. My curiosity, my working-class affection for practicality, and the tools I was getting at the university combined to make him my perfect sociological mentor. It didn't hurt that he was charming and had a delightful sense of humor. At the time, neither of us could know that he'd receive multiple nominations for the Nobel Peace Prize and worldwide acknowledgement as the founder of the new field of nonviolent studies—also called civil resistance.

In Oslo, Gene found it easy to convince me that when I entered grad school, my master's thesis should be on nonviolent struggle.** He continued to advise me on nonviolent research for decades, and after I moved on to other challenges we continued to be friends, each always eager to know what the other was up to.

---

* Gene Sharp's report summarizing his Norway research has been put online by the International Center for Nonviolent Conflict: Gene Sharp, "Tyranny Could Not Quell Them," (London: Peace News, 1958), available at https://www.nonviolent-conflict.org/wp-content/uploads/2016/08/Tyranny-Could-Not-Quell-Them1.pdf.

** George Lakey, *The Sociological Mechanisms of Nonviolent Action* (Toronto: Canadian Peace Research Institute, 1969). An abridged version of this work was published as a pamphlet, "Nonviolent Action: How It Works," pamphlet 129 (Wallingford, PA: Pendle Hill, 1963) and as an article: "Sociological Mechanisms of Nonviolence: How It Works," in *Nonviolent Action and Social Change*, Severyn T. Bruyn and Paula M. Rayman, eds. (New York: Irvington Publishers/Wiley, 1979).

≈ ≈ ≈

As Berit and I settled into our cozy Oslo apartment, we had few discussions about where we would want to plant our family for the long run. We were taking one step at a time. In Norway, I was like a kid in a candy store—all these new things to learn and adventures to be had!

By wintertime, each of us acknowledged an orientation to the future that tipped us in favor of settling in the United States rather than Norway. While Berit's family of course wanted us to stay, the cultural inclination of Norway was outward bound, from the Viking days ("Viking" means "expeditioner") to the early-twentieth-century mass migration to North America. Norway still produces a remarkable proportion of staff for international relief agencies, the UN's civil service, and UN peacekeeping forces.

For me, there was that deep sense of personal calling to address peace and justice through social movements. After just half a year in Norway, I knew that country was much farther along in addressing injustice than was the country of my birth; I could be far more useful in the United States than I could ever be in Norway. And Berit knew that for her own considerable skills, the need in the was much greater in the United States than at home.

The next step for me would be to finish my degree at Cheyney in the fall and do some graduate work to prepare to get a job teaching social science. Despite the enjoyment I was finding in Norway—with its promise of a great place to raise a family and growing old in peace and security—we finally decided to settle in the violent and raggedy heart of an empire.

After our Christmas with the family in Skien, we realized we'd like to see more of Europe together before returning to the United States in September. We already lived simply and couldn't cut back more in order to save for summer touring; I would need to find a job to earn that extra money. In August, I'd played cocktail piano for a couple of weeks in a tourist hotel to sub for the house pianist, but those opportunities weren't likely again until the summer. I applied to be a substitute teacher, and a secondary school quickly turned up where I could teach English and music part-time. It helped that in Norway I'd kept a hand in music by directing the University of Oslo's summer school choir, including a concert on national public radio, and then later joining the university's men's choir.

Teaching in the secondary school motivated me to work even harder learning the language, because I had to use Norwegian to teach the younger students. The older ones could handle English. To prepare the music classes, I also learned more Norwegian music, and then, for the fun of it, started a choir to give the young people the experience of performing.

Of course, I couldn't avoid innovating in the school's music classes. The tradition was to focus on learning to sing traditional Norwegian classical and folk songs. I internationalized the curriculum, giving each class the responsibility to access—from an embassy—photos, graphics, and a folk song. Each week we focused on a different country, decorated the classroom accordingly, learned a folk song in that country's language, and listened to a classical recording from that country as a group. The various classes found themselves in friendly competition with each other and broadened their musical knowledge considerably—and mine, too! My approach proved effective, so the national teachers' pedagogical magazine published my article with ideas I'd tried out in the music curriculum. Teaching more than six hundred youngsters also gave me more exposure to Norwegians of all social classes, stimulating my sociological studies at the university.

I was surprised to discover that the oldest member of the faculty had taught at the school during the German occupation. He told me that after multiple refusals by the national teachers' union to go along with Nazification, the Nazi dictator Vidkun Quisling decided to retaliate by arresting about a thousand teachers—one in twelve—sending them to a concentration camp north of the Arctic Circle. By arresting at least one teacher from each school, Quisling calculated that the other teachers would be under pressure on behalf of their suffering colleagues to reconsider their union's resistance, and knuckle under.

The arrests were to be done by the Norwegian police, most of whom were not Nazis and resented being used to enforce edicts of the regime. The police tipped off the schools, telling them the date they would show up to make the arrest, which gave faculty members time to plan. In faculty meetings all over Norway, the staff considered which of their number would be best suited to undergo the ordeal: single, young, healthy, teachers were the obvious choice. After collective discussion, a volunteer was found in each school, who presented himself to the police officer on the appointed day. That teacher was promised by his colleagues that they would do everything possible to get him released—except give in to Nazi demands.

"How did it work?" I asked.

"Brilliantly," he replied. "After our colleague was arrested, we teachers organized our communities—first through the children's parents, then expanding the circle. We aroused a more intense level of opposition to the regime, so much so that Quisling realized that holding teachers in the camp actually worked against his interests and released them. Only a few had died from the winter cold, exposure, and overwork."

He took a moment to stare out of the window. "Those were awful times, and I remember them like yesterday. A small country up against seemingly overwhelming might. I take pride in the victory I told you about, one of the many victories we pulled off against Nazi tyranny. We wanted our children to learn from us. We wanted them to know that even in an extreme situation, they should be creative and look for the power they do have. I believe people can always find some way to refuse to cooperate."

8

North Philly and the Ivy League

The move from Oslo to Philadelphia in August was made easier by knowing I wanted to start my graduate work at the University of Pennsylvania after finishing up at Cheyney. Happily, inexpensive housing near Penn was easy to find.

I had earlier visited West Philadelphia's Powelton Village, a tree-lined neighborhood of three-story Victorian houses a short walk away from campus. It was said to be the only neighborhood in Philly where interracial couples could hang out on the street without worrying about racist taunts. There were several housing co-ops in Powelton, along with a nonprofit real estate firm dedicated to keeping the neighborhood from being gobbled up by slumlords.

Berit took a job as associate for the director of intake at Philadelphia's pioneering therapy center, the Child Guidance Clinic. We quickly found a cheap, vacant fourth-floor walk-up apartment where the owner agreed to buy the paint if we gave it the makeover. My Cheyney friends Marybelle and Earl joined us in a mini work camp to fix the place up. Friends raided their attics for furniture to give us, and we borrowed two canvas cots from the American Friends Service Committee warehouse until we could hunt down a used bed.

I then asked Berit to meet me after work at the corner of a fancy shopping street downtown for a surprise. We walked a few stores down the street, and I escorted her into a piano shop to show her the new piano I'd just bought on the installment plan. I heard in Berit's belly laugh a combination of delight and exasperation: "What can I expect next from this husband of mine?"

In Powelton, there was a small Quaker Meeting that met in an Episcopal parish house, where folk dancing also took place once a week. We came to love the weekly worship of the Friends and getting to know the community of other regular attendees. The wide theological embrace of Quakers supported me in my relationship with Jesus without requiring it of everyone, and the emphasis on peace and social justice was strong. Berit had been brought up Free Church Lutheran, which meant a worship style considerably less formal than the Norwegian state church's liturgical version of the Lutheran service. She was willing to hang with the Quaker preference for silent worship with occasional breaking into brief vocal ministry or song. In decades to come, she found herself more attracted to a strong liturgical tradition and chose membership in the Episcopal Church.

≈ ≈ ≈

Cheyney had a challenge waiting for me in my last semester before finishing my degree. The school assigned me to practice-teach at the Reynolds School, in the heart of poverty-stricken North Philadelphia. In my third-grade classroom, we had forty-four children. I was the only white person in the school.

I watched my supervising teacher, Corinne Archer, work the room, supporting the children in their wide range of abilities. I helped a child learn to spell c-a-t, grinning with his sense of accomplishment. I listened to a boy tell me he wanted to be a nuclear physicist when he grew up, and noted that he had some understanding of what that work might be. I was moved by the dedication of my colleagues, who were paid little while facing enormous obstacles. I doubted I could learn to match their skills. For me it was a relief to finish the term and get ready to enter Penn; I imagined there would be little reason for me to return to North Philly.

I was very wrong. North Philly became big in my life, right into my eighties. Over the years, the combination of movement organizing and my biracial family has had me running back and forth to North Philly as often as several times a week. These six decades of connection have included times of inspiration, despair, and most everything in between. Next to where Berit and I settled, West Philly, North Philadelphia is to me the most significant part of the city.

≈ ≈ ≈

My graduation from Cheyney was a high point in my life. My dad, after years of opposing my going to college, surprised me by coming to my graduation. Maybe my mom insisted, but he seemed genuinely reconciled to my having done this thing called college. He still didn't like teachers—in his working-class experience, they too often came across as condescending—but he may have been hoping I wouldn't actually join the profession. This surprising boy of his never did anything right, so why would he become a teacher just because he'd graduated from a teachers' college?

I was surprised by how comfortable my parents seemed to be, as virtually the only white parents at graduation. They greeted my Cheyney friends warmly and surrendered to the general atmosphere of parental pride. In the weeks following graduation, I thought a lot about my dad. He was brought up a Methodist, and the name of that denomination is not accidental: Dad felt there's method to living right, and everyone needs to learn how to do it. At work or at home, he frequently debriefed his performance and tried to do something differently in order to get it right. (I'm the same way.)

What upset me for years was that my dad didn't come to my performances, at school or my piano teacher's annual spring piano recitals. Maybe he was wary of the effect of performance on my ego. The right thing for a working-class boy, he signaled, is to serve, not to lead. I wondered what was so problematic for Dad about leading. After all, workers need leaders for their unions.

Then I remembered a story he'd told me from his first factory job. A couple of union organizers got jobs there, sub rosa, and began to agitate. Management found them out, fired them, and mounted a machine gun on the roof of the factory, pointed toward the area where the men assembled before the whistle blew to start the shift. I could tell from the way he told the story that he'd been badly frightened.

Perhaps he didn't want his firstborn son to be in an exposed position, where he might be badly hurt or killed. He'd no doubt seen my willingness to put myself forward. My mother wouldn't have allowed him to *forbid* me to preach a sermon as a twelve-year-old, or take the lead role in the senior play, or to enter extemporaneous speech contests and student-conduct the high school band. But he could at least refuse to give his blessing and hope this would be just a phase.

I'd been deeply hurt by his absences at my performances, too hurt even to ask him about it. Seeing him at the Cheyney graduation, with pride on his face, I wondered if, in his protectiveness, my dad was loving me.

א א א

Berit's enthusiasm for me to go to graduate school included her offer to support us both, as she had done in Oslo.

The University of Pennsylvania's willingness to consider me was due to my having spent the previous year in Oslo reading sociology. Study at a European university opened a door that would likely have been closed to someone with only a degree from a state teachers college. To hedge its bets, the sociology department asked me to take the Graduate Record Exam for sociology, on which I scored at the 99th percentile.

One of the many things I loved about my studies at Penn was the reinforcement I was getting for the systemic view I'd seen operating so well in Norway: it pays to look beyond the parts of something to begin to get a view of the whole. One witty professor at Penn acknowledged that there might be a temperamental difference among sociologists between the "splitters" and the "lumpers." If so, I was a "lumper," which helped me see why so many partial solutions (for example, to the problem of poverty) didn't work. In contrast to Scandinavia, the United States remained mired in poverty after many decades of reformism that never aimed to take on the system as a whole.

I applied the same way of thinking to my ethics. I decided there's not a "moral truth" and a "practical truth," so that we can say that while killing is wrong, we do need to get practical and kill someone—or hundreds of thousands of people—to defend and protect. I concluded there is only one truth, which is both ethical and practical, and when there appears to be a divergence between morality and practical outcome, that's what our brains are for: we then need to dig into research, innovate, and go beyond the apparent contradiction presented by our limitations of vision. Thanks to the spaciousness of my Penn experience, I gained a fuller appreciation for the combination of research and action.

At this time, in the early 1960s, I was spending time on picket lines at Philadelphia's Woolworth stores, in solidarity with the students in the South staging widespread sit-ins against segregation. I did find this generated some tension with some of my courses, still geared to the fifties myth of societal consensus. As I got required courses out of the way, I took seminars and independent studies that allowed me to follow my activist passion. To match my increasing time spent demonstrating and organizing, I researched issues that affect the success of social movements.

One semester, to learn more about dynamics of repression, I chose to study inmate organizing in Nazi concentration camps. Immersing myself in the documentation of the Holocaust kept me depressed for months, but I came out of it with even more respect for the resilience of the human spirit. Knowing that people actually organized themselves for resistance under the extreme conditions of a concentration camp built my confidence in our ability to organize anywhere.

I found deep meaning in pursuing this kind of intellectual work, and continued to make eccentric choices for papers, like a study of the social fabric of the Germantown Monthly Meeting of Friends. My studies weren't teaching me much about the broader field of sociology; I'd find out later, with mixed feelings, that I was educating myself for a virtually non-existent field of activism, instead of the existing field of sociology.

The department head, Dr. Vincent H. Whitney, thought it time for a conversation. "George, my colleagues and I know that you are very active in protests here in the city and, while not everyone agrees with every stand you take, most would say that an engaged intellectual is a good thing." He paused to light his pipe and smiled when the tobacco caught satisfactorily. "At the same time, we've also had the advantage of years of practice in advancing the field of sociology, and we've had a great time doing it. What I'm wondering, George," he said, pausing to give me his most earnest look, "is if you are giving yourself the chance to experience the satisfactions of becoming a professional sociologist."

We sat in silence.

There are so many silences between people: the cowed silence, the expectant silence, the grieved silence, the hopeful silence. The brief silence Dr. Whitney and I shared that day was the silence of curiosity: a question hanging in the air, its answer unknown to either of us.

I was emphatically aware of the investment the department had made in me, an investment not in the future of activism but in the future of *sociology*. My working-class family had taught me a sense of obligation: if someone gives us something, we owe them. Our rules require that we hold up our end of the bargain.

In the months that followed, I wiggled out of Dr. Whitney's challenge by a simple expedient: I fooled myself. Clinging to my excellent grade point average, I convinced myself that I could have it all: I could get my PhD in sociology without fully taking on the identity of a professional sociologist.

9

jailed in the civil rights movement

Philadelphia's media were full of pictures and breathless reporting. A mass civil rights campaign— usually associated, in the 1960s , with cities in the deep South—was happening only half an hour away.

In November 1963, I knew little about Chester, a shipbuilding city on the Delaware River, except that it was heavily Black and segregated. Berit and I watched with hope as a campaign began in Chester to seek equality in schools and city hiring: the sit-ins, the daytime mass marches that escalated into nighttime marches despite the heavier violence that city police and state troopers meted out after dark. We were disturbed by the stories we heard: for example, that police sometimes chased demonstrators into buildings to continue clubbing them. Jails were filling, and the movement called for more volunteers to participate. The campaign was almost entirely Black people, which concerned us; people might think that racism was Black people's problem, but we knew it was white people who had invented racism and therefore it was our responsibility to get rid of it.

I dressed in khakis, a white shirt, and a tie—in those days, there was a dress code for civil disobedience because it helped to swing public opinion our way. After a long hug from Berit, I jumped into our little Volkswagen bug and headed for Chester. I found the campaign's organizing center, a storefront in the Black part of town. There were rows of metal folding chairs, partly filled. I signed in with my name, address, the contact information of the person to be notified when I got arrested, and my car's license plate number, then took a chair next to some young people. We chatted until my name was called. I went to the sign-in desk.

"Take three other people in your car and go to City Hall," the organizer said. Despite the atmosphere of urgency, she smiled. "That's where you'll sit in."

She read out the names of three other volunteers. The four of us shook hands and hurried to the car.

I then made my first mistake of the day. I drove directly to City Hall, where there was no chance whatever to park. The front of City Hall, with its imposing façade and rows of concrete steps, had a lot going on. Police stood around, demonstrators held their signs, and media people carried their cameras and notebooks.

"Stop the car—let us out!" my comrades said. "Look, there's Audrey! See her with the sign over there?"

I pled with them: "I need to find a safe place to park the car first. Please don't go inside until I come back!"

It took ten minutes to find a safe place to leave the car, and another ten to return to City Hall. By then, my comrades were nowhere to be seen. *They must have tired of waiting and gone right inside*, I thought nervously. *How could they not have waited for me? I don't want to be alone in the middle of all this!* (Later I learned that the police in front of City Hall had already turned them away—they were Black—and they had gone to the school district headquarters to join a sit-in there.) I walked up the broad steps through the reporters and TV cameras, through the demonstrators, through the police (who ignored a white man like me), and through the steel-and-glass doors into the building. I came into a very large, quiet, and darkened lobby with a series of office doors around its edges. I was alone, except for three police officers hanging out in the far corner from me.

Where is my team? I fretted. I began circling the lobby, looking through the windows in the office doors to see if my comrades were inside an office. The offices were deserted.

The trio of officers sauntered over to me. "Can I help you?" inquired one of them; I guess he figured I'd come to pay my water bill and didn't know that city workers had been told to stay home.

"I'm looking for the sit-inners," I said. "I've come to sit in."

The three smiled incredulously. "You what?" asked the first one.

"I'm with the movement," I said nervously. "I've come to sit in."

The officers started to grin. "Well," said the first one, "why don't you just go ahead and do it?"

"What?" I said. This action was not turning out anything like what I had expected. I continued: "Right here?"

He gestured toward the lobby floor. "Pull up a tile and sit down."

And so I did, grateful for one action I could take in the midst of my bewilderment.

"All right," he said. "Now you can go home and tell your friends you're a hero." He paused as I continued to sit. "Go on now, go home."

"Oh, no," I said, my voice getting stronger. "I'm serious about this. This is about civil rights. I'm sitting right here."

"Okay," he said, turning to the other two police officers. "Arrest him!" he said.

The two grabbed me by my armpits and yanked me up. They threw me against a wall, patted me down, and handcuffed my hands behind my back. At last, something was happening the way I imagined it would!

The policemen walked me toward the back exit of the lobby, one on each side; I remember the echo their shoes made in the empty space. I suddenly felt very alone.

Behind the lobby was a stairway that led to the back door of

City Hall. "You wanna walk him over to the station to book him, or call the wagon?" one asked the other.

I heard the tension in his voice. I knew the police had been working absurd overtime hours because of the protests, and on some level they probably hated being in the public eye these days. They were working-class men like my dad and uncles; they were being used in this conflict, and I didn't think they were my enemy.

That's when I made my second mistake of the day. "I don't mind walking," I said.

Calling attention to myself triggered their fatigue and resentment. One of them started to beat me.

Immediately I remembered what Dr. King and others had been saying for the past few years. I took a deep breath, unlocked my knees, opened my hands, and prayed. After a bit, the other officer spoke up. "Let's use the bus," he said. "Let's get this over with."

They led me to the parking area behind the building, where a yellow school bus had drawn up. They half pushed, half threw me into the bus.

I sat down in the first empty seat I saw, next to a young man who was holding to his nose a handkerchief that was matted with blood. He was wearing a shirt and necktie and was the only other white guy on the bus.

"What happened to you?" I asked.

"I'm a reporter for the *Bulletin,* but the police thought I was a Swarthmore student, and they hate the students. I guess I look really young. So they broke my nose. "

He seemed eager to talk—he was trying to make sense of the sudden attack on him. I knew that Swarthmore College was near Chester and that some of the activist students had been involved in the campaign from the start.

"Wait 'til my editor hears about this," the reporter said. The blood had begun to drip from his sodden handkerchief, so I offered him mine.

The reporter and I got separated when we arrived at Broad-meadows Prison, and I wondered if he got medical attention at the jail before the newspaper bailed him out. I later learned one result of the broken nose: the Philadelphia *Evening Bulletin* changed its attitude toward the movement from negative to positive. It was a pleasure to get fair reporting and friendly editorials for a change.

My bed was in a block of about thirty single-person cells arranged around an open space. It was easy to communicate with neighbors, and we had two exercise times each day to mingle in the open space. Campaign leader Stanley Branche was in our block, and during exercise time he quickly set us marching back and forth, singing freedom songs.

> *We are soldiers in the army*
> *We've got to fight, although we have to cry,*
> *We have to hold up the Freedom Banner,*
> *We have to hold it up until we die.*

The warden became nervous about the possibility of our high spirits infecting other prisoners, so he took an exercise period away from us. That set us to banging our metal beds up and down, clanging our cups against the bars, and howling like banshees. We refused to stop until the deputy warden came and, after negotiating with Branche, gave us back our second exercise period.

The week went by quickly: singing, conversations, marching, and spontaneous actions of resistance to prison authority. I was experiencing the surprising power of collective determination. If people can empower themselves through solidarity, even with the harshness of a prison, the excuses given in the outside world for timidity wear pretty thin.

After a week in jail, my day in court was as surprising as every-thing else had been. I was charged with trespass. My arresting officer turned out to be the deputy chief of police, and he told the judge what happened. The judge asked me to tell my side of the story, which I did briefly.

The judge leaned forward and turned to the deputy chief. "Did you say to Lakey, 'Pull up a tile and sit down'?"

"Yes," said the deputy chief.

"Then the charge is invalid." The judge glared at him. "When a police officer invites someone to break the law, we call it 'entrapment.'"

The judge snorted. "Case dismissed."*

≋ ≋ ≋

There was no way ahead of time to know how I might be useful as a civil rights demonstration unfolded. Earlier in 1963, in May, protesters had gathered outside of a school construction site in North Philly's Strawberry Mansion neighborhood. The workers building a new junior high school for Black children were entirely white, a reflection of discriminatory practices in the unions of the construction trades. As a white son of the working class, I felt a particular responsibility to get over to North Philly and join the movement, so after turning in the semester's last term paper at Penn, I went to the site. Unusually for me, I went alone.

Because I knew that we do better in mass actions when we're in an affinity group or at least have a buddy, I felt very alone in the middle of a crowded street full of Black people from the neighborhood. There was such a big turnout that the nearest I could get to the entry gate to the building site was still a distance away. Many more people were joining the protest, piling up behind us. I

---

* For a bigger picture of that Chester civil rights campaign, see the case study by Carl E. Sigmond, "African American Residents of Chester, PA, Demonstrate to End Segregation in Public Schools, 1963–1966," Global Nonviolent Action Database, August 29, 2011, https://nv-database.swarthmore.edu/index.php/content/african-american-residents-chester-pa-demon-strate-end-de-facto-segregation-public-schools-19.

began to look around me to see if I could connect with at least one person near me, and made meaningful eye contact with a man a couple of yards away.

Shortly after, a giant roar came up from the demonstrators immediately next to the entry gate; apparently the opening time had arrived and white workers were being ushered in with protective police on hand to create an aisle for them. It was an inflammatory moment: I could picture the newcomers restlessly piled up behind us pressing forward in the narrow street to get in on the action at the entry gate, and the potential for a riot that would leave a lot of demonstrators hurt.

I eyeballed the guy I'd spotted earlier, who was obviously thinking the same thing. He nodded and we quickly approached each other, reached out to join hands, and stretched our other arms to block the oncoming rush of bodies.

It worked. We slowed the rush considerably, long enough to avert a stampede and remind someone to start singing a civil rights song many people knew, "Freedom!" Another riot averted—one of many such stories that emerged from the civil rights movement.

The ongoing protests gave the city's Commission on Human Relations the clout to negotiate an agreement to employ Black workers on the site. It was a small step, but there were also civil rights songs to remind us that it's a long road to freedom.

א א א

Along with studying at Penn, I was working with the Friends Peace Committee, an official Philadelphia Quaker agency promoting disarmament. However, I found I couldn't stay away from the racial justice issue. Martin Oppenheimer was a sociology grad student a couple years ahead of me who was as passionate as I was about activism; together we participated in the local chapter of the Congress of Racial Equality (CORE), the civil rights group most experienced in using direct action. Since the early 1940s, CORE had been desegregating public facilities in the North using sit-ins, stand-ins, and swim-ins.

As the 1960s civil rights movement reached what activist writers Mark and Paul Engler have called the "whirlwind" stage, Marty and I grew concerned that the movement had no way to adequately train the thousands of people who kept joining in from all over the country.* Risks were high.

We dreamed of a civil rights action manual that would at least share information about tactics, strategy, how to handle tear gas and violent threats, and the pros and cons in the recurring argument about violence and nonviolence.

When, on April 7, 1964, Rev. Bruce Klunder was run over in Cleveland by a bulldozer while protesting the construction of a segregated school, Marty and I faced a sudden quandary. Yes, Klunder, who had two small children, would probably still be alive if he'd gone into that situation knowing more about the tactics of direct action. Yes, a manual could convey that kind of information. And yes, the appropriate writer of such a manual would be a Black civil rights leader like Bayard Rustin, or an experienced member of the Student Nonviolent Coordinating Committee. But the reality was that all the appropriate people we knew of were at capacity, organizing and coping with almost daily emergencies. How could they take the time required to write a manual?

We looked at each other. Marty was working on his PhD dissertation on the civil rights movement. Both of us were activists picking up valuable information from civil rights organizers. We could put together a manual—we grad students had that kind of discretionary time. Marty could lead the project, and I could draft some chapters, too.

---

* Mark Engler and Paul Engler, *This Is an Uprising: How Nonviolent Revolt Is Shaping the Twenty-First Century* (New York: Nation Books, 2016).

We gave ourselves a short timeline. We put off everything we could and wrote furiously. The book includes a short historical sketch of the movement; Americans are famously ahistorical and therefore prone to make the same mistakes over and over again. We described how to set up an organization, conduct training workshops before venturing into action, choose among various action tactics that have proven useful, and set up methods of reducing risk while maintaining the offensive, as well as key things to know about arrest and the courts, and tips on jail conduct that preserves dignity and a sense of one's own power. The manual closed with a debate: nonviolence, or armed defense?

I found a Quaker printer willing to work overtime to get it out, and Friends Peace Committee fronted the money. Bayard Rustin agreed to write the foreword. He said, "At long last here is a much-needed practical training manual for nonviolent direct action . . . a pioneering endeavor in this field for some years to come. It should be carefully studied by every activist in civil rights and related causes."

Our goal was to bring *A Manual for Direct Action* to the movement via the June 1964 training sessions for the Mississippi Freedom Summer. Up to a thousand students were being recruited in the North to come to the Western College for Women in Oxford, Ohio, for the training. From there they would be dispatched to Mississippi to do voter registration and teach in Freedom Schools. I'd been recruited to be a member of the training staff.

The pages for the manual arrived from the printer just in time, their ink barely dry. Friends Peace Committee volunteers took shifts at an all-night collating session, walking around large tables where the pages were stacked and manually assembling the copies for distribution. Our goal was to load the bundles of books onto a Greyhound bus; the company assured us a thousand copies would get to Cleveland in time for a staffer of the National Council of

Churches, which had organized the training, to pick them up for opening day.

When I returned to the Friends Peace Committee office after the training in Ohio, I saw a trail etched in the linoleum of the office: long ovals marking the path the valiant volunteers took, hour after hour, to collate the book. Now it seems like the Stone Age.

The manual was a success. The two thousand copies we'd printed disappeared quickly, and we printed more. In Chicago, a commercial publisher, Quadrangle Books, heard about the manual, called us up, and offered to publish it as a trade paperback. Marty and I disappeared again for a week to revise the manual in light of the feedback we'd gotten from our first version, and sent it off to Quadrangle with considerable relief.

The book stayed in print for many years, continuing to help the civil rights movement, and was also used by the antiwar movement, as well as in other struggles. Five decades later, I wrote a successor called *How We Win: A Guide to Nonviolent Direct Action Campaigning.*✳ That book addresses our present context and includes key lessons about organizing and strategy learned since the 1960s. The Rev. Dr. Bernice A. King, daughter of Martin Luther King Jr., endorsed the book and described the original manual as "literally a lifesaver for many during the height of the struggle for Black freedom and dignity in the 1960s."

In June 1964, I joined the Freedom Summer training staff in Ohio for the first week's batch of nearly five hundred volunteers. It was my first chance to work with the Rev. James Lawson, who had studied Gandhi's work in India before training the founding leaders of the Student Nonviolent Coordinating Committee (SNCC). In Ohio, we relied heavily on role-plays, giving participants nonviolent combat training to orient them to conflicts they might encounter.

✳   George Lakey, *How We Win* (Brooklyn: Melville House Publishing, 2018).

The staff included a number of SNCC workers fresh from the field in Mississippi, who shared sometimes brutally honest stories of violence and degrading jail conditions. The songs and group spirit in the jails buoyed them, however, and kept them in touch with their passion for justice. At the end of the week, I watched them excitedly board the buses headed for the South again.

After a day to debrief and relax, the training staff welcomed another batch of hundreds of volunteers. This project was the idea of its coordinator, Bob Moses—a high school math teacher in New York who left his job to go to Mississippi and organize poor, illiterate, and rural Black residents to register to vote. Bob believed that if close to a thousand mostly white, young people from the North came to Mississippi to accompany the embattled SNCC workers, the sheer danger of their exposure would activate their parents and communities. He envisioned them compelling a reluctant Democratic administration in Washington to intervene and force Mississippi to desegregate.

On the second day of the second week, we were all called to the college auditorium. The students from the first week were already distributed around Mississippi. I found a seat in the second row of the auditorium along with others on the training staff, guessing we would get a progress report. But when a federal official who'd been observing the training came to the center of the stage, he appeared upset. He looked around, then stared at the paper he had placed on the rostrum. "We've just received word that three of the Freedom Summer workers are missing together in Mississippi—James Chaney, Andrew Goodman, and Michael Schwerner. Chaney was an SNCC field organizer. Goodman and Schwerner were student volunteers."

I was stunned. Chaney, along with other SNCC organizers, had been at high risk for months, I knew. But Goodman and Schwerner had been here in our training the previous week—volunteers like the students sitting around me—and they might already be dead. Looking around, I wondered what the students were imagining. How many of them would quickly return to the northern suburban homes that many of them came from?

Over the next few days, I watched the SNCC workers take on the role of older siblings to these frightened students. We built an invincible container, strong enough to hold the shock and grief and fear that rocked our training. Under the old trees of the campus, stories and listening, freedom songs and prayers were shared.

Very few students went home. At the end of the training, most got on the buses and took their turn to head toward Mississippi.

SNCC's 1964 campaign turned out to be one of the boldest and most brilliant strategic moves of the entire civil rights movement, with lessons for today. Their primary target was the federal government, led by a Democratic administration highly reluctant to support racial integration in the South. SNCC joined Bayard Rustin, Dr. King, and others in believing that federal pressure was needed to force change.

≈ ≈ ≈

Eager to learn more about strategizing, I found a moment during the training to ask Bob Moses a burning question. I wanted to know how it was that he and most other SNCC workers in Mississippi had survived, considering that they were all surrounded by people who wanted them dead and had an organized instrument in the Ku Klux Klan to make that happen. Local law enforcement was useless—police were often KKK members. The state government of Mississippi declared SNCC to be its enemy. The federal government's Justice Department, run by President John F. Kennedy's brother Robert, refrained from intervening, while a rogue FBI under J. Edgar Hoover actively worked to undermine the civil rights movement.

Bob's answer to my question about survival was simple: "Because we don't have guns in our freedom houses, and everyone knows it."

"I don't get it," I replied. "I don't see the mechanism. I don't see how that actually protects you."

"Maybe this story will help you understand," Bob said, in his low-key, patient tone of voice. "I think this is the sort of thing that happens: A worker in a small-town hardware store shows up at the store one morning all excited. He tells his boss, the owner, that 'the guys'—meaning the local KKK—have decided to kill the SNCC workers and burn down their freedom house on the outskirts of town. They plan to do it that night. His boss says, 'No, you're not.'

"The worker is stunned, knowing that his boss is active in the White Citizens' Council and hates SNCC as much as the worker does.

"The boss goes on: 'You guys have no idea what the consequence would be. Mississippi already has enough economic trouble. Getting investment from the North is really tough. So you kill up a bunch of n*****s, and it's all over television in the North, and Mississippi looks to the banks up there like an out-of-control shithole of an investment. There's no way I'm going to let you do it."

I walked away from Bob marveling at the political sophistication of the SNCC strategy. They used their own vulnerability to force the professional middle- and owning-class White Citizens' Councils to control the working-class KKK, with the result that they kept themselves, the hated SNCC workers, alive. Identity politics is too simplistic in its moralism to support this level of strategic thinking.

Once more I found myself wishing for more academics at Penn and elsewhere to go beyond the violence paradigm, to complicate their thinking, and to create more theory to support nonviolent strategizing for life-and-death situations.

violence greets opposition to the Vietnam War

During my studies in graduate school, I'd been watching my blue-collar Bangor classmates being drafted into the Vietnam War. My academic work gave me a draft deferment; the American empire, like other empires before it, was all about using working-class conscripts to do the bulk of its killing and dying.

The national draft system was to some degree decentralized, administered by local draft boards of civic leaders. My draft board realized that I was the kind of conscientious objector who would refuse to join the army even as a noncombatant, so the board would likely assign me to some kind of nonmilitary alternative service for two years. However, the matter was only a technicality as long as I was in school.

As 1963 arrived, I realized that I would be turning twenty-six in November, which was the cutoff point for draft eligibility. All I had to do was stay in school until November—no problem, since I still had years to go to get my PhD—and the government would then set me free of my obligation.

The trouble was that cruising along and making my As at an Ivy League university is not what a working-class person would call "doing my part"—certainly not in comparison with high school classmates being sent to Vietnam. That fracture in solidarity was more than I wanted to live with.

The draft board sent me the draft order. In those days, some draft boards were open to a conscientious objector's own proposal for their two years of service. Mine agreed to my proposal of working for Friends Peace Committee. I'd been counseled that there might be some pushback from the draft board about that proposal, but they accepted it. Maybe my board felt I was such an oddball to volunteer to be drafted that they wouldn't bother to order me to a placement I didn't want.

From its side, the Friends Peace Committee liked the idea. I'd been volunteering with them for a couple of years, helping to build the organization into the premier Philly peace group for demonstrations and youth work. The Friends Peace Committee worked across some differences that other groups did not: the committee endorsed both world federalism and unilateral disarmament, did both discrete lobbying and mass media work, included both older people and youths, and conducted both essay contests and direct action. It wasn't something I would later advise groups to do, but Friends Peace Committee was making it work.

The group's director was way overdue for a sabbatical year and decided to take two years off to make up for it. He persuaded the board that I should take his place while he was gone. He set off for the Rocky Mountains and promised to return in the summer of 1965.

Friends Peace Committee represented—and sometimes mobilized—Philadelphia Yearly Meeting, a constellation of a hundred Quaker congregations in the Delaware Valley, which includes eastern Pennsylvania, New Jersey, and Delaware. Quaker organizational structure was fairly loose at the time; each of the Yearly Meeting's agencies, which we called "committees," developed its own program under the guidance of a steering committee of Friends.

It was the perfect spot for someone who wanted to "do his part." With Berit's support and my Vietnam-bound classmates in the back of my mind, I cranked up the group's budget and grew its staff while also taking my graduate courses at Penn. I also increased Friends Peace Committee's mass media presence.

Philadelphia's Black-owned radio station, WDAS, aired interviews with Jackie Robinson, Martin Luther King, and other breakthrough Black leaders. Joe Rainey's late-night show included a phone-in feature and had a wide listenership in the Black community. Rainey realized early that developments in Vietnam could threaten the civil rights movement, which is why he often invited me to join him on the air.

"I have a question for your guest," said a caller one evening. "Mr. Lakey, how do you get away with dodging your responsibility to go to Vietnam to fight, then getting the government to give you draft credit for protesting the war? That's outrageous! You are a disgrace to this country!" This was the fourth time a caller had denounced me on these grounds. How had the right wing dug this up? I was popular on the talk show circuit because I could get the phones to ring, but now the invitations could dry up.

"When Quakers settled here, we already believed that war is wrong," I countered, "and our principles go way beyond the Vietnam War. Peace is patriotic no matter what mistake the government is making at any given moment. Century in and century out, somebody's got to question the military way."

The media work was one of the many reasons I felt productive with Friends Peace Committee; still, I was never entirely easy with the life I was living. My days, I knew, weren't anything like those of my high school classmates in Vietnam.

Fast forward to 1975: I'm at my high school class's twentieth reunion and hear someone say "George, I gotta talk with you. I've been avoiding it."

Richard D'Eduardo stared at me while his body swayed unsteadily. We were in the crush around the bar, and he'd obviously been there for a while.

He took another swallow. It looked like whiskey, on the rocks.

"I knew," I said quietly. I hoped it wouldn't turn physical, not in the middle of an otherwise cheerful night, surrounded by our peers.

"Okay, so it was hell, and none of us wanted to be there, but we thought we had to serve our country, right? And I'm one of the lucky ones because I didn't get shot up. It was hell, George, hell." Another swallow. "I've got no words for what it was."

While I was listening, I was subtly moving my feet apart to give me better balance. I was glad I'd had only one beer—the advantage of being brought up a teetotaler!

"And we're all there because we're trying to serve our country, right? It's our fucking country, George, it's our flag, and we're gettin' shot, and we're gettin' booby trapped, and we're losin' our limbs and losin' our minds, George, our fucking *minds*."

I knew I didn't need to say anything. Richard was into it now, this thing he'd avoided that had come between us. My high school class was small—maybe 115 students. We knew each other and had school spirit and class loyalty.

Richard wasn't swaying as much—maybe the intensity of what he was saying was sobering him up. I knew I was plenty focused. "I'm finally home on furlough, and I'm trying to forget everything and pig out on my mom's pasta and get into the pants of every Italian girl who will let me. But I can't skip the eleven o'clock news, not unless I'm screwing, and even then I think about it, I think about the news. One night I'm watching it, and they're showin' another antiwar demonstration, and I see people gettin' arrested and loaded into the paddy wagon, and I see *you*." He paused, and his stare got even more intense. "I see George, my classmate, gettin' in the fucking paddy wagon. My classmate. And if I'd been there"—he paused again, then lowered his voice— "if I'd been there, I would have killed you."

I no longer heard or saw the other people at the bar. Our eyes held each other as though the two of us were so alone that no desert or beach or wilderness could provide as much solitude as now surrounded us. I was ready, and curious, and scared, and also wondering what this loyalty challenge would demand later when I got the chance really to think about it.

Our stare held, and then Richard's eyes shifted. He looked at his drink, shook his head, put the glass on the bar.

"All right," he said, eyes suddenly tearing up. "That was then. I've been home for a while. Time to think. I can hardly do much else, but I do hold down a job. Now I figure I know what you were doing when you got arrested."

He paused again, then continued. "You were on our side. You wanted me home."

I slowly exhaled, and found my eyes were wet, too. I had to ask: "And the rightness of the war?"

"Sure, I figured out it was bullshit. Didn't everybody? But that's not the main thing, not between us. The main thing is that you weren't stabbing me in the back."

Richard suddenly looked shy, and very sober. "So I gotta shake your hand, okay?"

I grabbed his outstretched hand, ready to make an emotional response of my own, then saw that he was already looking away. He'd done what he could do. I let go of his hand and half turned away, grateful, wanting to support his dignity. I clapped his shoulder lightly. "You're a helluva guy, Richard," I said, "and this is a helluva class."

He smiled for the first time, reached for his glass, and raised it in a wordless toast.

‫ ‫ ‫

Back in 1965, when I was still stirring controversy for my antiwar views, I found an unusual opportunity to forward the Quaker message.

Albert Bigelow—the captain of the *Golden Rule*, which had sailed to the Marshall Islands to oppose nuclear testing—became available for media appearances in the Philly area. I offered him to Joe Rainey for a radio interview. However, on the day of the scheduled show, Joe called me: Malcolm X was in town for the day and eager to be on WDAS. No way could Joe refuse that opportunity, so he'd have to pass on Bert.

I quickly filled Joe in with more on Bert's history, including his participation in the famous Freedom Ride, when the Greyhound bus was bombed at Anniston, Alabama, and the Freedom Riders on board were mobbed. "Bert's a white guy who combines the peace and antiracism causes," I said. "Like Malcolm X, he has a background in serious boxing, and during World War II he was commander of a US warship in the navy. Both guys are warriors. Why not put Bert on with Malcolm X and let them dialogue? Maybe they'll duke it out on the nonviolence question!"

Joe promised to run the idea by Malcolm X, who agreed.

At five minutes before 11:00 p.m., Bert and I were in the WDAS studio with Joe, seated around the table with mics, when Malcolm X strode in, surrounded by tall, muscular bodyguards. He took his seat between Joe and Bert, and the studio light flashed on.

As his guests responded to Joe's questions, I watched them warm to each other, each picking up on the other's energy. Bert told Malcolm X about his friend Jim Peck, a white pacifist, who had his head battered so badly at a Greyhound stop that he required more than fifty stitches, and then challenged Malcolm X about his consistently heaping scorn on white allies. Malcolm X, in turn, demanded that all white peace people abandon their pleas for polite dialogue about racism and put their bodies on the line as Jim Peck had.

The table they shared let me observe their body language, their folding chairs edging closer to each other as they argued. Their sparring struck me as a subtle, intimate dance. At one point, Bert posed a poignant question while putting his hand on Malcolm's knee, and there was no shrugging away on Malcolm's part. I wished the radio show could continue into the night, and so did Joe as he watched his switchboard lighting up with phone calls.

Since those days with WDAS I've been on many interview programs—including with hosts Terry Gross, Leonard Lopate, and arguably the greatest of them all, Chicago's Studs Terkel. But I continue to hold Joe Rainey and his show in a special place: a broadcaster taking chances and believing that his audience wanted to go there with him.

ҡ ҡ ҡ

I realized that the US military escalation in Vietnam was on a collision course with the civil rights movement. I remembered reading that the United States, in joining World War I, derailed much of the social activism of the preceding decade. The same happened when the United States joined World War II. Despite President Lyndon B. Johnson's boasting about his projected anti-poverty program, I could see that the Vietnam War would provide a convenient excuse to lose track of the deep changes needed to end poverty and racism in America.

Maybe this time we could do something about that. I wanted the peace movement to get ahead of this situation and run alongside the civil rights movement as an ally, asking concerned people at the grassroots to walk and chew gum at the same time. That was one reason why I'd gotten arrested in the Chester civil rights struggle: trying, as a known peace leader, to provide an example.

When I took the Friends Peace Committee job, the larger peace movement was preoccupied with the intention of the United States to rearm West Germany as a NATO member, which would add to tensions with the Soviet Union. I was also worried about the arms race, but more concerned about Washington doubling down on its determination to keep Vietnam within its empire. To me, going up against rising nationalism in Vietnam was a foolhardy and bloody course, terrible for the Vietnamese and for Americans, including the damage it would do to aspiration for racial justice.

Education was needed: most people hardly knew where Vietnam was on the map. Friends Peace Committee was a player in the regional peace movement, and I also had access to national peace organizational conferences; I wanted to encourage more peace people to raise the Vietnam concern.

A few high school students inspired to be activists asked Friends Peace Committee for training, and youth worker Michael Yarrow agreed to organize a summer project in 1964 called Students for Nonviolence. I shared with Mike the view of longtime activist Charlie Walker that one of the most empowering activities for arousing a movement is street speaking. I told him about the spontaneous street meeting I'd started at Penn during the Kennedy-Khrushchev confrontation. Mike agreed to try it out, but said I would need to "sell it."

When meeting with the high schoolers, I told them that Malcolm X developed his movement by speaking on street corners in Harlem, and that Alice Paul did the same for woman suffrage in the early 1900s in Center City Philadelphia.* The teens were both scared and fascinated, and agreed to try a series of street meetings. Mike assured them we would first practice before going out to the street. Each Tuesday and Thursday afternoon, we took a milk crate to the same spot across from City Hall, and the students took turns standing on the box and talking about Vietnam.

The students knew little about Vietnam at the start of the summer, not unlike most members of Congress. Study was essen-

---

* I interviewed Alice Paul in the course of researching my first scholarly article: George Lakey, "Technique and Ethos in Nonviolent Action: The Woman Suffrage Case," *Sociological Inquiry* 38, no. 1 (January 1968) https://doi.org/10.1111/j.1475-682X.1968.tb00671.x.

tial, but our pedagogy was far more lively than a classroom's. I told the students they would be studying "in dialogue with the people." Early in the summer, our students were easy for passersby to stump: "What gives the North Vietnamese the right to invade the South?" "What about the Geneva accords? Didn't the accords give the United States the right to be there?"

Mike and I loved watching the students dive into scholarly books and articles to learn more and figure out their own positions on the controversies raised on the street corner. The mainstream mass media were of little help; as usual in the beginnings of wars, the mass media simply parroted the government line. (They later would do the same on Iraq.)

In the beginning of the series of street meetings, Mike or I broke the ice by being the first speaker, then each of the students mounted the milk crate. Several said it was the scariest thing they'd done in their lives. As I watched their power grow, I realized that street speaking was the activist equivalent of a high ropes course in Outward Bound. After a couple of weeks, students began to volunteer to be the first speaker.

The students designed a leaflet to hand out that had a coupon on the bottom, and were delighted to find an increasing number of bystanders sending in checks, asking how to volunteer, and telling us they were recruiting friends to come to our street corner at the end of the day. The students realized that on the street they encountered many people who wouldn't go to a church basement or union hall for a meeting on Vietnam, but would stand for an hour on the street learning and discussing the issue with strangers.

Midway through the summer, after a turn on the milk crate, I found a spot in the middle of the crowd to listen to a student take a turn. Out of the corner of my eye, I saw a hard-faced man edging closer to me. I couldn't miss the tension in his body language. When we were almost touching, he turned to face me, then looked down. I followed his eyes and saw he was holding an open knife. "I'm on leave from 'Nam," he said quietly. "Fuck you."

I took a breath and looked deeply into his eyes. "I know you can hurt me," I said, "but first, take a minute to think about the consequences for you."

He blinked, then blinked again. He slowly put the knife back in his pocket, edged his way out of the crowd, and was gone.

≈ ≈ ≈

"Now the high school students want more, George." It was Mike Yarrow, starting our weekly staff meeting. "They want to stage an all-night vigil protesting the Vietnam War down at Independence Hall to climax their summer."

I liked their choice of site, remembering a dramatic moment in the history of the women's movement, the 1876 centenary celebration of the Declaration of Independence. Soon after the lead speaker began, feminist leader Susan B. Anthony disrupted the assembly by leading a team of women to distribute to the listeners a Women's Declaration of Independence.

"I'm not sure an all-night vigil is a good idea," Maureen Parker said. Maureen was our office manager and a parent who often felt protective. "Remember that street meeting a couple weeks ago, George? It was broad daylight. And even so, that soldier pulled a knife. You had to talk him down."

After intense discussion, the staff agreed that we should say yes to the students as long as their parents agreed and gave signed permission. Mike and I would stay with the students all night, and other adults could join us in shifts, staying in the background so the students wouldn't feel their action was being taken over.

The students started their vigil in the late afternoon, pleased with the tourist and media attention. By midnight the area was quiet, with only an occasional couple passing on their way home from a nearby tavern. The street was empty of pedestrians at 2:00 a.m. when a young man appeared across the street. He walked toward us with a strange intensity; my street sense moved me forward to head him off.

I saw that he noticed my movement; he slightly slowed his pace, although he didn't look at me. My heart beat faster; I intentionally relaxed my arms and opened the palms of the hands at my side. I put my body almost-but-not-quite in his path. "Can I help you?" I said with a smile.

"Who are you?" he asked, looking directly at me for the first time. His facial muscles were tight, and his blue eyes glared at me.

"I'm an adult sponsor for these high school students. They're holding a peaceful vigil to show their concern about the war."

I emphasized the word "peaceful" as I said it.

"I can see that," he said with a sneer, sweeping his eyes over the students' signs. He turned back to me, and said more softly, as though exerting great self-control, "I can also see that none of you has a fucking idea what you're fucking talking about."

"We want to learn more," I said, trying to sound relaxed even though warning bells were clanging in my head.

"I'm a marine," he said. "Just got here from 'Nam, on leave." He seemed to study my face, then shook his head. "No fucking idea," he said as if to himself.

I felt myself opening. A congenial Quaker silence moved into my belly to join the jitters.

"Have you ever killed a man?" he asked suddenly, peering into my face.

"No," I said simply.

He shook his head slowly. "You have no idea. I used to be like you, like other people. I thought the greatest thing was sex, the biggest thrill a man can have."

It suddenly seemed important to him that I understand what

he felt. He probed my face. A chill ran down my spine as I looked at his wild, cold eyes; then he seemed to go away, far away.

"Yeah," he continued, "I thought it was sex, that was the height. But now I know different. When I killed my first it was self-defense, you know? On patrol. But, man . . . Then I started to look for chances. That's what I looked forward to."

He paused and looked at the teens, sprawled in sleeping bags now, signs propped against the red bricks. "Peace Heals," one sign said.

I was conscious now of my love being bigger than my fear, and at the same time I was noticing details. Unlike the soldier at that earlier demonstration, this one wasn't putting a hand in his pocket. He was right that I couldn't imagine getting turned on by killing, and he was right to try to find someone to tell about it, even me.

"They're really tired," I said. "They're kids."

"Yeah," he said heavily, turning back to me. "Just tell them tomorrow they can do their protest shit because we marines are there to protect them."

I slowly raised my hand in the gesture of a handshake, as Quakers do at the end of Meeting. He looked at my hand, then at my face. Slowly, he turned away, then made his way down the street.

11

my baby helps to save the trees

In 1964, Berit was enjoying her job assisting admissions at the Philadelphia Child Guidance Clinic, but we'd been married five years, and she was ready to quit and be a mom. After a year of hoping to conceive, however, we discovered that we were both relatively infertile.

We applied to the largest adoption agency in the state, Children's Aid Society, and were told we would have to wait a very long time for a match. However, the agency had just expanded its range of eligible adoptive parents for Black babies to include white married couples. They'd been feeling the pressure of so many unplaced Black children going to orphanages and decided, in light of the gains of the civil rights movement, that white couples might be suitable for Black babies. Would we be interested?

Taking this step would be consistent with our values. My parents would accept a Black grandchild, and Berit's, too. The civil rights movement was rising, and racial barriers were falling. And we were eager to start a family. We told Children's Aid yes.

September 10, 1965, was a fateful day, but we didn't know it. The baby girl who would become ours was born that day. In early December, we got the call from Children's Aid and went to meet her. She cooed and we cooed. It was a match.

Paperwork was quickly done, and we soon brought her home to an unforgettable Christmas. Appropriately, we named her

Christina, as the name she would go by. We inserted as her first name Esther, after Berit's mother, knowing that in Norway she would be called "Esther Christina." We were so happy that we didn't even mind taking turns getting up during the night to feed her, holding her just so in order that, as she sucked, she'd be staring into our faces.

In early spring, a different kind of excitement affected our domestic life. We'd bought a house on Spring Garden Street, half a block from a stone gothic Catholic church on the edge of Powelton Village. It was a long street stretching out of sight, lined with tall, old trees planted close enough for their massive branches to touch each other.

The street's three-story Victorian twin houses were no longer the splendid homes of yesteryear; signs of deferred maintenance were everywhere. But I liked the floor-to-ceiling front windows, the bays on the side, the elegant double front doors, the bits of stained glass here and there. No longer the pretentious neighborhood it was built to be, Powelton Village retained architectural graces, mixed with the signs of young families struggling to pay the bills.

"George," called Berit from upstairs, as I let myself in the front door one day after work.

I called back. "Where are you?"

"In Christina's room, changing her diaper. You've got to do something!"

I heard the urgency in her voice and took the stairs two at a time. "What's going on?"

"Did you see the tree being cut down on the corner?" Berit asked. "Pat found out that they are starting to take down all the trees on Spring Garden Street! So we decided to go out with our babies and stand under the trees to stop them."

"Hold on!" I said, unable to take all this in. "Why would they cut down all the trees? And why would you try to stop them with our babies? Are you crazy?"

"They won't hurt us," she said confidently, "and the reason they plan to cut down the trees is to make it easier to repave the street. They're the ones who are crazy. We've got to stop them!"

Our neighbor Pat Fallon and her baby spent a lot of time with Berit and Christina. Pat was at least as stubborn as Berit when her mind was made up, and I knew it was hopeless to try to talk them out of it.

"So what am I supposed to do?" I asked, surrendering.

"Get on the phone and stop the tree cutting. Pat and I are your leverage. You teach this stuff, so you're supposed to know how to do it! Tell them you've got some crazy moms on your hands!" With that, she started down the stairs with our baby.

Scared now, I jumped on the phone without taking off my jacket and started calling city bureaucrats. I worked my way up the organizational chart, in each case explaining that there were a couple of moms with their babies standing under trees and the cutting had to stop immediately. Finally, I reached someone with the authority to call the crew and stop them in the middle of their bringing down the third tree. I rushed out to find Berit and Pat nervously jiggling their small bundles, and told them the news.

"Now what?" Pat said.

"Now we need a mass meeting tonight," I said, "inviting the city, and we need publicity."

"The easiest church to get will be the Lutherans, over on Haverford Avenue," Pat said.

"I'll call them," Berit added. "And I'll start calling the media."

"Okay," I said, "I'll start door-knocking and mobilizing people to come to the meeting. Let's just order out for pizza—there's no time for us to make supper."

As I knocked on doors, I thought of Berit's remark: "You teach this stuff, so you're supposed to know how to do it!" This was 1966, and I was teaching movement organizing and social change theory—my first teaching job in higher education. A graduate program for activist organizers was hosted by Crozer Theological Seminary, in nearby Chester. Earlier, I'd been drawn into the circle of leaders who outlined the curriculum—people like Bayard Rustin, A. J. Muste, and CORE director James Farmer. I felt privileged to be on the weekend retreats, participating in discussions about which content was most important for young organizers to learn. I used the chance to get closer to A. J. and Bayard, then followed up by having them come as guest lecturers once we were in gear at Crozer.

We named the program the Martin Luther King School of Social Change. Dr. King had gained his first graduate degree at Crozer, and older faculty there remembered him vividly from his student days.

While teaching, I was still taking graduate sociology courses at Penn, and being a new dad. It seemed to me a busy enough life—who needed to organize a direct action campaign, too? But I'd never seen Berit more determined.

Later that evening, the Lutheran church basement was full of tension—angry neighbors, defensive city officials, reporters, and staff representing several politicians. "How do you think you can get rid of a street full of trees without even telling us?" one woman demanded.

"And really you should ask us," said another woman, "because we live here and you don't."

"Right," shouted a man. "I'll bet no one rips up your trees without asking!"

Since I was chairing the meeting, I let the anger build without allowing the officials to say very much, so they could learn what they were dealing with. The politicians' staff sat quietly, taking notes. Clearly, the city had blundered into a hornets' nest, and I wanted them to know it.

Finally, an official from the streets department conceded that there was another way of repaving a street without cutting down the trees, but he argued that many of the trees were diseased anyway, and our neighborhood would benefit from a complete replanting.

"I'm a gardener," one of the older neighbors said, "and I challenge this statement that the trees are in bad shape."

It looked to me like the time to consolidate our gains. "Maybe we can make an agreement," I said. "The city could agree not to continue cutting while we ask an expert from the University of Pennsylvania to study the trees. We can meet again tomorrow night to work out our negotiating position. The city sees now how strongly we feel."

"Yes, but what if the city just goes ahead and cuts them tomorrow anyway?" a neighbor demanded. "Then it's over and done with. We need a way to protect the trees while we're negotiating!"

"Let's set up teams of people to rove up and down Spring Garden Street, and if any crews come near a tree, the team can stand between the crew and the tree and raise a shout. The rest of us can come out and stop the crew."

A burst of positive enthusiasm came from the crowd. "Organize it, George," someone called, so I asked volunteers to come forward to take slots of time, and we closed the meeting.

Berit and Pat were pleased that they'd ignited such an enthusiastic campaign. The nonviolent teams roved the street, and the phone rang off the hook with minor politicians seeking ways to ally themselves with motherhood and apple pie.

The mayor, on the other hand, already hated us. A few years before, he'd wanted to build a sports stadium at the edge of our neighborhood, and our feisty civic association had blocked it. He'd never forgiven us.

The media portrayed us as a gallant little neighborhood defending ourselves against insensitive bureaucrats. A daily newspaper ran a huge photo on the front page showing some of us beside a felled tree trunk. TV crews followed our teams up and down the street and showed footage of glum tree cutters. One reason the media loved the story was the suspense of the campaign: Who would win—David or Goliath?

Berit cashed in our credits with a babysitting cooperative to get good care for baby Christina while also mobilizing the botanist from Penn and developing our vision for the future of Spring Garden Street. She drew on her charm to get information out of reluctant sources. The same analytical skills that got her a summa cum laude degree from Midland College paid off in sorting and sifting information.

After a turn supervising the nonviolent intervention teams or handling a news conference, I'd come into the house for coffee and find Berit at a paper-filled dining room table, her brown, curly hair tidy and blue eyes calm in the middle of the storm around her. I was to see that centeredness again when she joined the staff of Women Organized Against Rape and navigated through the high winds of feminist pushing and male resistance.

Our tree fight turned the corner when the mayor bowed to the necessity of negotiating with us. The UPenn professor found that many of our trees were indeed diseased, but also that many were sound. The media pronounced us the feisty little neighborhood that cared about its trees the same way it cared about preserving its reputation as a multiracial, multiclass bastion of progressive politics. I was contacted by a Democratic Party leader to see if I might like to run for something. (It was just as I was teaching my students: the Democrats' role is to co-opt successful social movements!)

We went into talks with the city armed with Berit's homework, so there were no surprises. The outcome? An agreement to preserve the healthy trees and plant the rest of the street with trees of our choice. We chose—no surprise, considering Berit was the daughter of a florist—flowering trees.

The neighborhood rejoiced in its victory and in our increased solidarity and reputation. Berit and I finally got to put our feet up in front of our living room fireplace, glasses of sherry at hand and a sleeping baby Christina in my lap.

"You know what I've loved about this campaign?" Berit asked, with a tired and satisfied look on her face.

"You mean besides winning?" I laughed.

"I always thought we'd win," she said. "What I've loved is that for a change we were fighting alongside mainstream people. Our trees weren't one of those quirky, marginal causes that takes forever to be taken seriously. Now I know what it's like to be one of those people who position themselves to be on the side of 'truth and the American way.'"

We laughed together. As I stared into the flames, I remembered our home in Oslo and our first year as a married couple. Just half a decade before, Berit seemed so contented to be back in her native land after two years in the United States getting her sociology degree. The more Norwegian language and culture I learned, the more Norwegian she seemed to me to be. And now it tickled her to identify with grassroots Americans fighting the bureaucrats!

I agreed it was reassuring to know that we weren't compulsively eccentric; we did have the skills and ability to be mainstream when we chose to. Even Berit and I could sometimes be "just folks." Then I remembered something I'd learned a few days prior.

I was taking my turn on one of the tree-protection teams with a woman from the other, more upscale, end of our street. We were barely acquainted, but I knew her as a friendly, upper-middle-class woman; I assumed she had fairly conservative politics.

"George, I'm glad we're getting this chance to work together," she said. "You know, I've always admired you."

"What do you mean?" I asked guardedly.

"Well, I know that you go downtown to City Hall and join those protests where people hold signs against the Vietnam War.

You are so courageous! I'm against the war, too, but I'd never be so brave as to go down there and hold a picket sign."

"Woman!" I burst out. "Do you know what you're doing right at this moment? You are walking on this street ready to stand between a tree and a chainsaw! And you think it's brave just to hold a sign?"

She stared at me for a moment, then began to laugh.

"I never thought of it like that. This . . . what we're doing now . . . it just seems so natural, just defending ourselves, like a mother bear defending her cubs. Somehow it seems very different."

12

community deepens the Vietnam movement

One of Bayard Rustin's favorite phrases was "people in motion." I'd heard him use it over and over in strategy discussions, and remembered that this emphasis was what drew him to Montgomery, Alabama, in 1955—to advise the boycott's very young and inexperienced leader, Martin Luther King Jr.

In 1965, Quakers were also a people in motion. After years of being inspired by the civil rights movement, more Quakers were becoming anguished that the escalation of the Vietnam War had not yet stirred a mass movement. The American Friends Service Committee—by far the largest Quaker organization working at home and abroad—was giving medical aid in the form of prosthetic limbs to civilians in South Vietnam hurt by the war. However, many Quakers were concerned that the US government was preventing them from extending the same aid to North Vietnam by threatening prosecution. The situation was preventing us from continuing the historic Quaker practice of humanitarian relief for civilians on *both* sides of a war.

The man who was replacing Gary as my best friend, Ross Flanagan, deeply wanted to do something about this government interference. He and his wife, Dorothy, had recently moved from California to New York City so that Ross could work with a Quaker agency there. Ross was a romantic like me, had a crooner's baritone voice, and loved Broadway songs as much as I did. He radiated earnestness but also had a wicked sense of humor. His handsomeness and eloquence made his speaking much easier to listen to than mine, so he was very popular on the speaking circuit. Among Quakers, we both shared—without competition—the adjective "prophetic." Ross moved people; I organized them.

Ross thought of a way to confront the US government's limitation on Quaker aid: have people buy first-aid packages and take them to their local post office addressed to the Red Cross of the Democratic Republic of Vietnam.

Rebuffed in each case by the post office, Quakers then sent the packages to Ross, who mobilized people to attempt to carry them across the Peace Bridge at Niagara Falls to Fort Erie, Ontario. We knew the Canadian postal service would mail the packages to North Vietnam. From the US government's point of view, however, this was an illegal dodge, equivalent to smuggling goods across the border that were deemed illicit because of their intended use by the "enemy."

Publicity about the US government blocking humanitarian relief at post offices began to raise more questions in the minds of mainstream people about the rightness of a war against people who never did anything against Americans and were no threat to us. The action supported dialogue, in which peace activists could point out that the war was intended to protect the US empire, a new concept to many.

Ross's dramatization of this antiwar work, building on what I'd been doing through the activism-oriented Friends Peace Committee, increased Quakers' motivation. Some groups of Quakers began to propose to their local congregations that they formally send medical aid to North Vietnam through Canada, claiming responsibility for the act after they'd done it. This idea, however, was immediately controversial—even though it built on centuries of Quakers breaking laws for the sake of conscience.

Eventually, Ross's proposal came before the Philadelphia Yearly Meeting, the denominational structure that supports individual congregations in the Philadelphia region to work together. The body's annual session, which thousands of members are eligible to attend, was forced to wrestle with a hard question: In this proposal to violate civil law in a democratic country, what is God's will?

As far as I could tell, only a few idealistic young Quakers believed that the proposal would pass. I wasn't one of them; I simply couldn't see how so many Friends would come to a consensus on such a controversial issue.

The large Meetinghouse was full of members from a hundred local congregations. People spoke passionately for and against the Philadelphia Yearly Meeting, as an organization, violating federal law in this way. No one tried to justify the war, but a number of Friends thought this action to be a step too far.

Several times, the presiding officer, a widely respected man whose day job was as a US federal judge, stopped calling on the next speaker and invited us back into silent worship. The profundity of the silence became deeper each time. (Just as the Inuit people are said to have many names for snow, Quakers notice many kinds of silence.)

After hours of this back-and-forthing, the presiding officer once again read the proposal. He paused, then asked how many Friends agreed. "I agree" was voiced strongly from all parts of the Meetinghouse. As before, he also asked how many Friends disagreed.

This time, no one spoke.

He held the moment, then announced the conclusion: the Meeting agreed to take this step.

I heard hundreds of people release their held breaths simultaneously.

"I must speak personally," I recall the presiding officer saying, in effect. "Our procedure would be for me to sign the letter informing the government of our action. However, my role as a federal judge forbids my assisting someone to break the law. I must therefore resign, ceding that office to our assistant clerk."

A rumble of sympathetic approval could be heard as the assistant clerk, who was also sitting at the table in front, took the place of the clerk and declared a short break before we came back to hear the reading of the minutes from the afternoon session.

On my way out of the room for the break, another Friend turned to me and asked, "George, did you expect us to make this decision today?"

"No way." I grinned. "A lot of individuals in the room had to put ego aside and do deep searching and earnest listening to be able to come to an agreement, and that's the Spirit at work. In a way," I said, as my smile got wider, "what it really felt like to me was that the Holy Spirit took us by the scruff of our collective neck and shook us until we lined up with God's will!"

ﬡ　ﬡ　ﬡ

None of this was lost on Larry Scott, whose strategic brain and powerful energy had so inspired me as a college student, when I'd ventured into his successful campaign against atmospheric nuclear testing. Like Bayard Rustin, whom he had worked with, Larry knew the importance of seizing the moment when "the people are moving." He sensed that Quakers were now ready to launch a national group that would specialize in direct-action campaigns that used civil disobedience, and the issue to begin with was medical aid to civilians suffering in Vietnam.

Just as Larry had done in his previous organizing, he kept an eye on the ecology of the movement. Every social movement has differentiated parts within it: youths and older people; radicals and reformists and conservatives; gender- and class-based groups. Each segment is likely to organize itself in ways that are consonant with the life situation and point of view of the individuals within it. Without this knowledge, activists are likely to upset themselves at the lack of unity in a social movement.

Like a biologist looking at a forest, Larry expected social movements to contain an ecology of differentiated parts. His aim was to respect the ecology and organize something new in that spirit of respect. Now, as in his anti–nuclear testing days, he wanted to start something new—and to be successful, he would be mindful of what was already there.

I was a member of the national peace education committee of the American Friends Service Committee and, with others, I'd been urging the organization's board to turn to civil disobedience to demand that the government allow it to work in North Vietnam. With his ecological perspective, Larry knew that the AFSC would not jeopardize its many other worthy projects underway in the United States and abroad by picking a fight with the US government. However, it might welcome the formation of a new national Quaker agency to do what it could not do. Likewise, the national lobbying arm of Quakers, Friends Committee on National Legislation, counted on its respectability for access to members of Congress and could not take a defiant posture. Again, if more radical Quakers organized an alternative voice, a division of labor might seem somewhat reasonable.

༄ ༄ ༄

Among Friends, the increasing anguish about the war was profound. On November 2, 1965, a young Baltimore Quaker and father, Norman Morrison—moved by earlier acts of self-immolation by Vietnamese monks and nuns opposing their government's role in the war—took gasoline with him to the Pentagon and, finding a spot outside the building within view of the office window of Defense Secretary Robert McNamara, doused himself with the gasoline, lit himself on fire, and died.*

When the news broke, Norman Morrison's name was not immediately identified. Some people actually telephoned my house to find out if it was me.

How do people handle their anguish? I was not about to make a judgment on Norman Morrison's action, but I naturally wondered whether I would do what he did. I, too, had prayed over the sacrifice by Vietnamese monks and nuns. I'd asked myself what more I could do and wondered if it was my fears that held me back. I had baby Christina to take care of, but Norman also had a little girl, plus two older children. The questions multiplied.

Early the previous year, Berit and I did something that may have prevented me from reaching a point of desperation. We already enjoyed friendships with several young families who had strong Quaker identities—the Arvios, of course, but also Ross and Dorothy Flanagan, as well as a young Quaker family from nearby Wilmington, Delaware. Berit and I noticed that during our visits with these individual families—in addition to having fun and catching up with each other's achievements and challenges—the conversation usually turned to the condition of Quakers, which invited a series of complaints.

I have a longtime aversion to complaints that don't go anywhere; to me they seem a boring self-indulgence. My practical working-class nature wants to move to action. Berit agreed, and together we came up with a possible solution: we'd invite those three families to gather with us for a family-fun weekend. The ten children, as well as the grown-ups, would enjoy each other, we figured. And in that atmosphere, maybe the complaining about Quakers would either stop or would go somewhere.

---

* In filmmaker Errol Morris's 2003 documentary *The Fog of War*, McNamara talked about Morrison's action and acknowledged that he was moved by it. *The Fog of War*, directed by Errol Morris (Sony Pictures Classics, 2004).

We got together, and we clicked. The children formed a posse and had a wonderful time. The adults found themselves singing and dancing together, laughing much more often than crying, and having splendid worship times. We continued to gather every few months, shared joys, angers, doubts, and fears. As our anguish about racism and the war increased, so did our solidarity. Each of the weekends released us into calm and purposeful actions that, we thought, just might make a difference.

Of course, many others beyond the Quaker community were deepening their opposition to the war at the time. Champion boxer Muhammad Ali announced he had "no quarrel" with the Vietnamese. Other religious groups were stepping up, including members of the Catholic Worker movement, a radical Catholic group that distinguished itself by its service to the poor. One of them, Roger LaPorte, followed Norman Morrison's example with a public self-immolation. Again, friends of mine were concerned. Some thought Ross and I might consider taking the same action. Looking back, I think our little Quaker community kept Ross and me so fully in touch with life and love that we wanted to stick around for the changes we might help happen. If we want to dance with history, we'd better keep on dancing.

One of the changes needed, our group of families thought, was to make a Quaker contribution to an emerging movement for religious renewal. Cynthia and Ray Arvio both loved to write, as did I. Why couldn't our little group write a pamphlet?

The result was "Quakerism: A View from the Back Benches," self-published in June 1966. It became the focus of a Sunday article by a *New York Times* columnist, and we brought copies to a major Friends gathering in Cape May, New Jersey. Ross and I also hoped that a gathering of more than a thousand Friends in one place would help us take action on the war to a new level. Our pamphlet urged a stronger commitment to the peace testimony, especially in times of war, such as now.

As the gathering began in 1966, the United States escalated again, now bombing the population centers of the seaport city Haiphong and the capitol, Hanoi. That was too much even for British prime minister Harold Wilson, who had been trying to contain his opposition to the war within diplomatic channels. This time Wilson's bold public denunciation was a major story in US papers and on TV.

A couple of us quickly asked some activists attending the Cape May conference to an emergency meeting, resulting in a determination to carpool our way to Washington, DC, the next morning. There, we would worship in the Senate gallery, to pray for that body to rise up and call for a cessation of the bombing. If the senators adjourned without doing so, we would remain until arrested.

Larry Scott stayed behind in Cape May, to talk with the leaders of major Quaker organizations that had a stake in the peace issue. His goal was to use the opportunity to gain their tacit agreement that a new national Quaker group should emerge to focus on direct action against the war, even though that might subtract from the Quaker energy and donations that currently supported them.

In DC, we filed into the Senate gallery and were shocked to find only a dozen senators on the Senate floor. Oregon senator Wayne Morse and Alaska senator Ernest Gruening passionately denounced the president's escalation, while the others had different matters on their minds. It was a travesty—anything but how one would expect a responsible parliamentary body would respond to aggression on the scale of Hitler's bombing of London. The Senate soon adjourned, and about thirty of us stayed in our seats, continuing to pray. The Capitol police handcuffed us and led us away, soon to begin serving our seven-day sentences.

Now there was no turning back. The willingness of Congress to accept President Lyndon Johnson's escalation erased the illusion that Congress could bring its maverick, hawkish president to heel—since declaring war was, after all, its responsibility under the Constitution. Democracy plainly wasn't working. It was up to the citizens, once again, to generate a mass movement that would force the government to do the right thing.

threats and cheer on the home front

The thermometer read 102 degrees. Our baby, Christina, lay in bed crying, her face red with fever as she turned her head from side to side, trying to find a cool spot. Berit hung the phone in its cradle and turned to me. "The night nurse said we should give her Tylenol."

"We don't have any in the medicine chest," I said. "I'll go pick some up."

Christina was our first child, and we were still learning the ropes. As it turned out, we would always be learning the ropes.

One lesson from this moment was that just because your baby doesn't have frequent fevers is no reason not to keep a supply of Tylenol just in case. It seemed to me the number of "just in case" situations for babies was limitless—we couldn't stock enough for all the possibilities. Fortunately, we had an all-night drugstore only a couple neighborhoods away from Powelton Village.

I found a parking place on a residential street about a block from the store. It was past midnight; we'd been asleep when Christina woke up crying with fever. I hurried inside, made my purchase, and started back along a dark and nearly deserted street of typical Philadelphia brick row houses. Ahead of me I saw a group of young men hanging out on the sidewalk. For a second I thought it might be smart to cross the street to avoid them; this was a solidly African American neighborhood and for all I knew they might be turf-conscious and not that friendly toward a white guy. I shrugged my shoulders: *It's my right to walk wherever I want to, so I'll just continue on the direct route to my car.*

There were five or six of them, pretty much occupying the whole of the narrow sidewalk. As I walked into their space, one of them stepped up to me and pushed me against the wall of the closed-in porch attached to someone's row house. Surprised, I stared at him as he pushed me again and said something I was too scared to understand.

Oh, shit! I thought to myself. *I'm in trouble, and I'm clueless about what to do.*

This felt really different from earlier confrontations, when I was threatened for my political views. At least I knew what *not* to do: show belligerence or, on the other hand, play the helpless victim. My activist training told me there's always something creative to reach for, a way of being assertive, being human, and coming from a place of goodwill. What was it?

My heart pounded so loud that my ears didn't seem to hear anything the young men were saying. My eyes registered the others in the group stepping closer to me, and I felt my anger rise closely behind my fear. My brain said something like, *George, think of something to do!*

Instantly I was transported back two years, to the Freedom Summer training in 1964. Rev. James Lawson, a battle-scarred veteran of the civil rights struggle, was explaining to four hundred of us trainees some techniques of response to attack.

"Let me tell you about John Wesley, the English Methodist preacher," Lawson said. "He was used to being mobbed by hostile crowds and developed a technique for handling it. Wesley, first of all, threw off his hat so the crowd could see his face and he could see everyone in the midst of the chaos. He then scanned the mob to identify the 'leader.' Wesley believed that every mob, however disorganized, had somebody within it who was a potential leader.

"Once he got an intuitive sense of who that was, he forgot about everybody else and put all his energy into communicating with that one person. If the shouts were too loud for him to be heard, Wesley just did eye-to-eye contact, completely focusing on this person who was a potential leader. And, every time, that person would do something to turn the mob away from beating Wesley, and in effect save his life."

Lawson's story was what I remembered in that split-second, as the men held me up against the wall. Since I didn't have any other ideas, I decided to try it out. I scanned the group of young men and, trusting my intuition, decided the "leader" wasn't the guy who was pushing me and getting in my face. (What *was* that guy saying? Why were my ears not working, only my eyes? And why were the others in the group coming in closer to me?)

I decided the leader was another young man, who was standing back a bit, with a thoughtful expression in his eyes. Channeling Wesley, I focused my energy on him. "Why are you doing this to me?" I asked. I allowed my anger to show in my voice and, at the same time, held my hands out and down, palms open. "I came out to get some medicine for my baby." My voice rose. "She has a fever! She needs the medicine. Why are you hassling me?"

The guy who'd taken the initiative hit me a couple times in the shoulder, not very hard, as if mainly to get my attention. My heart went on pounding, but my backbone was straighter, and a calm was growing inside. I had a plan; I was acting. I looked more intensely at the guy I hoped was the leader.

"I'm a dad," I said, raising my voice some more. "I'm trying to do right by my baby. She needs the medicine. I came to the drugstore over there." I motioned with my head in its direction. "Why are you stopping me? I need to get home!"

"Hey, man," said the thoughtful-looking one to the guy who was pushing me. "Let him go."

The pushing guy turned around to address the other. "Why? He got no business on our block."

I suddenly realized I could hear what they were saying again. And I noticed the bodies: something was shifting.

Another guy stepped into the argument. No one was looking at me anymore; they were looking at the pushing guy and the leader. My hearing faded out again as I continued to focus on the leader. He glanced at me, then turned back to the pushing guy and said something. Somebody seemed to agree with him—judging from the body language—and a couple of them turned their backs on me. It was all about their argument now, and I started to edge away.

I'm a huge white guy, and I'm pretty sure I wasn't suddenly invisible to them, standing in a small circle three feet away. Still, no one did anything about my continued edging across the sidewalk into the street. Then, walking more rapidly, I headed down the center of the street to my car.

My heart gradually calmed down as I drove home, praying my thanks to Jim Lawson and John Wesley and the entire tribe of Methodists—but most of all to the guy who, whether or not he really was the leader of his friends, stepped up at an excellent time.

"George! I'm up here," Berit called as I entered the house. I took the stairs two at a time, bringing the Tylenol to Christina's bedroom, where Berit was waiting. She looked at me closely, then said, "What happened?"

"Berit, don't ever let someone tell you that nonviolence training isn't useful. I have a story for you."

More times would come in my life when I would have to manage violent threats and tough situations, and I did feel a level of confidence going forward because of the stories of others who came up with creative, nonviolent ways to respond. These stories can be a guide to anyone wishing to practice nonviolence. Role-plays in training workshops are helpful, too. For stories, the civil rights movement is a gold mine, easily accessed through movies and books.* I'm no fan of being reckless, but we don't have to stop taking chances for justice because of fear of violent threat.

צ‍ צ‍ צ‍

If it's possible to fall in love with a house, we'd done it. After five years of apartment living in Powelton Village, we now shared with the bank and two third-floor tenants a three-story brick-and-stone twin, complete with small yards front and back and an iron fence. It was 1966.

When we heard the predictions for snow on Christmas Eve, our happiness was complete.

"I'll go out and forage for more firewood," I told Berit early that morning. Our fireplace in the living room had a marble front and mantel of the classic sort made famous by Manhattan brownstone town houses. Powelton Village was mostly built in the same period and for the same social class as the New York brownstones, with nine-foot ceilings on the first floor (ten feet in the show-off parlor room) and floor-to-ceiling front windows.

"I saw a tree branch down a few blocks away," Berit called from upstairs. "The tree was dead already, so it might make good firewood."

I jumped into my Volkswagen bug, eager for the chase. As it turned out, the branch had already been scavenged, so I cruised

---

* Some short articles on meeting violent threat: Antje Mattheus, "How I Fought Off a Motorcycle Gang," *Waging Nonviolence*, July 2, 2013, https://wagingnonviolence.org/2013/07/how-i-fought-off-a-motorcycle-gang/; Antje Mattheus, "Nonviolent Self-Defense and Race–a Personal Story," *Waging Nonviolence*, August 13, 2013, https://wagingnonviolence.org/2013/08/nonviolent-self-defense-and-race-a-personal-story/; George Lakey, "Rewriting an Attacker's Script–Getting in Practice," *Waging Nonviolence*, September 19, 2013, https://wagingnonviolence.org/2013/09/re-writing-attackers-script/; George Lakey, "You, Too, Can Stop a School Shooter," *Waging Nonviolence*, August 27, 2013, https://wagingnonviolence.org/2013/08/you-too-can-stop-a-school-shooter/; George Lakey, "Defense on the Streets–Stepping into Conflict," *Waging Nonviolence*, June 26, 2013, https://wagingnonviolence.org/2013/06/defense-on-the-streets-stepping-into-conflict/.

the neighborhood hoping for another windfall. Tonight, we would as usual celebrate the Norwegian way, with a Christmas Eve dinner of pork and Norwegian-style sauerkraut, potatoes, and cranberries. We'd sing American as well as Norwegian carols by the fire.

Our usual practice was to invite someone to join us on Christmas Eve who didn't have much family around; this year it would be Lois Bertholf, an elderly Quaker in the neighborhood Meeting we attended. Our toddler, Christina, would be having the second Christmas of her life, and already her laugh filled the house every time we turned on the Christmas tree lights.

At last I saw it: a rickety fence was being torn down in a nearby alley. I told the owner I had a saw in my trunk. Could I carry some fencing away for my fireplace? "Be my guest," he said and laughed, glad to have less to dispose of.

The first flakes began to fall as I finished sawing, and by the time I'd driven the ten blocks to my house, the street was already white. "Did you hear the latest prediction?" Berit asked as I walked in with a stack of wood. "They expect the biggest snow we've had in years! I'm going to put the roast in the oven early and ask Lois to come sooner than we planned," Berit said. "Who knows how hard it might be to get her back home?"

I agreed, although Lois only lived a few blocks away. Everyone in Powelton Meeting lived a few blocks away, which was one reason I loved it. We saw each other at the folk-dance parties at the Episcopal parish house, at the grocery store, while waiting for the Number 10 trolley going to Center City. At that time in my life, I was attached to the concept of "having it all." Living in Powelton Village—the one place in Philly where interracial couples could relax and artists could count on being respected by their neighbors—gave us the advantages of a friendly neighborhood and a big city at the same time.

I also liked commuting to teach at the Martin Luther King

School on the campus of Crozer Theological Seminary in Chester. A number of faculty members lived on the campus, but I wasn't attracted to the academic version of community. The bubble seemed small and confining to me, and it lacked a certain grittiness that Powelton's fight for survival offered. Our neighborhood was always under threat, it seemed. As I joined the fight, I learned more about what we were up against: slumlords bought large single-family houses and turned them into tiny apartments, then allowed them to run down. Drexel University eyed our blocks as sites for building new dorms and classrooms. We'd barely succeeded in saving our trees.

The King School's mission was to teach skills for social change, but its placement in a seminary surrounded it with students studying ancient Greek and Hebrew on a graceful campus on a hill. I felt that living in Philly and being active in the feisty community organization that fought off slumlords, Drexel, and the mayor, were more consistent with what I was teaching.

"I'll get Christina," I called to Berit when I heard her beginning to cry in her room upstairs. "Ja så, er du ferdig å sove?" ("Are you finished with your nap?") I asked Christina, who was already standing up in her baby bed. Berit and I spoke only Norwegian to Christina, figuring that she would pick up English from other people. We wanted her to be able to communicate with her Norwegian family, most of whom didn't know English.

I carried Christina down to the living room to see the tree. She reached for the ornaments, so I gave her a Norwegian straw wreath to play with. We were soon on the floor, Christina on my back, singing and laughing. Then it was a quick foray to the porch to taste the snowflakes falling down.

"Lois!" I started, glancing at my watch. Depositing Christina in her high chair in the kitchen with Berit, I bundled up for the three-block drive. Volkswagen Beetles were the perfect winter cars; the engine's weight was where it was most needed, in the rear.

Simple and useful, if you didn't mind driving a car that sometimes sported the bumper sticker, "Made in der woods by der elfs."

By the time I got Lois back to Spring Garden Street, our house was filled with the smells of a Norwegian Christmas.

Lois, Berit, Christina, and I ate dinner in front of the fire, where the fence wood burned beautifully amidst a few logs. For me, the scene was magical: the light in Christina's eyes, Berit's happiness at being back in Norway—if only through smells and tastes—and Lois telling us anecdotes about her favorite authors. The time arrived for Christmas songs, but the storm and Lois's fragility were on my mind.

After hugs and kisses, she wound her scarf around the collar of her long coat and I half walked, half carried her through the snow to our car. The three blocks turned into six, as I avoided blocks where someone had abandoned their car that had slid into a drift. Mentally, I was debating whether I could carry Lois all the way if I needed to, but we finally arrived at her doorstep. Her tears glistened in the streetlight as she said goodnight; I guess it was a magical time for her, too.

When I finally got out of the car in front of our house, my nervous energy became ecstasy; I turned my face upward and reached for the flakes with my tongue as Christina had done earlier in the day.

Every year, Christmastime reminds me how much I love life; the celebration of Jesus is also a reminder of our capacity for joy and celebration. It's fine with me that its date on the calendar was moved from when Jesus really was born to when the pagans were already celebrating; I want to get away from the association of Christianity with asceticism and self-denial. My personal calling to be willing to sacrifice even my life for the cause, if it came to that, is no contradiction to how much I say yes to our ability to connect with others and laugh and sing and make love and be at peace with Creation.

14

piercing a naval blockade with medicine for Vietnam

Before making the most complex campaign move of my life, I flunked my PhD orals exam. It was not a great combination.

Heading into the exam, I was glad to know that my advisor, Philip Rieff, was on my orals committee. He was the closest thing to a mentor that I had found at Penn. Although I didn't admire him in the way I did A. J. Muste, Bayard Rustin, or Lillian and George Willoughby—older activists I got as close to as I could— Rieff stretched my mind in ways that alternately stimulated and scared me. I took every seminar he offered, and he supported me to pursue my out-of-the-mainstream activist research each time. As I waited in the corridor to be invited into the room for the orals exam, I reassured myself that he would be in my corner.

The exam began with an optimistic tone, professors relaxed in their chairs, me with my legs crossed. The examiners had a simple task: to determine whether I had mastered the length and breadth of the field; obviously my good grades would make this a short and pleasant exam. It may have been short, but it didn't turn out to be pleasant.

As I flubbed one question after another, the committee sat up straighter, and I uncrossed my legs. Sweat pooled in my armpits. Committee members' eyes glanced increasingly at the floor. Dr. Rieff was visibly perplexed: How could my knowledge of the field be so patchy? The ritual nature of the exam prevented him asking that question, but it might have saved us all some puzzlement.

A few days later, still shaken, I had a talk with Dr. Rieff. His skillful questioning revealed the answer: I'd used my courses to educate myself for activism rather than for academia. He offered some advice: "Take a year off from everything else, George, and catch up with the field. Then take the orals again."

ℵ ℵ ℵ

Larry Scott and George Willoughby believed in dancing with history. On the occasion of President Johnson's war escalation and our jail-going response, they called the founding meeting of a new Quaker organization that would play the rebel role in the ecology of Quaker organizations. We called it A Quaker Action Group (AQAG, for short), its name indicating a lack of pretension that we were *the* Quaker Action Group. Larry became executive director, and I was asked to be co-chair along with George, bringing the next generation into a leadership role.

I was tickled by the name AQAG, which we pronounced as if it was short for "a quagmire." Since our mission was to be trouble-makers—hopefully the "angelic troublemakers" that Bayard Rustin asked for—I figured that if the feds came down on us heavily, seizing our bank account and padlocking the door, we could move across the street and start "B Quaker Action Group." We could have many more lives than the proverbial cat.

For our first project, we decided to further dramatize the Quaker confrontation with the US government over sending medical aid to Vietnamese civilians suffering because of the war. We knew that Vietnam was, to most Americans, simply a remote trouble spot on the map, where there was some kind of threat to the United States that required military intervention. The belief seemed to be that we were the world's police and had shown in

Korea—where another "racially inferior" bunch had gotten out of line—that we meant business.

The small experiments with medical aid to North Vietnam had already expanded the peace movement by portraying the Vietnamese as actual human beings who were suffering. This was a smart idea, because mainstream America's responsiveness to suffering— as with earthquakes and hurricanes in other countries—was legendary and could be tapped if our fellow citizens could see the Vietnamese in that light.

With that strategic goal, we turned to nonviolent direct action and its capacity to dramatize issues.* Almost immediately, we invented a project that would escalate the drama by attempting to break through the US naval blockade of North Vietnam and bring medical supplies to civilians suffering under our country's bombs. It would mean somehow sailing through the Seventh Fleet, which sounded to me beyond bold—almost into the realm of suicidal. I'd already had my life threatened by angry veterans; what might an armed fleet of fighters do to a bunch of peace activists in the middle of a war zone?

I was counting on George Willoughby's judgment on all this, since he'd been on the *Golden Rule*'s defiant voyage into the Pacific Ocean's nuclear testing zone. George said that voyage taught him some advantages of that form of direct action. For one thing, a sailing ship is slow, giving time for a buildup of support and for the mass media to catch up with the importance of the story. There's a drawn-out drama as people begin asking, "What will happen? Will it be seized, or worse? What will happen to those vulnerable activist sailors?" As people and the media ask those questions, the political message of the action starts to sink in.

---

* For a more recent example of the intentional use of drama to encourage change, see my article on the Sunrise Movement's use of a sit-in to put the Green New Deal on the political map and note their use of suspense: George Lakey, "How Movements Can Use Drama to Seize the Public Imagination," *Waging Nonviolence*, July 9, 2019, https://wagingnonviolence. org/2019/07/movements-drama-seize-public-imagination-sunrise/.

Additionally, George said, the image of a sailing ship is a gallant one, carrying a romantic background of vulnerability and courage; it underlines the conviction involved in taking bold, nonviolent action for peace. All of this is why we didn't just take a plane or send medicine as freight via some third country—which might be possible and easier. Our eye was always on the domestic movement-building process.

 ﬡ ﬡ ﬡ

Earle Reynolds, whose family and sailing ship *Phoenix* had followed up George's voyage toward the nuclear testing area back in the fifties, offered his ship and volunteered to captain the first voyage himself. Earle was an anthropologist who'd been in Hiroshima for years, working for the Atomic Energy Commission, studying the lasting effects of the atomic bomb dropped on that city in 1945. He offered to sail the *Phoenix* from its home in Hiroshima to Hong Kong, establish a base there, then sail to North Vietnam.

After that voyage was completed, the *Phoenix* could leave again from Hong Kong to take medical supplies to South Vietnam, where the situation was even more complicated.* In addition to the South Vietnamese Red Cross, we also wanted to deliver medical supplies to their opponents in the south: the National Liberation Front—the armed insurgency movement supported by the north and often referred to as the Viet Cong—and the Unified Buddhist Church. This was the church whose monks and nuns had engaged in the self-immolation protests that inspired Norman Morrison and Roger La Porte. These mass-based Buddhists were staunchly opposed to the war and to the South Vietnamese government.

---

* Jessica Reynolds Renshaw tells the story of the history-making sailing ship in *The Reynolds Family, the Nuclear Age, and a Brave Wooden Boat* (CreateSpace Independent Publishing, 2017).

Bringing supplies to the civilian medics of all four major forces in the north and south would be consistent with the centuries-old commitment of Quakers to give humanitarian aid to all sides in a war. Doing it all, however, might be impossible to achieve.

To start, the North Vietnamese were less than thrilled with the idea. I met with government representatives in Stockholm during an international peace conference and then again in their offices in Paris. They emphasized the danger to us of the trip and explained a strongly held Vietnamese norm that hosts are responsible for the safety of their guests. As they saw it, receiving supplies from us for the North Vietnamese Red Cross made them hosts, so the risk of our being hurt or killed by the United States during the project fell on them. They didn't see any way they could protect us.

I tried my best to explain that we were not expecting protection; we were willing to give our lives if it came to that. I knew that Norman Morrison was highly honored by the North Vietnamese for immolating himself outside the Pentagon in protest against the war. His was a household name in North Vietnam, and they knew he was a Quaker. I linked our willingness to die to his conscientious action, his witness, but I emphasized a difference: in this mission we saw death as a risk rather than a certainty.

I also joined AQAG's delegation to inform the government in Washington of our intentions. Quakers strongly prefer to follow the practice of informing an opponent what to expect if our plan involves intense confrontation. In that way, our practice conforms with those of Gandhi and Dr. King. Our team entered a room with staffers from the US treasury, the State Department, and the Pentagon; all three had a stake in how to deal with the *Phoenix* voyage.

After we described the nature of our group, the Quaker practice of nonviolence, and our intentions for the project, they described their threats: ten-thousand-dollar fines and five years of jail time, seizure of our bank account, taking away our passports. We said we understood their point of view, and that we intended to go ahead anyway.

By this time, we'd gone through the substantial list of volunteer applicants and selected our crew. I'd taken myself out of the running—too much else to attend to, including a young daughter. Bob Eaton, a recent grad from Swarthmore College who'd grown up in Annapolis learning to sail, would be Earle's first mate. We agreed that the Canadian Broadcasting Corporation could add a news team to make what became an hour-long TV documentary. *Look* magazine added a journalist to do a major photo story. We bought ten thousand dollars' worth of medical supplies and were ready to sail—even though the North Vietnamese had not yet given their approval.

That gave us pause. I knew from conversation with North Vietnamese officials that they were highly knowledgeable about how the US government worked; they understood that the war wouldn't end until American social movements forced the issue. What they didn't know as well as we did was how to stir public opinion and build US movements.*

For one thing, we understood the level of public ignorance about Vietnam, American racism, and the nation's difficulty in seeing Vietnamese people as human beings. We were confident that our taking medical supplies for civilians suffering from the war gave peace people an opening for persuasion, especially since we were bringing medicines in a dramatic, risk-taking way. The media portrayal of peaceful Americans defying a military blockade for humanitarian reasons would invite a reappraisal of the victims of US bombs and question the US governmental portrayal of the "evil enemy."

---

* Much later, another possibility was suggested: the North Vietnamese might have understood at the time the value of the voyage but wanted to be seen as discouraging us because, should the *Phoenix* "disappear," the North Vietnamese government would not be criticized for encouraging us to take an ill-fated trip; they would have plausible deniability.

We were also confident that our project took all the risk on ourselves; we weren't endangering North Vietnamese people by their accepting our medicines once we arrived in Haiphong under our own sail.

ֶ ֶ ֶ

The stakes were high; accelerating the growth of the American antiwar movement was imperative. We decided to risk the lack of courtesy involved in the lack of a North Vietnamese invitation. The *Phoenix* set sail for Haiphong harbor.

We had more confidence in the receptivity of the North Vietnamese than we had in the US Seventh Fleet allowing us through its blockade without arrest, harm, or both. We had no way of knowing what decisions had been made inside our own government after it had threatened us if we went through with the voyage.

As the *Phoenix* sailed into the South China Sea in the spring of 1967, our AQAG gang in Philly held our breath; would US forces stop or fire on our ship? After all, they could make the small ship simply disappear in the vast sea—then shrug their shoulders when asked where it was.

Nevertheless, our ship arrived safely in Haiphong. The crew was greeted by North Vietnamese government officials who accepted the medical supplies for their Red Cross. Crew members were taken to the capitol, Hanoi, and hosted for a few days before returning to the ship. Later, crew members told us they were exhausted—first by the tension of the voyage and then by the unaccustomed attention of officialdom, who honored them in a formal, ceremonial way.

Still, some were able to manage quiet conversations on the sidelines, where they related in a person-to-person way with Vietnamese civilians and heard about how people's families were coping with the current bombings on top of years of attack by a superpower. Living under the French empire had been bad, our crew members were told, but the scale of violence coming from America was almost beyond comprehension.

Back in Philadelphia, we kept praying for the *Phoenix* crew as they sailed once again through the Gulf of Tonkin and the possibility of vengeful attacks by upset US combatants. We notified the families that the crew members were on their way home.

Mass media coverage was enormous: nightly news on television networks plus many newspaper stories. One reason for the extensive media coverage was the duration of the drama: day after day the question was asked, "What will happen to the *Phoenix*?"

Afterward, doors sprang open across the country to hear the story.* *Look* magazine's long photo story was a hit. Pro-war people reconsidered their views. Peace-inclined people who'd been inactive were stirred to action. America's best-known activist Roman Catholic priest, Daniel Berrigan, wrote that he wished he'd been on the *Phoenix*. Then, the following year, he made a trip by air with professor Howard Zinn to Hanoi to bring back three American pilots who'd been shot down over North Vietnam and were then released by the North Vietnamese government.

In the Philly AQAG office, we began organizing for the second voyage—destination South Vietnam—reading applications for positions on the crew. The *Phoenix* would sail from Hong Kong with medical supplies for the South Vietnamese Red Cross, as well as for the clinics at the pagodas of the Unified Buddhist Church. Delivering to the National Liberation Front remained on the agenda as well, but we were still trying to figure out whether that was logistically possible.

As before, we would seek to raise ten thousand dollars for the

---

* One of the crew members for that trip published her account as a book: Elizabeth Jelinek Boardman, *The Phoenix Trip: Notes on a Quaker Mission to Haiphong, North Vietnam* (Celo, NC: Celo Valley Books, 1985).

medical supplies—not much, but about what our small ship could carry along with the crew. And I, who had been contentedly fundraising for the project while co-leading AQAG, teaching at the King School, and playing with baby Christina, felt compelled to offer myself for the next voyage. It wasn't a conscious change of mind but rather a sudden inner calling that was unusually clear, as if God was tapping me on the shoulder.

It seemed that everyone in the situation had a choice except me: the selection committee of AQAG could decline to put me on the crew, my Quaker Meeting could refuse to support me, and the King School could fire me. But if AQAG chose me, I would go—and I would have Berit's support, even though she admitted it would be hard on her.

The clarity of the summons didn't stop me from thinking about consequences, of course. Entering a war zone in the South China Sea would be dangerous—even if it was in South Vietnam's waters this time. I wanted to live a long life, and certainly didn't want to die in my twenties in an ocean halfway around the world. I found myself reviewing what I'd thought and discussed about risk and sacrifice, staying strongly in touch with my feelings and with the beliefs that shaped my actions, including the Quaker tradition of sometimes being led by God into situations that pragmatic and/or self-interested calculations would strongly advise against.

I considered the young people killed in the civil rights movement and in the many other movements where activists surely wanted to die as little as I did. I even thought of my dad's brother in the navy, who was killed during World War II, and others in the armed forces of the world who don't make it back home alive. I thought I was no one special in that life-and-death way.

All of us have a responsibility to believe in something larger than ourselves, something so important that we're willing to die for it if that's what it takes. I would so much rather die for a cause than because a drunk driver crashes into me, yet many people do take the risk of going out at night, even drinking themselves and heightening the chances of catastrophe.

When considering the *Phoenix* voyage, it helped that in my earlier think-throughs on risking, I'd come to the place where I made my peace with the possibility of dying "before my time." That matters: a specific occasion of lethal risk is easier to face if one is already in some sense at peace with dying for a cause. Having come to that place, a new time of decision was a matter of integrity, a matter of follow-through on what made me, me. After all, I might not act with clarity, or even keep my wits about me, if I went into a dangerous situation not having resolved the question of whether I was prepared to give my life.

I'd become a dad, and that was huge for me. There is, however, a priority responsibility even for dads—one that my own dad and uncles and, indeed, so many millions of fathers who died in combat—fulfilled when they joined the military. Being a dad is another reason to be a member of a community, as I am with Quakers, a community that includes a web of shared responsibility for young ones.

When considering an action, I also think about the strategic occasion for a risk. I don't want to risk injury or, for sure, my life, for ill-considered, unstrategic emotional venting, which is what too many protests are. I'm constantly amazed by activists who go about their jobs and lives thoughtfully and then become irrational when it comes to protest. Surely building campaigns that can win change is worth as much thoughtfulness as our job, or planning to build a house.

Finally, I'm responsive to a Source that is greater than rational strategizing, a creative knowing that sometimes emerges and says, "This is it." I'm inspired by the Friends who have made break-throughs by following what we call "leadings," and I aim to stay open to that possibility. Centuries of Quaker practice have shown the wisdom of creating a committee that assists an individual who experiences a leading. The committee assists the individual to discern whether they are experiencing a valid leading or simply an impulse that appears so.

I asked my Quaker Meeting for what's called a "clearness committee." A handpicked group of Friends from my Meeting sat with me and asked probing questions, including about my responsibilities to my child. We sat in silent prayer. My leading was clearer than ever. The Meeting united to support my leading, delegating a Quaker elder to provide ongoing liaison to Berit, and said that, if I didn't return, my family would receive support.

AQAG decided to put me on the crew and named me project director for that voyage to South Vietnam. Bob Eaton would be skipper, responsible for navigation and ship safety.

The King School was a different matter. Crozer's president was well aware of the negative reaction among some of his board members to the first voyage of the *Phoenix*—"giving aid and support to America's enemy." He'd already tried to forestall a dip in donations. The idea of a Crozer faculty member joining the crew of that so-called peace ship—it would not do. He asked Bayard Rustin, knowing my deep respect for him, to call me and talk me out of it.

Bayard's charm and the deftness of his arguments, which emphasized the importance to the movement of my staying here and teaching my students, were lost on me.

Since Bayard was the best chance they had, Crozer's president let me know that I would be fired if I joined the *Phoenix* crew. I quickly called George Willoughby, who told the students.

I guess the seminary president had forgotten that we were in the business of sharing with students the skills of direct action. The King School students quickly spread the word among seminary students, many of whom had taken my classes or in other ways knew me. A critical mass of students was soon reached, and the president was informed by the King School director that he'd better retract quickly before he had a publicity-generating student revolt on his hands, along with a faculty making noises about academic freedom.

The message was quickly sent to me: I wouldn't be fired, but I'd best get from Asia back to the classroom as soon as I could.

ᘓ ᘓ ᘓ

As I sat in a window seat in the plane over the Pacific, my thoughts drifted back home. Before leaving, I had made a decision on my PhD. Rather than retake the orals exam, as Philip Rieff had suggested, I would drop my pursuit entirely.

It had taken some time to sink in, but the department chair had intuited correctly: I'd been using Penn's excellent resources not to become a professional sociologist but to become an evidence-based social activist with skills to do homework for the movement. Also, as an activist, I was one of the many whose theory of change was shifting toward a more radical stance. I knew that my friends in the Graduate Sociology Club with a professional middle-class background would likely find my giving up the PhD—and distancing myself from their class identity—to be incomprehensible. It reminded me once again of how strongly I still identified with the working-class me.

Despite my having reached this decision before the trip, the many hours on the plane gave me the solitude to think it through carefully again. This time I had additional evidence: based on behavior, I clearly heard the calling of a revolutionist, not the calling of a professional sociologist. So, thirty thousand feet above the ocean, I wrote my letter withdrawing from Penn, with sadness, relief, and gratitude to my mentor, Dr. Rieff.

My first stop in Asia would be what was then called Saigon, the capitol of South Vietnam, to negotiate visas for the *Phoenix* crew, so we could bring our medicines to the South Vietnamese

Red Cross and the clinics at the pagodas of the Unified Buddhist Church. Since neither had invited us, though, the first order of business was to try for a meeting with the government's minister of health, then go see the head of the Buddhists.

I expected a hostile reaction because of the previous *Phoenix* voyage to their supposed enemies in the north. To my surprise, the Saigon government's minister of health had a big smile for me. "You represent the people who sent a ship with medicine to North Vietnam?" he asked. "Please tell me what you found in North Vietnam. A branch of my family lives there, and it is so very hard to get news from them."

His request stood against the barrage of US propaganda alleging North Vietnam to be a separate country from the south. He knew better than I that "South Vietnam" was an artificial construct created at the Geneva Conference in 1954, meant to be dissolved in an election two years later throughout all of Vietnam. President Dwight Eisenhower admitted that the United States had monkey-wrenched the plan, refusing to allow the election because it would certainly be won overwhelmingly, in the south as well as the north, by Communist leader Ho Chi Minh. Democratic process was to be allowed only when the result pleased the empire, according to the arriving Americans, as well as the departing French.

Our meeting ended amiably, with the health minister's hope that our crew would receive visas to bring our medical aid.

ॠ ॠ ॠ

The An Quang Pagoda was half an hour away from where I was staying in central Saigon. It was surrounded with military spies, my interpreter, Cao Phuong, told me as we approached. "They don't usually bother us on the street; their function is reporting."

This young biology professor at the Buddhist Van Hanh University was later to became well known as the nun Sr. Chan Khong—right hand of Thich Nhat Hanh, the organizer of a peace movement of young Buddhists in Vietnam. Exiled by the Saigon government, she and her cohorts would build the internationally famous meditation retreat center Plum Village in France.

At this moment, however, in October 1967, Professor Phuong went by her birth name, which just so happened to mean "Phoenix" in Vietnamese. Needless to say, she was the perfect person to take me to the An Quang Pagoda to meet Thich Tri Quang, the head of the Unified Buddhist Church, which was famous for its opposition to the Saigon government's complicity in America's war.

In the simple monastery room where Thich Tri Quang slept and worked, I explained AQAG's mission to bring medical aid to civilians of all the major political factions, including the clinics at his pagodas. He quickly showed he understood the nuances of our politics, as well as our spiritual grounding as Quakers. He said that when our ship reached the port in Da Nang—five hundred miles north of Saigon, on South Vietnam's eastern coast—he would have representatives there to receive the aid.

As I left the pagoda, Cao Phuong asked if I had time to visit her campus and have a meal with a friend. I was delighted; it was far more than I expected from a stranger with so many responsibilities. At the campus, she chose a plaza where students liked to hang out and walked to an informal group of them, including some she knew. She immediately introduced me. They eyed each other, and each found some pressing reason why they needed to leave just then.

Shrugging her shoulders, she led me to another group, where the same thing happened. She turned to me with amusement in her eyes. "As you see, they want nothing to do with an American. We'll try once more, and I'll use a different strategy."

I understood the students' hostility to a random American

wanting to talk with them, so I wondered what Cao Phuong had in mind to break down the barrier. We slowly walked to another group in animated conversation, where she greeted them warmly and asked what they were talking about. She joined their conversation and, after a while, threw a quick translation in my direction. She continued, and then another quick translation came my way. The third time, she turned it into a question for me, quickly translating my answer back to them. One of them responded to what I said and asked me a question about the US role in their country, to which I responded. The discussion warmed, with Cao Phoung playing facilitator and translator at the same time. The students leaned in, sometimes serious and sometimes smiling, with appreciation that a visiting American professor actually had a clue about the devastating impact of his country's actions.

I remember they were especially surprised that I understood my country's imperialism, and responded vulnerably with their own fears of Chinese domination when the US eventually would lose its war in Vietnam. Long ago, Vietnam had been part of the Chinese empire, and the students did not want that to happen again; they were as keen for independence as the Americans who'd fought our own revolution against the British.

༅ ༅ ༅

The meal with Cao Phuong was as memorable as the discussion with the students. Again, I felt privileged to be present for a conversation that an American could rarely, if ever, be a part of, given the political tensions between our peoples. She'd invited one of her oldest friends, a woman who agreed with Cao Phuong on many things but had affiliated herself with the National Liberation Front—the armed opposition force fighting the US military in South Vietnam and supported by North Vietnam. During our conversation, conducted in English, Cao Phuong deliberately brought up the subject of armed struggle. As the huge white American male in the room, I made my points infrequent and short. Besides, maybe this was an argument that these close friends had been wanting to have, and my presence gave them an excuse to have it.

They argued about the comparative effectiveness of violent and nonviolent struggle, passionately and on a level of political sophistication I rarely heard—on or off of a university campus. They were respectful and conceded valid points made by the other. Neither seemed to make headway in the debate.

As I sat with the two Vietnamese friends, listening to the intensity of their debate, I was very aware of my being an outsider—a citizen of a country that, at that very moment, was destroying their country. I wasn't going to intrude with an opinion. Still, it was a question I'd looked into because of how shaken I was by the amount of violence my country was unleashing. I hadn't done the broad research on empires that was needed, but even so, I had done a few comparisons that were useful. I'd looked at the British Empire and the strategy choices made by three colonial independence movements—in India, Ghana, and Kenya—and how that empire struck back.

In India and Ghana, where nonviolent struggle was the force that drove out the British, minimal life was lost—perhaps fewer than a thousand killed.* By contrast, in Kenya, where an armed struggle emerged, the British reportedly killed more than 12,000 militants and incarcerated 150,000 others in concentration camps, including children. It wasn't until the empire's loss of India and Ghana, along with rising pressure in its other colonies, that the British finally yielded independence to Kenya.

To me, it was quite clear: a violent struggle unleashes the poten-

---

* Adriana Popa, "Ghanaians Campaign for Independence from British Rule, 1949–1951," Global Nonviolent Action Database, last updated May 17, 2011, https://nvdatabase.swarthmore.edu/content/ghanaians-campaign-independence-british-rule-1949-1951.

tial violence of an empire, while a nonviolent struggle inhibits that violence. And this same dynamic was at work in Vietnam.

In fact, the United States unleashed more tons of explosives on Vietnam than was dropped by the allies during all of World War II—about five hundred pounds of ordinance per resident of South Vietnam.* A low estimate of war dead in South Vietnam is nearly half a million,** but a 1975 US Senate subcommittee estimated 1.4 million Vietnamese civilian casualties.*** And those numbers cover only South Vietnam, not the north.

Sitting in that apartment in Saigon in 1967, I was aware of the ongoing violence by the American empire, feeling guilty—yet transfixed by the intensity and intellectual rigor of the dialogue between these two friends who disagreed so strongly about strategy. Then Cao Phuong boldly asked a question I'd never heard raised in the midst of struggle, a question informed by her own wisdom but one that I was able to understand because of what I'd learned comparing struggles against the British Empire.

"I want you to think for a moment," Cao Phuong said to her friend, "of all the Vietnamese who have been killed in the armed struggle that's been going on for a decade. And consider the alternative tactics of nonviolent struggle. Here is my question: If our people who've been sacrificed in the armed struggle had instead died while using nonviolent tactics, would the Americans still be here?"

Her friend became silent. She took a sip of tea. "Cao Phuong," she said, "you have asked a very good question."

---

* Melissa Dell and Pablo Querubin "Nation Building through Foreign Intervention: Evidence from Discontinuities in Military Strategies," August 2017, https://scholar.harvard.edu/files/dell/files/vietnam_war.pdf.

** Estimate from R. J. Rummel, "Statistics of Vietnamese Democide," lines 777–85, http://www.hawaii.edu/powerkills/SOD.TAB6.1B.GIF, quoted in Wikipedia: "Vietnam War casualties," https://en.wikipedia.org/wiki/Vietnam_War_casualties, last updated June 2, 2022.

*** Nick Turse, *Kill Anything That Moves: The Real American War in Vietnam* (New York: Metropolitan Books, 2013), 12, quoted in Wikipedia, "Vietnam War casualties," https://en.wikipedia.org/wiki/Vietnam_War_casualties, last updated June 2, 2022.

gunboats surround me in the South China Sea

At last I could meet the crew of the *Phoenix* in Hong Kong. Whether or not I was going to return alive to my family would depend a lot on them and their individual courage, competency, and ability to work together as a team.

At the airport, I was met by Michael and Marilyn Payne, New Zealand Quakers who were living with their children in Hong Kong while Michael designed architecture for the city's housing developments. They told me that the Friends Meeting had turned itself into a support team for the *Phoenix* crew; I could look forward to showering in one of a number of homes, since our little ship had no such provision.

Marilyn laughed easily and teased me about the *Phoenix* being moored at the Royal Hong Kong Yacht Club, between elegant sailing ships and old Chinese junks. "I think they put you on the edge next to the junks so people wouldn't assume you belonged to the yacht club," she said.

Nevertheless, the yacht club did have the benefit of attracting major newspapers like the *Guardian* and *New York Times*. In fact, the crew was able to hold a news conference right when they arrived, which was a relief to me. I didn't want them holding back and waiting for their project director to show up. AQAG's image was in good enough hands with our captain, Bob Eaton—a self-possessed, highly verbal guy, capable of holding his own with any reporter.

"Any sign of the visas from Saigon yet?" I asked.

"No, but the South Vietnamese consulate says they should arrive any day now," Marilyn said.

I heard stories in Saigon about the government's bureaucracy being corrupt and incompetent, so I already figured we'd need to increase the pressure. "I'll ask the crew how soon we can be ready to leave," I said, "and announce the date via the media. That might hurry up the bureaucrats—after all, the minister of health said permission was pretty much a sure thing."

It was hugs all around when I met the seven other crew members for this voyage of the *Phoenix*. Nearly everyone was younger than me—and I was still just twenty-nine. There were two women: Kyoko Koda, from Tokyo, representing the major anti–Vietnam War movement in Japan; and Maryann McNaughton, who I knew from the youth program of Philadelphia's Friends Peace Committee. Chris Cowley was a veteran British pacifist who'd been living in Japan. Beryl Nelson brought his extensive sailing experience to the role of first mate.*

While we received some much-needed gravitas from Ohio University English professor Harrison Butterworth, John Braxton was still just a student at Swarthmore. I knew him from a young Friends workshop I'd led several years earlier on civil disobedience—and could not believe he'd managed to convince his parents to let him join this mission into a war zone.

---

* Beryl Nelson's sister Marge was, at that moment, working as a doctor at the American Friends Service Committee's medical unit in Quang Ngai; her work in Vietnam served Vietnamese casualties no matter their political affiliation. She was a member of my Friends Meeting in Philly. Marge was later captured by National Liberation Front soldiers when they overran the entire province, and she was held as a prisoner. After being marched through various parts of Vietnam, she was safely released and wrote a book about her extraordinary adventures: *To Live in Peace in Midst of the Vietnam War* (self-published, 2019), available on Amazon.

Finally, there was Bob Eaton, the only holdover from the *Phoenix* crew that had sailed to North Vietnam. Bob and I already had an easy, trusting relationship. In our catch-up meeting he showed me his charts and estimate of a five-day sail to get to Da Nang. "We're really crowded, George," he said. "A fifty-foot ketch doesn't really have room for cargo plus a crew of eight. Philadelphia appointed eight! I know adding the internationals builds connections for the movement, but still." He paused. "I guess we can stand it for five days."

Little did we know that it would be almost a month before we could step off the ship.

≋ ≋ ≋

My visa strategy worked. We announced a departure date and held a large news conference at the Hong Kong Hilton the day before the announced departure. On the departure day, just as we were about to push off, a Vietnamese official came running down the dock toward us waving a large envelope and yelling, "The visas! The visas!"

The wind picked up and the waves grew taller before anyone had a chance to get used to the sea. By the time the waves reached twenty feet tall, everyone was sick, even Bob. Beryl was the only exception. Crew members usually took our turn at the wheel even when we were sick, but Bob made sure there were always two of us in charge of holding the course. I vividly remember a night when John and I were sharing the steering, the Phoenix ploughing through heavy seas. We were talking deeply about nonviolence theory when I said, "John, please take it." He moved quickly to the helm while I staggered to the rail and threw up. On my return, we continued our conversation, but it wasn't long before I grabbed the helm while John lurched for the railing. We continued thusly through the whole of our shift, every once in a while pointing to the humor in the situation but not quite able to laugh.

A rainstorm swept through, and we learned that our ship had seams that leaked. All our sleeping bags were soggy. A particular misery was to be cold and wet after serving our shift, then crawling into what felt like a wet sponge to fall into exhausted sleep.

Someone found out that the cider helped with seasickness. We quickly drank up our supply and achieved a happier state on more than one count.

When the sun returned, we lugged our sleeping bags to the deck and dried them out while we sunbathed. Bob said we would arrive on time, and sure enough, by sundown on the fifth day, we were closing in on the bright green coast of Vietnam. A South Vietnamese gunboat was waiting for us. The English-speaking captain said we'd arrived too late for the reception of our medical supplies, so we would spend the night in a safe anchorage and in the morning be escorted to the docks of the port of Da Nang.

We followed the gunboat to a tree-lined cove with a gentle beach and put down our anchor for the night. We were soon startled by a whizzing sound, followed by an explosion, and rushed to the deck to see that a gunboat was shelling the cove. We could actually see shells hurtling over the top of our masts and exploding on the beach.

This was their definition of "a safe anchorage"? I'd learned in Quang Ngai that a frequent strategy in this part of the world, with unlimited money flowing from Uncle Sam, was to set off random explosions to keep a place "safe." Apparently the cove was sometimes occupied by National Liberation Front soldiers, the so-called Viet Cong.

The sociologist in me had made sure that we had a tape recorder on board to record our crew discussions. I thought something might be learned about how a team makes decisions under stress, and this Quaker-led crew hoped that it could make tactical decisions by consensus. As project director, it would be my job to decide if we didn't all agree, but when we had the time we'd first try to decide collectively. To increase the chance of that working, I frequently called meetings of the crew to do contingency planning for possible future decisions. We came up with a range of possibilities and gamed them out, listening to each other while ideas were tried out when there was no urgency.

I was proud, at the end of the voyage, to realize that we had indeed made all our decisions by consensus, even when time was limited and we were stressed. I'm no longer attached to consensus decision-making for an action situation—it can reduce creative flexibility—but I remain proud of our achievement.

Now, the tape from the voyage is held by the Swarthmore College Peace Collection and is publicly available online.* Fellow crew member John Braxton and I listened to it together in 2019. One of my favorite parts is during the shelling of the shore. A crew member expressed frustration that our ship's radio had broken and we couldn't call our families to let them know we were safe.

On the tape, we hear a loud explosion.

A brief silence is broken by someone saying, sardonically, "Thank God we're safe!"

~ ~ ~

Along with the morning came a second South Vietnamese gunboat to join Number 602. (Numbers on this class of warship were prominently displayed on the stern.) It seemed odd that a second ship would be dispatched to escort us to the docks in Da Nang, which looked to be only a couple miles away. The unspoken question was

---

* The tape can be publicly accessed through the Swarthmore College Peace Collection: A Quaker Action Group, "Strategy Sessions On Board the *Phoenix* During the Trip to South Vietnam," digitized audiotape, reel 0205_01a, 02:09:02, 1967, https://archive.org/details/AudiotapeReel020501a.

soon answered by officials in a small boat motoring out to us. I grabbed our envelope of visas, in case they wanted to see them.

"Everything has changed," the lead official said without boarding the *Phoenix*. "You are to return to Hong Kong."

I waved the brown manila envelope. "There must be some mistake," I said. "The visas are right here."

"They are no longer valid," he said. "Your visit has been cancelled."

Impatiently, I said, "We need to have an explanation. What is the explanation?"

"We will give you no explanation," he said. "Return to Hong Kong." And with that, the boat motored away.

Our crew gathered at the rail and looked at each other with surprise and dismay. All that buildup, and seasickness, for this?

It was easy to agree that we wouldn't turn around. The second gunboat was obviously sent to help the first prevent us from sailing to the docks. They were much bigger than we were and made of steel. We were not interested in our wooden ship turning into splinters. But what to do?

We were sitting around our table below deck, lamenting our failed radio, when Beryl called from the deck: "Someone's coming!"

We saw the press boat getting closer, with an array of civilians holding cameras. "Communication is coming!" Kyoko shouted with relief. But a moment later a crew member on the nearest gunboat shot machine-gun fire across the bow of the press boat. It stopped, turned, and headed back toward Da Nang.

The isolation was a blow. I continued our meeting, searching for options, and we came up with a plan: We would refuse to leave without an explanation of the reversal. Having visited a South Vietnamese hospital during my trip to get the visas, I'd seen for myself a shortage of medicine. Once we knew what the government's problem was, we could decide what to do about leaving.

Bob pointed out that they could simply tow the *Phoenix* out beyond their three-mile boundary and patrol us until we left for Hong Kong. We developed a plan: if their crew came aboard the Phoenix to tie a towing line, we would begin to jump overboard to swim to land. Whoever made it could walk into Da Nang to confront General Lam, head of the province. He would likely know what was behind this reversal.

We were in no mood to weigh the risks of our plan—it was a relief even to have one. Bob maneuvered the *Phoenix* close enough to Number 602 to talk to its captain. The captain appeared, and they talked across the water, with Bob explaining our intention.

"That is a terrible idea!" the captain said. "There are sea snakes in the waters here, and you will be bitten and die." Bob intuited our response: "We will take that risk. Do not put your crew on our deck."

The captain, of course, had to report to General Lam, and a stalemate began. John got out his guitar, and we sang favorite movement songs, improvising new verses. I remember one of them, for the civil rights song "Hold On":

> *"To the crew of 602,*
> *Don't you know that we love you,*
> *Keep your eyes on the prize,*
> *Hold on."*

We got close enough to throw some candy bars to crew members on deck. They threw fresh fruit to us, with smiles all around. Unfortunately, those smiles were no guarantee of their officers' competency; on the second day of waiting, their ship passed us too closely and collided with us, snapping our mizzen boom as if it were a matchstick. That left our mainsail intact but reduced our maneuverability and also opened numerous small leaks in our hull.

After three long days of waiting, the captain finally got his orders and closed the distance to put a couple of crew members on our ship. We already had a plan for who would go overboard first, second, third, and so on. Bob had volunteered to be first, but we reminded him that a captain should not be the first to leave the ship! We settled on Harry as the first because he was the most venerable, and in Asia, venerability counts. But that was the extent of our venerables. If Harry failed to reach the shore, I was the next up.

It was dusk when Harry dived in. The warship's partner gunboat switched on floodlights and moved between us and the shore to block him. Harry tried swimming around the bow of the gunboat, but the captain moved the ship to nose him out. Harry then reasoned that if he tried to get around the stern of their ship they might hesitate to back up, lest they mangle him in their propellers.

He was a good swimmer, and it worked. Instead of backing up, the captain ordered three crew members to dive into the water and capture Harry. The last we saw of Harry in the penumbra of the floodlight was him heading toward shore, with South Vietnamese sailors swimming in hot pursuit.

"It's your turn," cried the crew, and I jumped in. As a certified romantic I knew what to expect at such an existential moment of high drama: I would have a profound revelation about the meaning of life. Instead, as I bobbed up to the surface of the water, my thought was that the water was lovely and warm.

"Come on in," I yelled to the *Phoenix* crew members standing at the railing, "the water's fine!"

I turned toward shore but was quickly surrounded by four Vietnamese sailors who'd dived at the same time as me. One of them held a line. "Take this," he said, "and you will be pulled to the deck." He motioned with his head toward the gunboat deck high above us.

"No," I said, "I want to go to Da Nang." With a smile, I continued, "But I won't try to hurt you—I'm nonviolent."

I'm guessing the others didn't know English, but they began to smile in return, and I suddenly saw in my mind's eye a floodlit picture of us from above, treading water and smiling and nodding to each other as if we were at a party. Bizarre!

The man with the line swam to me and tied it securely around my waist, saying, "Excuse me," and signaled to the gunboat crew on deck to haul me up.

On the deck, I stood watching the gunboat maneuver closer to the *Phoenix*. The captain was careful, mindful of the previous day's collision. Disabling our ship was apparently an accident rather than a part of his orders.

The Vietnamese first mate came over to me to say that I was lucky to be saved because on the shore were National Liberation Front soldiers. He added, "The VCs do not like Americans."

"I don't want to be 'saved,'" I said. "I want to be on land, to go to Da Nang!"

By then the gunboat's deck was looking down on that of the *Phoenix*. I was lifted by strong arms and handed down to our crew members, who gave me a big hug. I was confused—where was Harry?

"He's on shore!" they told me. "He got to the beach first, and their sailors were afraid to pursue him because it's a free-fire zone and NLF soldiers might be there."

Later we learned what happened next: Harry found the dirt road we'd glimpsed that paralleled the shore and walked toward Da Nang. As we'd agreed ahead of time in our planning for whoever made it to shore, he kept on his bright orange life jacket, walked in the middle of the road, and sang and whistled as he walked. Our idea was that if there were NLF soldiers in the area, the sight of such a spectacle would be so curious that they would hold their fire until they found out more, and that would be our margin of safety.

A mile or so down the road, Harry ran into a couple of US Marine sentries in their jeep, who had been told to be on the lookout for "a couple of drunken sailors who'd jumped off the SS *Phoenix*."

The marines offered to put him up in their post overnight, and Harry accepted the offer. He kept them up most of the night arguing about what they were doing in Vietnam, and in the morning, they actually agreed to drive him to General Lam's office in Da Nang. It couldn't have worked out better.

Because Harry jumped out of a US Marine vehicle, no one stopped him as he entered the building. He strode confidently through the outer offices and found General Lam, who gave him an explanation for why our mission was rejected at the last minute: The strength of the peace movement led by the Unified Buddhist Church was growing again in Hue and Da Nang. The South Vietnamese government didn't want the Buddhists to get even the small amount of support and recognition our aid would provide.

Soldiers were ordered to put Harry back on our ship. Our own sources had also indicated changes in Buddhist strength that might make Saigon the better destination, now that Da Nang seemed closed. We told the captain of Number 602 that there was no reason to tow us away; we would sail on our own to the Saigon area. There we would vigil at the three-mile-line denoting their boundary. We said we'd wait there for a reasonable length of time—three days—awaiting permission to proceed into Saigon to offload our medicines.

The weather treated us well, and our crew arrived in the Saigon area in good shape despite the disabling of our mizzen sail. The next three days were highly stressful. None of the gunboats that greeted us got close enough to enable human contact with the captain or crew. By day, they repeatedly sailed across our path to invite a crash by us; we knew the consequences for us and the plausible deniability for them if such happened. There were some narrow misses, and Bob spent long stretches at the helm.

Their favorite tactic at night was to shoot tracer bullets parallel to our ship, waking up those trying to get some rest and reminding us that they could destroy us if they wanted to.

On the third day, a US Navy patrol boat joined, to increase the pressure. It circled slowly around the *Phoenix* with a sailor manning the deck-mounted machine gun. He kept moving the gun as the boat changed position, in order to keep us as his target.

I was disappointed that the Quaker-style prayer meetings that we had and our brainstorming sessions didn't generate practical tactics supporting human-to-human connection. We sang no songs to Vietnamese crew members, whose faces we couldn't see. It was frustrating to experience repeated hostile actions and not respond with expressive, positive actions of our own.

Although disappointed that the Saigon government didn't relent, we were also glad when our three-day commitment was done and we could sail onward to Cambodia, a neutral country next to Vietnam and the closest safe haven. We were low on food and water, and our ship needed repair work before returning to our base in Hong Kong.

When we arrived in Cambodia, I left the crew to fly to Saigon and meet with Thich Tri Quang. I had no idea how the media were reporting the story, but for my part I was disheartened by what felt like the failure of our mission. As I walked into his cell, he looked at me, and through me. "I see you are discouraged, my friend," he said.

"We didn't succeed in bringing you the medical supplies," I replied.

He smiled. "I see you misunderstand our situation. First, I will give you the name of a freight agent in Hong Kong. He will send your medicines to us via a regular freighter, and we will get them, no problem."

Relieved, I smiled. We already assumed that the Buddhists had a regular channel they'd been using to obtain medicines for their pagoda clinics. The amount we could carry on our small ship would only supplement their supply. Our highly political protest peace voyage was—as with the trip to the North—intended to help build the crucial US peace movement by assisting my fellow American citizens in seeing the Vietnamese as human beings under attack, rather than as "threats." And we were intent on trying to reach all sides; no one could correctly say we were simply "aiding the enemy." Still, I was intently curious about what Thich Tri Quang meant by their "situation."

"It will help you to know more about my Buddhist people. Few of us Buddhists have a class analysis as the Marxists do.* Because they understand that the owning class of a country can make war without the true understanding or support of the people, they know it is incorrect to blame the people as a whole for the decisions of the few.

"My South Vietnamese Buddhist people, however, are left to invent an explanation for the war. Many therefore imagine that all Americans are devils, attacking us when we are in no way a threat to them. Your voyage contradicts the 'devils' belief, and that contradiction is to us a big contribution. Now, the clergy in our pagodas have begun teaching that many Americans are good and compassionate people, and to prove it they tell the story of the voyages of the *Phoenix*. The *Phoenix* truly is a bird that arises from the flames. It helps no one to struggle well if they believe another people are evil. Your brave voyage lifted a spiritual burden that was holding us back from self-realization, from enlightenment. It will make us stronger to tackle the tasks that are ours to do. Thank you."

---

* Marxists provided the leadership of North Vietnam and presumably of the National Liberation Front in South Vietnam that aimed for the unity of north and south.

~ ~ ~

As I packed for the trip home, I realized how much our planning back in Philly had turned into improvisation when we faced the reality on the ground (or water, as the case may be). So far, we at least had some assurance that our aid was reaching people represented by two of the four major players here: the North Vietnamese, and now the Buddhists. We still hoped to find some way of reaching a third—the Red Cross of the National Liberation Front—but that would have to wait.

At the very least, we'd issued a very public challenge to our government's attempt to dominate through killing and hurting people who were in no way a threat to us. I could hardly wait to get back to the United States and jump on the speaking circuit to tell our story—and, in that way, help build the antiwar movement. But even before the speechmaking, I needed to get home and see my family.

sharing strategy lessons in Britain

In Saigon, my next challenge was logistical and also sentimental. I needed to fly from Saigon to Tokyo to Sidney to Honolulu to Los Angeles to Philly in order to get home. Could I get back to my family in time for Christmas 1967? That's always been such an important, renewing holiday for me. Some connections would be close but, thanks to the international date line giving me two December 24s, I made it in time!

Even my exhaustion couldn't distance me from the bliss of being home for Christmas with Berit and two-year-old Christina. "Your baby saw your picture while you were in Vietnam," Berit said.

"How could that be?" I asked.

"We were at the Arvios' home in November for a gathering of the Back Benchers," she said, "and you know we were all praying for you that weekend. On Sunday morning, we were dawdling over our breakfast coffee with the *New York Times* spread out on the table. Christina was in my lap and suddenly said, "Daddy!"

"She pointed to the paper, and there was a grainy picture of the *Phoenix*, and you were at the deck rail with some other crew members. I couldn't have told it was you if Christina hadn't seen it."

I started to laugh. "It was that boatload of media people trying to reach us when we were stuck outside Da Nang! The gunboats wouldn't let them near us. They sent machine gun fire across the bow of the press boat. One of the journalists must have had a telephoto lens."

"Now you know your little girl was really missing you," Berit said. "You know, all along I somehow had this confidence that you would be okay and return to us safely. Maybe I think my prayers are that powerful! And now"—she snuggled closer—"they're answered."

≈ ≈ ≈

Larry and George, the senior leaders of A Quaker Action Group, said I could let go of the *Phoenix* project as I resumed my classes at the King School in January 1968. Most of the crew stayed with the ship, with Bob continuing as captain and Beryl as first mate. The *Phoenix* once again sailed through the blockade of the Seventh Fleet of the US Navy, arriving on January 29 in Haiphong harbor to deliver the supplies for the National Liberation Front's Red Cross.* We'd finally reached three of the four major forces in the war.

AQAG and the American Friends Service Committee wanted me to speak about the *Phoenix* trips and the war across the country during breaks at the King School. On one of those tours, I learned something new about the first *Phoenix* voyage to Vietnam. It was the fall of 1968, and the leaves were turning. The man I encountered was shorter than I was but heavily muscled, leaning toward me with a scowling face. His buzz cut suggested he might recently have been military. He stepped in front of me on the walkway leading to the chapel at the Midwestern campus where I was about to speak about my sailing to Vietnam with medical supplies.

---

* Jessica Reynolds Renshaw, *The Reynolds Family, the Nuclear Age, and a Brave Wooden Boat*, (CreateSpace Independent Publishing, 2017), 181ff.

"Are you George Lakey, the guy who was on the *Phoenix*?" he demanded.

"Yes," I said looking squarely into his eyes. "What's up?"

"I saw the story in the paper, about you speaking here." His tone of voice was threatening. "You should be ashamed of yourself for doing what you did—and now you're going around speaking about it!"

"I don't know what you're getting at," I replied with an even tone, putting my weight on both feet, getting ready to be slugged. I figured he might be referring to the first *Phoenix* voyage, since that was the most famous and, in some circles, infamous because it was "aiding the enemy." I wanted to hear him out.

"I was a navy pilot on a carrier in the Seventh Fleet when *your ship* was sailing toward North Vietnam," he said, curling his lip. "We were scheduled for a flight training exercise when you were near us—and we were laying bets on which of us would sink you."

He paused. On his face I saw a mixture of emotions as he remembered the moment.

"But when we got into our planes, the commander got on the loudspeaker and said the exercise was cancelled, on direct orders from the White House!"

This information—news to me—was too much to take in while this guy was in my face. First, I had to deal with him.

"Look," I said, "lots of Americans have differences about what we did and, man, you can come on into the meeting and share with the folks your point of view." I put on as welcoming a face as I could. "I mean it."

He hesitated, looked surprised, and dropped his eyes. I shrugged my shoulders, suggesting it was his move and I would accept whatever that would be. He hesitated some more, turned, and walked away.

That's when I allowed his news to begin to sink in. Those of us organizing the project had known the trip would be high risk.

The pilot's story confirmed it. Our crew came *that close* to being drowned in the South China Sea!

Later I learned what transpired behind the scenes: The three departments of government involved—State, Treasury, and Defense—couldn't agree on what to do with the *Phoenix*. They punted the decision to President Lyndon B. Johnson's White House. There it was decided that the *Phoenix* would be allowed to sail unimpeded to Haiphong harbor. National Security Advisor Walt Rostow was given the job of making sure the *Phoenix* got past the ships of the US Seventh Fleet safely. The implementation of his memo to ship commanders came just in time.

When I got back home and told Berit about my threatening encounter with the navy pilot, she smiled and said, "I wonder if it's your size that gets you threatened so often; maybe tough guys want to take you on for the glory of it!"

We laughed together.

"I wish there were a simple formula we could offer for what to do in a variety of situations," she said. "At Women Organized Against Rape, we hold training workshops instead of handing out a formula, to prepare women to handle themselves. The martial arts people have no simple formula either, so they offer training, and that's what we offer in the nonviolence movement. Getting trained sure beats walking around in fear."

≈ ≈ ≈

The *Phoenix* project continued to generate articles and speaking tours for several of us, helping to build the growing peace movement. We heard some inquiries about doing more voyages, but within AQAG we were clear that we'd made our point; there would be zero drama in continuing to do the same thing. Attention is more often gained from creativity.

Fortunately, activist creativity was alive and well. In 1968, the draft resistance movement was growing rapidly, and draft boards were receiving an abundance of attention. In Maryland, the Catholic activists known as the Catonsville Nine raided a Maryland draft board and burned the files of the young men liable for the draft. In Philadelphia, a Quaker activist had gotten hold of a list of names of members of the US armed forces who'd been killed in Vietnam. Larry, George, and others joined him in taking the list to a draft board's office and—with the media tagging along— group members took turns reading the names out loud with a short pause after each one. The draft board staff was shocked, the police were called, and the Quakers refused to leave. They were arrested.

Media coverage was intense. Many who had a knee-jerk reaction against antiwar protests had second thoughts as a result. The emotional impact of remembering fathers, husbands, brothers, sons who'd been killed in the war raised the question: What was it that they died for? By April, the reading-the-names tactic had been tested in several places and was campaign-ready. President Nixon, who'd been elected on the promise that he had a "secret plan to end the war," had yet to produce one.

AQAG decided to take the nonviolent tactic of reading the names of the war dead national by launching a weekly reading of the names on the steps of the Capitol in Washington, DC. Regulations at the time said the Capitol steps were forbidden for demonstrations, so each week those who read the names were arrested. I waited until May, when I'd turned in my grades at the King School, before taking my turn on the steps, by which time several members of Congress joined us. The police acknowledged congressional immunity, while taking the rest of us into custody.

Numbers grew. Influential *New York Times* columnist James Reston wrote that our campaign officially ended Nixon's honeymoon: Vietnam was once again a hot issue. The tactic's power to cut through the war propaganda was so great that, in October, a giant nationwide peace effort included thousands of readings of the names of the war dead—on the steps of courthouses and municipal buildings in towns large and small.

A strength of the rapidly growing peace movement was its profusion of creative tactics. More draft-eligible young men were refusing to cooperate with military conscription, and one way to take the offensive was blatantly to break the law requiring us to carry a draft card. Men of draft age routinely carried their card along with their driver's license in their wallets; an open refusal to do so often triggered retaliation by the government including imprisonment. The government asked for, and got from judges, longer prison sentences imposed in its vain attempt to keep the lid on the antiwar movement.

George Willoughby, with other older Friends, reached into Quaker practice to encourage more refusal to cooperate with the draft. Our worship style involves waiting in silence for the Spirit to lead; even Quaker weddings are influenced by that practice. George and the others agreed to hold, on May 5, 1968, a similar worship service at which any attendee who might be moved to do so could turn in his draft cards. The committee said that any cards received would be sent to the government in Washington along with the wish that, if retaliation was to be taken by the government, the committee members should also be sent to jail.

John Braxton, who'd crewed on two *Phoenix* voyages and was now safely back studying at Swarthmore, stopped by my house on the appointed day to go together to an old brick Quaker Meetinghouse in Center City for this unusual meeting for worship. On our way we teased each other: "Tonight's your big night! Tonight is when you defy the government once again!" We laughed our way downtown, each of us confident that no way would we open ourselves to possible imprisonment for draft defiance so soon after the stressful time we'd had in Asia.

It was a deep and powerful meeting for worship. In the end, both John and I turned in our draft cards.

I was called before my local draft board to explain myself, which I welcomed. This same draft board had, a few years earlier, given me an order to report for two years of alternative service under the Selective Service Act. I had requested the service because I didn't want the privilege of attending grad school to distance me from my high school classmates who were being drafted into the war. So I'd already "done my duty," and now had a small child, and they were intensely curious about my motivation for tackling the conscription system once again.

I was in the middle of telling them what I'd seen in Vietnam, when suddenly the secretary from the Selective Service storefront's outer office burst through the door to the conference room in a panic: Quakers from the local Friends Meeting had showed up to picket in solidarity with my protest. The board hurriedly dismissed me, and I never heard from them again.

John's outcome was quite different. He was prosecuted, convicted, and sentenced to two and half years in prison. He was paroled after four and a half months, however, as the American people increasingly turned against the war.*

Not everyone focused on developing creative, nonviolent tactics for the struggle. Many of the antiwar organizers fell into the habit of a traditional march or rally—by nature fairly boring and less likely to carry the indignation, sadness, and even rage felt by the growing movement. King School students found themselves being called on to travel and train people in nonviolent technique; increasingly, the call was for peacekeeping skills to reduce

---

* John Braxton's powerful statement to the judge at the point of his sentencing, and their remarkable back-and-forth about it, is shared by Wayne R. Ferren Jr., in his book *Conscientious Objector: A Journey of Peace, Justice, Culture, and Environment* (Bloomington, IN: Archway Publishing, 2021), 369–75. Ferren also includes some of Braxton's account of his two Vietnam trips on the *Phoenix*, including his experience of war-torn North Vietnam.

the number of those whose rage led them to act out with violence. Slowly, more people at the grassroots learned to isolate trouble and de-escalate when police and right-wingers attacked us. The King School had become an engine for distilling knowledge, along with deepening commitment and sharpening skills by passing them along to the growing network of battle-ready nonviolent activists. Both the Philadelphia-based Friends Peace Committee and the national American Friends Service Committee were instrumental in growing the network.

≈ ≈ ≈

I was asked by British Friends to spend the academic year of 1969–70 in the United Kingdom, sharing what we'd learned in the United States from the civil rights and peace movements. Berit was delighted at the prospect of being closer to our Norwegian family. She also remembered enjoying England when, as a teen, she was there as a finalist in an international essay competition. I figured the King School would grant me leave for a year that included guest lecturing at British universities. George Willoughby was always more of an internationalist than I was and encouraged me to accept the invitation.

My three months in Asia had expanded my worldview considerably, and I'd already seen the influence of Prime Minister Harold Wilson's loud dissent on Vietnam in 1966. I began to grasp global systems and to see there are multiple locations from which to challenge the American empire. I'd done my share of organizing locally, and it was time to continue to interact globally, hanging out with members of War Resisters' International and others with a transnational perspective. As a way to learn, being around a lot of activists works for me.

And so we spent the summer of 1969 in Skien, with Berit's family, "on the way" to Britain. It was fun to introduce our new baby boy, Peter George Lakey. A very light-skinned Black child, Peter had been born in January 1969 and placed with us a couple months later. He wasn't in good shape when we got him—screaming when we left the room as if certain he'd been abandoned forever—but we figured he'd come around. His big sister, Christina, loved having a tiny baby to "help Mommy with."

In August of that Norwegian summer, I briefly returned to Philly in order to attend the 1969 War Resisters' International Triennial Conference, held at nearby Haverford College. The political atmosphere in multiple countries was burning with discussions of revolution, so I decided to make that my theme for my coming year in the United Kingdom. War Resisters' International—the global network that the US War Resisters League was part of—was considering developing a manifesto to add to the dialogue and wanted me to present, for consideration, a new writing project I was working on: a five-stage strategic outline for nonviolent revolution.

In addition to supporting the ventilation of new ideas for peace, the triennial conference was a great place for networking. I got more chances to talk with Daniel Ellsberg, whom I'd met earlier at Princeton University, at a conference on revolution, when he was an unknown academic consulting for the Defense Department. At Princeton, we'd shared anecdotes while trading experiences in Vietnam. At the triennial conference in Haverford, however, his energy seemed more intense, which I figured was natural for a US marine who'd been up to his neck in the war and was at this conference surrounded by pacifists.

Later I would learn more about what was on Dan's mind at Haverford. He was weighing a decision to risk professional suicide and considerable jail time by releasing the top-secret Pentagon Papers to the *New York Times*. After he'd done so and incurred the wrath of the Nixon administration, he said in a public forum that he was helped by his conversations at Haverford with me and two

of my draft-resister comrades: *Phoenix* captain Bob Eaton and
Randy Kehler, director of the War Resisters League's San Francisco office. The conference adjourned for half a day to witness, in
solidarity, the sentencing of Randy and Bob in federal court for
refusal to cooperate with the draft.

After that intensity, it was good to return to Norway and relax
with the Norwegian family before taking on the challenges of our
year in Britain. We told our Norwegian relatives that we would
spend next summer with them and, possibly even before that,
sneak in a side trip for a sentimental Norwegian Christmas.

≈ ≈ ≈

"On your first day at the office, George, you should wear this,"
Berit said, as we were unpacking in our third-floor apartment in
Hampstead, getting ready to make London our base for the year
of 1969–70. Berit held up my dark-blue suit. "If you wear it for the
first few days with a conservative tie and a white shirt, then later
you can wear anything you please and you'll get away with it."

Berit was often my advisor in the arcane ways of professional
middle-class propriety. She was brought up by working-class parents who had worked and saved their way into the Norwegian
middle class, finally owning a flower shop and garden center in
their small town. So Berit's mother had raised her to appreciate
the nuances of presentation.

Now we were in class-conscious Britain, and I was feeling
insecure. After all, in my own country I continued to feel the
ambivalence that often goes with upward class mobility, along
with a subtle feeling that I was an imposter and would soon be
exposed as the inferior person that classism told me that I was.
Well, we were in London now, and to share my message effectively I would need to respect the fact that appearance mattered.
Berit brought sophistication to the management of self-presen-

tation; I was happy to take cues from her. "Right," I said, "the dark-blue suit it is."

British Quakers wanted me to lecture and give workshops among Friends, university students, and a variety of activists. They'd spent the decade watching the United States with a mixture of fascination and horror: How could a society produce the likes of John and Robert Kennedy and Martin Luther King and also gun them down? How could its social movements make breakthroughs in nonviolence while its government killed Vietnamese people by the hundreds of thousands?

I was known as someone prone to draw useful lessons even from the drama of blood and heroism; my mission would be to share what we in the United States had learned during the turbulent sixties. I was feeling the pressure of high expectations. British Friends had brought on a staff person whose entire job would be to book me for speaking engagements and conferences and arrange my travel. They wanted to maximize the number of civic and movement groups, universities, and Friends Meetings that would hear my message.

I took their goals seriously and tackled the year with full energy. As it turned out, I spoke to six thousand people at 115 meetings in the United Kingdom, as well as leading a number of trainings for students, Friends, and the Fellowship of Reconciliation. British Friends decided to be generous and say yes to invitations in half a dozen other countries as well.

Berit's dark-blue-suit strategy worked at Friends House on Euston Road, the large building that housed a capacious room for worship as well as the many offices devoted to Quaker good works in Britain and around the world. As soon as I realized I'd been accepted, I left my tie at home and switched to pants and a sweater, only to move on to a new sartorial dilemma: What should I wear on my speaking trips? Again, this sort of question is real for someone as motivated by effectiveness as I was, knowing that an audience's reception of my message was likely to be influenced by my appearance.

A typical speaking trip by train would include an afternoon lecture at a university followed by an evening lecture at a church. Students, and the activist community of that town or city, were put off by anything resembling a dark-blue suit—it was a dead giveaway for the likely bourgeois and useless remarks that would emanate from the mouth of the tall Yank that no one had heard of and expose the fraudulence of the title of his talk, "Which Way the Revolution? Lessons from the Sixties." The church people, on the other hand, would be turned off by the clothes favored by young activists. I couldn't dodge these realities if I wanted my speaking trips to be worth the effort.

Berit solved that dilemma brilliantly as well. "Here, wear this voms," she said, holding up my Norwegian tunic. "It's made of quality gray wool, for the church people, but it has these folk patterns," she said, pointing to the red and blue embroidered decorations, "and these pewter clasps, so no one will be able to figure out just where you're coming from, and they'll have to listen to what you actually say!"

As word spread about my availability, the voms got a workout. Two lectures a day expanded to three, and I began to sleep overnight in other towns and cities. I urged my tour planner to make the university gigs at night, because the students were more likely to keep me lively and awake with their debates. My campus visits attracted a contentious crowd; each political faction on the left felt honor bound to make an appearance. After impatiently listening to my prepared remarks, the students sprang to their feet to tear my ideas apart. I found it more exciting than speaking at US universities.

ᚾ ᚾ ᚾ

I'd spent the previous four years investing strongly in skill- and leadership development for social movements, through the Martin Luther King School and what became an informal national training network. Somewhere I'd heard the phrase, "Most of what we need to know, we have yet to learn." I certainly thought that was true about making a nonviolent revolution, and I was eager to learn how to do this complex thing, while also knowing that I couldn't do it myself because its complexity demanded a collective effort.

In these early months of touring, I didn't notice much attention to social change training and education, which surprised me because the United Kingdom was famous for its pioneering development of worker education. I began asking organizations to convene training workshops and—from those—found individuals who themselves wanted to learn how to facilitate the experiential methods I was using. They were more than ready. By the end of a year's work, there was a network of British trainers.

The new trainers realized that educational work, using the skills of a facilitator, is substantially different from the lecturing and debating skills so well honed in Britain. They agreed with me that facilitation, as opposed to instruction, is much more consistent with the egalitarian values of nonviolent revolution. From that point of view, my work teaching facilitation helped me offset the inevitable round of lectures that were planned for me.

נ נ נ

The tempo of the year increased. I made a point of learning to nap. I wrote articles on train rides, gave lectures established in one or another famous name, and even attracted some groupies who traveled around Britain attending my lectures and workshops. Regrettably, I neglected my family even more, leaving Berit to the isolation of tending to two young children in a neighborhood not her own. By my own standards, that was inexcusable, so I used the signs of my tour's impact to push my neglect out of my mind.

I flew back and forth to the continent, speaking at conferences, leading trainings, and working with German students who were launching a movement called Grassroots Revolution, a precursor of the Green movement, which became an important political party in the German parliament. I redoubled my attention to training British trainers, hoping to leave some skills behind when I left. By connecting in the spring of 1970 with some of the best British trainers I'd worked with, I pulled a network together; years later I heard that activist training went to a new level there as a result. More facilitators were relying on experiential exercises and drawing out the strengths in the group they were working with.

≈ ≈ ≈

In early May, Berit and I took a mini-vacation as tourists in Bath, just paying attention to each other. We found delight in walking along the graceful Georgian terraces under blue skies with hardly a cloud. In the middle of a tour of ancient Roman ruins, I noticed a woman coming up to the group with her face contorted, eyes shining. "They're killing their babies now," she said to a friend in the group. Her voice rose to near-hysteria: "They're killing their babies!"

Berit and I moved closer.

"These young people were peacefully protesting at some university," she continued. "BBC radio said something like 'Kent State.' And soldiers opened fire on them. I don't know how many died."

Our tour fell apart as people gathered around her with questions she was unable to answer through her sobs. Berit and I headed for a telephone, and then the train for London.

The later editions of the newspapers were full of the news: Richard Nixon and Henry Kissinger had invaded Cambodia,

George as a baby.

Super-eager to join the band.

George dresses in solidarity with his dad during World War II, with mom, sister Shirley and brother Bob.

New baby Peter joins Christina in George and Berit's growing family.

George and Berit going to a formal wedding of friends, on Long Island.

A pensive moment in Hong Kong during the flurry of work getting the Phoenix ship ready to sail to Vietnam.

The second voyage of the Phoenix in 1967, a sailing ship protest action George led to bring medical supplies to the Buddhists' anti-war movement in South Vietnam.

A South Vietnamese warship stops the Phoenix.

Negotiating with naval officers on coast of South Vietnam during the war.

At a Movement for a New Society retreat with Peter and Ingrid.

Daughter Ingrid joins LGBTQ demonstration with proud dad.

A casual moment for Movement for a New Society in the 1970s, Berit is in pigtails.

Lakey communal household in Movement for a New Society.

Jonathan Snipes and Horace Godwin led with George a series of weekend retreats for gay and bisexual men in the 1970s.

Training for Change workshop for young leaders in Eastern Europe.

Leading another sing-in of Handel's oratorio Messiah.

Once we were five: with Berit, Christina, and Ingrid planting the memorial tree for Peter Lakey the year after he died.

Training for Change workshop for young leaders in Eastern Europe.

Taking a break with Zimbabwe host Gerald Gomani during training Training for Change trip.

Leading an impromptu training roleplay on the sidewalk in George's West Philadelphia neighborhood. People come from around the world for trainings.

Johnny Lapham and his son Adrian join George and Ingrid at demonstration for climate justice.

Speaking at rally for Bank Like Appalachia Matters.

George and some environmentalist friends join Bill McKibben (front center) to show determination in the struggle.

Mid-winter family portrait.

George with great-grandson Yasin, new granddaughter Ella, and Janice Robinson, Berit's partner (who fell in love with and married Berit).

George's family, including his mother, father, sister, and brother.

Training for Change lead trainers honor George's mentors Lillian and George Willoughby; Judith Jones far right; Karen Ridd far left.

Annual Messiah sing-in grows, moves to Quaker Meetinghouse.

George with
Michael Beer and
Ingrid.

A complex training exercise about stress and communication in a workshop in Canada in 2008.

Earth Quaker Action Team's march to stop PNC Bank to stop financing mountain top removal.

Grandpas and granddaughters both need naps.

George and Johnny.

Swarthmore College students learn more about their professor's campaign against mountaintop removal coal mining.

Swarthmore College graduation speech.

unable to tolerate a relatively tranquil country holding out against our domination. As a result, students protested on campuses across the United States. At Kent State University, the National Guard was called in and—at a distance of sixty feet from the peaceful demonstrators—aimed and fired their rifles. Four students died.

In London, I was asked to speak at a protest scheduled for the next day. Leading actor Vanessa Redgrave would be there as well, along with Peggy Duff, the brilliant organizer of the Campaign for Nuclear Disarmament—the largest peace organization in Britain at the time. I was amazed to see a hundred thousand people arrive at short notice. Huge banners dotted the crowd, while chants rose defiantly. Protesters were also arrested at the US embassy. I was racked with conflicting emotions as I spoke: there was grief and rage, but also pride in my country's peace movement, which was already stopping business as usual in hundreds of places. Most overwhelmingly, though, I felt tremendous shame at the cowardice of my country's political leaders whose policies killed young people at home as well as in Indochina. Only ten days later, two young Black students were killed and a dozen more injured at Jackson State College in Mississippi, gaining little attention compared with Kent State.

The next morning, I learned that the *Sunday Times* didn't think much of me as a speaker. I didn't either; I was choking on too much raw emotion. All day, the BBC continued to report on antiwar demonstrations throughout Britain and the rest of the world. As Berit and I held each other that night, our children sleeping soundly, we were grateful for the world's outpouring of solidarity with the victims of still more US violence. We knew global opposition rattled the US State Department and encouraged more centrists to come out against the war. Hopefully my work that year in Britain helped build a stronger link in the growing international chain needed to restrain the US empire's destructiveness.

Somehow or other Berit and I had managed to save our summer for recovery, a summer that we'd been looking forward to with longing. In the fall, we would return to Philly and an even larger volume of social movement activity than when we'd left. Now we would spend a few months in Norway, forget about lectures and workshops, share the parenting, and relax.

17

the tree of life, a book, and a new baby

The summer of 1970 was the most idyllic of my life. We spent it on a small island in a Norwegian fjord. Berit's oldest brother, Einar, invited our family to stay with him and his wife, Alfhild, on Sandøya, not far from Brevik, on Norway's southern coast. We stayed in the apartment Einar made in the basement of their house.

Berit and I quickly developed a routine of sheer bliss. We got up early with the children (Christina was five and Peter was one and a half) and had breakfast together. Then I opened my portable typewriter on the wooden table that stood at the window facing the fjord and settled down to write while Berit played with the children.

At that time, I was still working on my five-stage concept for revolutionary change, which I'd begun the previous year and introduced at the War Resisters International Triennial Conference at Haverford College. I still had much to write, but the basic framework was taking shape, with the five stages defined as 1. cultural preparation; 2. organization building, including the creation of alternative institutions; 3. confrontation via smaller-scale direct action campaigning; 4. mass political and economic noncooperation; and 5. assisting the alternative institutions to scale up and carry out the basic work of a complex society, in a way that lines up with the vision enunciated in the first stage.

Of course, the stages overlap and are subject to local and sectional differences. Feminists who studied the framework later pointed out to me that the sequence of stages might become cyclical. The main point I was making for movements is that there's strategic strength in sequencing, as opposed to the exhaustion (and impossibility) of trying to do everything at once.

This whole new way of thinking was the result of a challenge I received from an African freedom fighter who hailed from the British colony that later became Zimbabwe.

I met Nathan Shamuyarira at the International Student Seminar in Vienna, in the summer of 1967, where we were both speakers. He told me that as a younger man he'd been inspired by Gandhi and tried to figure out how nonviolent struggle could win his own country its independence from Britain. His Christian faith, he said, was added motivation, and he regretted that he couldn't come up with a plausible strategy in time for the rising revolutionary tide in his country. He joined the violent revolution.

"You," Nathan said, pointing his finger at me, "have the luxury of time and academic resources that enable you to advance the field, to make more options available for people like me! George, I want to challenge you to do that!"

I love "field-testing" a new piece of writing, so presenting my early concept at the triennial conference hosted by War Resisters International was a great opportunity to make sure I was operating in the same context as those I hoped to connect with and support. My conversations with people there—like Daniel Ellsberg, British activist leader Michael Randle, and others who'd been wrestling with questions of revolution for much longer than me—were encouraging.

Over the next few years, I would turn this concept into several pieces of writing. First came "A Manifesto for Nonviolent Revolution," which War Resisters International adopted for itself at the next triennial conference in 1972. That short piece was then translated and published in various countries, while in English it became the whole issue of a popular activist periodical, *WIN* magazine, and also the closing article in a scholarly book, *Toward a Just World Order.** The positive feedback from both activists and intellectuals fueled me as I then completed the more multidimensional book version, *Strategy for a Living Revolution,* published in 1973.**

Harvard sociologist A. Paul Hare teased me after it came out, saying that despite my writing in a popular style, he could tell that the book was "clearly the work of a sociologist." I'd allowed my research into the social dynamics of movements, leadership, team behavior, conflict, and oligarchy to influence my vision of life-enhancing, fundamental change.

While I was working on all this in the summer of 1970, at Alfhild and Einar's house beside the fjord, I noticed that my writing was taking a more and more global perspective. It really did pay to go to Asia and then plunk myself down in Europe for a year. I began to envision how the world could settle disputes without armies, emphasizing decentralization, evidence-based global coordination, and nonviolent enforcement. The part of me that I felt was fundamental—the visionary—was proposing how humanity could justly handle the severe environmental problems of the future.

ૅ ૅ ૅ

During the peaceful mornings on the island, I often paused as I wrote to watch the fishing boats returning with their catch, the shrimp already cooked on the way back. I saw the fishers offload the baskets of shrimp and clean the boats to be ready for the next

---

* Richard Falk, Samuel S. Kim, and Saul H. Mendlovitz, eds. *Toward a Just World Order*, vol. 1 (Boulder, CO: Westview Press, 1982).

** The book is still in print half a century later, now with the title *Toward a Living Revolution: A Five-State Framework for Creating Radical Social Change* (Eugene, OR: Wipf and Stock, 2016).

morning's departure. When the breeze came in my direction, I could hear them joking with each other as the workday wound down.

Berit and I most often used the conventional family arrangement of those days: Dad earns the bread, and Mom takes care of the children. Part of what made this summer wonderful was creating an alternative division of labor. After I wrote in the morning, our little family ate lunch together, and then it was my turn with the children while Berit rested or visited with Alfhild. Christina, Peter, and I roamed the small island picking and eating berries as we went: strawberries, raspberries, blackberries, and blueberries. Norway has such a short growing season that all the berries ripen at nearly the same time.

We climbed the small hills and pretended they were mountains. Christina delighted in rolling back down the hill if it was grassy. I laughed with her, this beautiful girl: tan skin framed by black curls, a killer smile, and large, dark eyes filled with light. Peter tried his best to roll after her, but couldn't quite figure out how to roll and ended up scrambling like a drunken crab. He'd bounce up ready for more fun, his bright blond curls waving in the breeze. I'd talked with Black friends about Peter's coloring, and they laughed at me and said that their young children came in all shades.

Christina was adventurous. She tested which trees were best for climbing, and yelled down from a high branch for approval of her skill. She bravely walked up to enormous cows and petted them; I kept her away from the bulls. I loved to hug her, but she wouldn't stay long; a quick squeeze was the most I would get before she ran off to explore a new spring or a raspberry bush we had somehow missed.

Peter liked to stay close and especially liked being carried. Even when I was walking behind him, I felt an invisible string that kept us connected. Maybe it was the anxiety that already haunted Peter when we met him as an infant in the adoption agency. We soon realized he was a child who struggled to feel secure, but didn't grasp until years later how profoundly vulnerable he felt.

Christina, Peter, and I explored for hours through those lazy afternoons. We hid from each other in the woods while I tried to convince Peter that the game includes staying quiet; he was very anxious to be found. Sooner or later, we'd return to the rocky beach and dare each other to stay in the cold water for more than a few minutes. At some point, Peter usually fell asleep from sheer exhaustion, and I'd hold him while watching Christina dig in the sand, her orange life jacket glowing in the bright sun.

We usually ate dinner with Einar's family and shared news from the day around their beautiful table with handmade tablecloth, candles, and Norwegian silver. Berit and Einar told stories from their childhood: about the scariness of the German troops who occupied their town, the defiant refusal of their dad to sell his potatoes to the German soldiers, the Norwegian Nazi family that was moved into their house over their protest, the hiding of Norwegian Jews until they could be gotten to the safe haven of Sweden.

Although the sun still shone brightly in that northern country after a summertime dinner, the heavy eyelids of our children said it was bedtime. Berit and I took our youngsters downstairs and tucked them in, then took time for each other. The sofa faced the window, and we watched the fishing boats rock gently at anchor in the calm water of the fjord, the seagulls browsing from one boat to the next. We made another pot of coffee and sat close together, reading. We cuddled and talked about our lives, dreamed about the futures of our children, and made love.

To our surprise, we made a baby.

Berit and I had already reached the number of children in our family that we wanted. We took no precautions because neither of us seemed to be fertile; years earlier, we'd tried hard to conceive, with doctors' help, before adopting Christina and Peter.

This might be a fanciful notion, but I believe I remember the night on Sandøya that we conceived. It had to do—as with many other things in my life—with activism.

During the year living in Europe that was now drawing to a close, I'd been following with keen interest the activities of AQAG. Formally, I was still cochair of the group in 1970, even though an ocean separated me from our office in Philadelphia. AQAG's current campaign was gathering momentum the summer we were on Einar's island; the goal was to awaken the public to the reality that the US government was busy building chemical and biological weapons.

Larry Scott continued to strategize brilliantly. He explained that the mass media are far more interested in a narrative that builds to a climax and has an uncertain ending than they are in a one-day protest. AQAG participants, therefore, started the summer campaign on the Capitol steps in Washington, DC, holding small evergreen trees and seedlings. "We are walking to the Edgewood Arsenal with these trees of life," they told the assembled media. "We intend to plant them on the grounds of the arsenal and thereby confront that center of death with the hope and reality of life."

The drumbeat of media attention grew as the mostly young campaigners walked northward, and more people joined them. Newspapers tried to find out, without success, whether the arsenal would allow AQAG to plant trees on its property.

On Sandøya, I was getting frequent reports; Larry had developed what's called a dilemma action, where AQAG would win with the trees no matter what the arsenal did. If the commandant allowed the trees to be planted, we would have achieved our stated goal and AQAG would declare victory. If the commandant used his military police to arrest our campaigners, he'd show that his arsenal was too death-centered even to allow some new evergreens on the property. Either way, our media coverage would put us where we wanted to be. The public would begin to wake up.

Excitedly, I shared the letters from AQAG members each day with Berit. We imagined how it was going for our activist friends, as they slept on the floors of churches, luxuriated in a rare shower, and consulted with lawyers about how much jail time they might get. On our Norwegian island, clustered with evergreens, we had no difficulty identifying with the campaign's symbolic focus on the evergreen tree.

Finally, the confrontation happened. On the first day, five people and four trees were arrested. On the second day, another eight people and six trees were arrested. In its lead editorial, the *Baltimore Sun* challenged the government to give up its chemical and biological weapons, and our small but dramatic campaign launched a national movement against biological weapons that succeeded before the decade was out.

Back on Sandøya, the campaign was vivid for me because of my tight bonds with the AQAG gang, plus each morning's book-writing about activist strategy. The way the campaigners centered their action with trees and life and joy harmonized with my wandering with children among the evergreens, followed by the evening's cuddling with Berit and laughing over the letters. One night, our lovemaking perfectly integrated the joys of the day; in our cozy bed I experienced myself as a tree of life, sturdy and abundant.

And that was the night, I believe, that our third child was conceived. We named her Liv Ingrid; "Liv" honors Berit's sister and is the Norwegian word for "life."

≈ ≈ ≈

In 1971, we were happily back in our home in Powelton Village, Berit again at work at the Child Guidance Clinic and me doing movement organizing. In the spring, Berit, heavily pregnant, entered the hospital to treat an infection, and her water broke. Thus began one of the best days I'd ever shared with Berit, although that's easy for me to say, since she did the work. Unusual for those days, I insisted that I be in the hospital's labor room. The attending physician predicted I'd get in the way. "You'll distract from our work." Then he doubled down, sneering that I'd have to be carried out of the room after I fainted.

Berit and I soon established our own energy and enjoyed a pleasant few hours. Her contractions were infrequent and light. I read short stories to her; we joked and kissed. Then the doctor advised inducing labor; Berit's touch of diabetes and the fact that her water had broken made an infection more likely, they said. They put medicine in her IV drip; Berit's contractions became hard and frequent.

"Do you want more ice chips?" I asked in the brief pause between contractions. She shook her head no, and another one hit her. As it subsided, she said, "Rub my back again."

Grateful for a chance to do something, I rubbed and rubbed, marveling at her stamina, her sheer grit as she panted through the contractions hour after hour.

"It's time to push now," the doctor said, and I propped her back more as Berit pushed. "It's crowning," one of the nurses said. "Looks like a redhead."

"You're doing fine," said the doctor. "Push real hard now."

Berit pushed mightily, and we heard an exclamation from the other end of the table: "The head is out!" I smiled; Berit was concentrating too hard at that point to manage a smile. "Push again!" said the doctor, but no more baby emerged. I heard the scary word "forceps" mentioned at the other end of the table.

"Let me try something," said the doctor, and then, "Push as hard as you can!" While the doctor put his hands around the baby's head and his foot up against the table for additional leverage, I leaned into her back. An exhausted Berit, gathering her remaining strength, pushed with all her being. The doctor pulled at the same moment.

"It's out!" came the chorus at the end of the table. I heard Berit's belly laugh of triumph and relief as the doctor held aloft a nine-pound, four-ounce Ingrid, covered with ooze and ready to cry.

building the Movement for a New Society

The United States experienced fierce polarization in the sixties: bombings increased, people stopped speaking to each other, young people fled to Canada and Sweden to refuse the draft. Polarization arouses more people to act, but those who've been acting become vulnerable to burnout. Some experienced activists were dropping out, taking their skills and hard-won lessons with them.

Larry Scott wanted a sabbatical, so when we returned to Philadelphia after our year away, I filled in and became interim executive director of A Quaker Action Group. The sociologist in me immediately started interviewing AQAG members, both the inner circle and the less frequent volunteers. I was especially looking for signs of burnout.

The AQAG activists I interviewed were proud of their track record and, at the same time, showing the strains of the increased force of the winds of change in the late 1960s and early '70s. Sexism was identified as a pressing issue by AQAG women. There was also burnout accompanying the endless war in Vietnam. Another issue was that the increasingly radical analysis of US military interventions was leaving activists impatient with working just one issue at a time, as the small-scale AQAG felt forced to do in order to have any impact at all.

I persuaded the AQAG leadership to proceed on two simultaneous tracks: to start an organizational planning process, which we tried to lighten by using slang and calling it "Whither AQAG?" and, at the same time, to join a new campaign that could give us a small but significant role. My diagnosis was that there was still some energy left for campaigning, even while the "Whither AQAG?" process designed changes that we hoped would avert burnout and help us retain people's experience and skills. I didn't expect the radical restructuring that in fact resulted.

The new campaign engaged us with a familiar opponent, the US Navy—except, this time, in Puerto Rico.

Culebra is a small, beautiful island with pristine beaches—minus the ones that were then being shot at and bombed by the navy for target practice. In addition to the danger inhabitants faced from stray shells and bombs, the practice also interfered with fishing, which was the livelihood of many residents.

Puerto Rico had another, larger island that was also a military target, Vieques, but the six hundred Culebran people had raised their voices so strongly that a coalition formed around them: a committee of clergy and the Puerto Rican Independence Party, which stood not only for independence but also for social democratic institutions that could curb the worst of the capitalist exploitation Puerto Rico was experiencing. Both the clergy and the party were committed to nonviolence and wanted a stateside nonviolent group to help them increase attention to their cause in US media.

In 1970, AQAG hired two Spanish-speaking field staff to go to Puerto Rico and start working there. They learned that a Methodist chapel had once stood on the beach the navy targeted. Why not rebuild the chapel on the beach, using easy-to-carry modules, and worship there in defiance of the navy's guns? It would be another dilemma action, like the planting of trees at Edgewood Arsenal. If the navy gave up target practice to spare the chapel (and the islanders' bodies), they would celebrate! If the worshippers were arrested, they would *also* celebrate, because arrests expose the government in yet another militarist excess and expand the movement. Either way, the drama makes the point and raises the campaign to a new level.

The clergy committee joined Culebrans' support for the idea. The biggest player, though, was the Puerto Rican Independence Party. Its leader, Rubén Berríos Martínez—a flamboyant young law school professor who favored nonviolent direct action over the failed terrorism of an earlier era—indicated some hesitation. Berríos' problem wasn't with the strategy but with the relative amounts of publicity AQAG and the Puerto Rican Independence Party should get. Berríos didn't want gringos getting any credit at all, enacting a kind of "colonialism of the left," in his eyes. While AQAG understood this and accepted its role as a secondary ally, it still needed to get enough publicity to do the fundraising that enabled the project in the first place.

I was asked to come down to San Juan to try to resolve the conflict. It was the dead of winter, and my friends teased me that I would find any excuse to leave cold and bleak Philadelphia!

I took an instant liking to Ruben Berríos. I also learned a valuable strategy lesson from him that remains relevant to this day. I asked Ruben, "Why wouldn't it be better, since the Puerto Rican Independence Party is an independence movement, to stay away from the Culebrans' struggle rather than 'contaminate it'—in the eyes of the moderate government—with your radicalism?"

"You're not seeing clearly enough the point of view of our opponents," he replied. "What the governments of Puerto Rico and the United States see are two things: first, a specific struggle to gain a navy departure from Culebra. The power holders also see an independence movement saying to our people, 'Do you see how the people and ecology of Culebra suffer because we Puerto Ricans don't run our own affairs? The US Navy could not shoot at Culebra if we were an independent country!'

"Now consider the dimension of time. Because our party enters the Culebran struggle to frame the issue as an argument for independence, that means the longer the United States continues to endanger Culebra, the more Puerto Ricans will agree with our point of view. Of course, that in turn strengthens the independence struggle. Does the United States want support for the independence cause to grow? Certainly not!"

He smiled and leaned in. He was getting to the heart of his argument. "Since the United States doesn't want the independence cause to grow, our participation in this reform struggle gives them added reason to give in and give the Culebrans what they want. If the navy leaves, Puerto Ricans will be less discontented with Puerto Rico's lack of power. This is an example of how radical participation in a single-issue struggle can sometimes hasten the winning of that reform, as well as raise consciousness in general! The Puerto Rican Independence Party's participation becomes a win-win; the people of Culebra win when the navy leaves, and we've won by using the very fact that we had to struggle to get the navy out as illustration of why we need independence!"

Even though I admired Rubén's strategic thinking and enjoyed his charm, I remained stubborn about the credit AQAG needed to be able to participate in the project. Rubén was also stubbornly against gringos taking what he saw as a "savior" role. We argued more, then brought in a bishop from the clergy committee to mediate, without success. As I got to know him better, I realized he was irritated that I didn't know his language, forcing the entire argument to be conducted in English.

At the end of the day, Rubén suggested that we take a break and go to his home for drinks and a meal. As we walked in, he called to his wife, who to my astonishment swept into the living room with a traditionally Swedish look, tall and with blue eyes and blond hair to match. I burst into a hearty Norwegian greeting and she, happy to speak her native language for a change, responded enthusiastically. Soon she and I were chatting merrily in Norwegian and Swedish (which are linguistically close enough to make that possible), and

I registered, out of the corner of my eye, Rubén's expression. All over his face was his surprise that this gringo wasn't a typical arrogant American who refuses to learn another language after all—I'd simply learned a different language than he'd had in mind and was now giving a moment's entertainment to his wife.

In five minutes, over drinks, we resolved our disagreement. Language matters.

In early 1971, the chapel was built on the beach, and the navy held off target practice. The US Naval Construction Battalions, or Seabees, were brought in from Vieques to make the arrests of the worshipping Puerto Ricans and their Quaker allies. We got the media attention we needed to continue to campaign with others against the navy, which then announced it would indeed give up and let the Culebrans have their island.*

א א א

While supervising our end of the Culebra campaign, I was also laying the groundwork for a new organization that would be more complex than any I had ever attempted. I brought to the project an enlarged interest in the value of decentralized networks, because in Europe I'd learned about the work of Shalom, a Dutch network of autonomous action groups, most of which were operating "Third World Shops," selling fair-trade goods. As I understood it, Shalom contained a variety of work and a common philosophy strongly backed by a communitarian training center in Amsterdam that serviced the whole network.

---

* Nathalie Schils, "Puerto Ricans Expel United States Navy from Culebra Island, 1970–1974," Global Nonviolent Action Database, July 6, 2011, https://nvdatabase.swarthmore.edu/content/puerto-ricans-expel-united-states-navy-culebra-island-1970-1974. A photo from the Culebra campaign and a brief description of the follow-up struggle on the larger Puerto Rican island of Vieques—also a US Navy target—are in George Lakey, "Puerto Rico's Lessons in Revolutionary Campaigning," *Waging Nonviolence,* June 20, 2012, https://wagingnonviolence.org/2012/06/puerto-ricos-lessons-in-revolutionary-campaigning/.

My big question was: Could I find ingredients for such a network in the United States that could become mightier than the sum of its parts? Much of the US left had become flavored with a hippy culture often hostile to structure, but I believed structure was essential to building a national organization that could support emerging movements with strategy, training, and the spirit of innovation.

It turned out the ingredients did exist, and they came together in the Movement for a New Society, a network that lasted almost two decades and impacted the larger social change scene in the United States. Three decades later, I still run into young people who ask me about the Movement for a New Society. But I'm getting ahead of my story. In 1971, the first task was finding incipient groups of compatible flavors and textures, and putting them together in the right way. That took a year of looking, listening, and encouraging.

The "Whither AQAG?" process flourished, thanks partly to *Phoenix* veteran John Braxton and others who were writing a study book to ground AQAG members and interested allies. The group organized the book around a medical metaphor: health practitioners have a picture of what health looks like, they do a diagnosis to determine what the pathology is, and they develop a treatment plan—in other words, they work with vision, analysis, and strategy. Activists often become stuck in complaints about symptoms, instead of developing a vision of what a healthy society would look like, an analysis that detects the source of the symptoms, and then a strategy for getting from sickness to health.

The new AQAG book-in-process reflected group study that continued to engage more and more people, whether previously associated with AQAG or not. Two former members of Martin Luther King's national staff, Bill Moyer and Dick Taylor, were very dissatisfied with American activists' tendency to avoid a big picture, in favor of reacting to symptoms. Bill and Dick joined activist Quaker Susan Carroll, progressive nurse Phyllis Taylor, and others in creating a "macroanalysis seminar" that cheerfully defied the tunnel vision characteristic of much social policy.

Another ingredient was a group of young adults who'd been picking apples together at harvest time each year in upper New York State. That group was sharing dreams and visions, and developed a yearning for a liberated community of Quakers committed to radical simplicity. They explored beyond the boundaries of private property, including the practice of monogamy, which they considered the private-property principle applied to sexuality. I reached out to them and found them interested.

In the Philadelphia area, there was a loose group nicknamed "the floating Meeting." They were mostly young adult Friends who moved from one location to another for worship, demonstrating their discontent with the stuckness they saw in mainstream Quakerism, with its resistance to giving up habitual racist and capitalist behaviors.

The latter two mostly young adult groups had in common a love for singing as well as for prolonged worship that continued as long as the Spirit let them. They planted seeds for what became *Rise Up Singing,* probably the most successful folk/activist songbook of the second half of the twentieth century.*

Soon, AQAG cofounders Lillian and George Willoughby added to the "Whither AQAG?" process by sharing a concept drawn from George's long connection to the Gandhian movement in India. Their idea was to create what they were calling the Philadelphia Life Center—a combination of close community living and training and activism. I thought this Gandhian ashram of theirs could function like the Dutch Shalom network's training center, feeding into the larger network.

As Lillian and George described it, the Life Center community would embrace radical simplicity. It would support prioritizing

---

* Hundreds of thousands of copies have been sold. Available from the editors, Annie Patterson and Peter Blood, Rise Up and Sing, 42 Jenks St, Amherst, MA 01002, or info@ riseupandsing.org.

our true vocation, which is service to the people rather than building a résumé. It would support radical activism: people can take more risk when we let go of mainstream career aspirations and reduce our income to fit our fewer needs. It would support liberated culture; our music and poetry and lifestyles would grow out of what Gandhi might call "experiments with truth."

ᴚ ᴚ ᴚ

I saw it as my job to integrate the more communitarian interests of these groups—spirit, lifestyle, and culture interests—with the more hard-edged campaign/organizing/macroanalysis interests. Bit by bit, each cluster of people drawn especially to one aspect of the project began to see the complementarity of the others; as usual, successful organizing lay in assisting people to understand that they need each other.

Forty or so people agreed actively to pursue the Life Center idea. After surveying several likely neighborhoods in Philly, we settled on an area just west of the University of Pennsylvania with inexpensive, semidetached three-story Victorians. On Forty-Sixth Street, Larry Scott found an old stone mansion in disrepair that we could buy, thanks to a loan from the Quaker Meeting several of us belonged to. The Willoughbys moved into the old mansion with others to form "the Stone House" and started to fix up the formerly grand parlor to use as our training space. The house would provide the "village well" for other cooperative households we began to form on the streets nearby.

Some of us donated our books to the collective library in the Stone House, as well as washing machines for the shared laundry, and pots and pans for the community's kitchen. Keith Miller, a young Quaker just released from prison for draft resistance, started a food co-op in the basement of the Stone House as a link between our needs and those of our neighbors.

Groups formed to buy or rent other houses, and each of the houses was given a name. "The Youngest Daughter" was started by a group that moved from the Quaker study center Pendle Hill. The household that was generating the macroanalysis seminars packed their boxes of economics studies and left their beloved Germantown to buy a house they called "Daybreak." Berit and I moved, with more than a twinge of regret, from our dear Powelton Village; one of Berit's favorite treats was walking down our street in the spring to see strong older trees intact while young ones flowered beautifully, the result of our tree fight. Still, every new venture means a departure of some kind, and ours included moving to the new neighborhood to create our new collective house that its members called "Trollheim."

At the same time as we set up group households, we began to form work collectives to get things done. Volunteers joined musician Peter Blood in compiling songs for our potlucks and songfests. A collective formed to start a printshop, for the use of ourselves and our neighbors. The macroanalysis collective launched a network of study groups across the country.

My close friend Ross Flanagan teamed up with Lillian Willoughby and others to organize a neighborhood safety program; it was partly the alarming crime rate in the area that made the houses we bought so cheap. The collective's organizing was effective in bringing down the crime rate in the neighborhood.*

As the word spread, more people without Quaker backgrounds showed up. Sandra Boston, a Methodist missionary single mom with three young boys, joined others to start a new house called "Rainbow Race," and created the Church Mouse Collective for mutual spiritual support and exploration. Berit promptly became a member of that collective.

---

* George Lakey, "How a Neighborhood in Philadelphia Learned that Real Safety Lies in Solidarity," *Waging Nonviolence*, July 15, 2013, https://wagingnonviolence.org/2013/07/fighting-neighborhood-crime-nonviolently/.

Meanwhile, Augustinian priest Paul Morrissey joined and celebrated mass each Thursday afternoon in the Stone House; he later became key in what we called the Bundling Brothers Collective–six or seven of us men lying on the floor together for an hour or more, making a kind of puppy pile while we told jokes and unwound. It was amazingly helpful in undoing the distancing and role-playing that keeps men hanging on to patriarchal behaviors. Humanist atheists launched dialogues to make sure the space we created was still safe for diverse philosophies.

There were also people who came and left, sorrowfully. There were communitarians who found us not communitarian enough; they accused us of false promises because in our slogan, "Living the revolution now," we didn't state our assumption, "while working to bring the revolution to all." There were vegetarians who were shocked that some members still ate meat; there were consensus enthusiasts who wanted the community that grew to a hundred members to decide everything together instead of leaving so much decision-making to individual households and work collectives. There were hippies who found us much too busy, and puritans who found us much too sensual and pleasure-loving.

Through it all, the Willoughbys provided an anchoring presence. When women's groups formed to cleanse the Life Center of sexism, Lillian participated, while George joined one of the men's groups that formed in response, working to unlearn patriarchal habits. All of this was the new wineskin that the Willoughbys hoped would hold the new wine while it ripened, and it did, thanks partly to their patience, wisdom, directness, ease with conflict, and confidence that it would all work out. They modeled eldership in a community of mostly young people.

In a few years, there were sixteen group households in the neighborhood, plus some people living in apartments, making it about a hundred and twenty people who identified with the Life Center.

ॠ ॠ ॠ

Berit and I recruited a couple of others to create a small team that would try to knit together a national network of like-minded groups called Movement for a New Society (MNS). We reached out across the country with an invitation for action collectives and alternative institutions that could subscribe to our policy and principles, while retaining their autonomy of action.

Individuals would be allowed to join MNS only as members of collectives and alternative institutions like our Life Center community in Philly. The benefits of joining included being part of a larger whole, easier access to the emerging training center, and increased support for influencing single-issue movements toward a holistic, nonviolent revolutionary perspective. The downside for many interested people was the high common denominator we demanded of groups interested in joining. One longtime pacifist leader even called us the "new Bolsheviks."

Our reason for being so rigorous was that once a collective joined the network, it gained the right to "call crunch." This was a mechanism groups could use when their work elicited more of a challenge than they could handle—for example, severe repression. When a collective called crunch, each MNS collective was expected to release someone to aid the beleaguered group. It was that kind of solidarity that had enabled member groups of Dr. King's network, the Southern Christian Leadership Conference, to move their campaigns forward at times of violent backlash, when a campaign in a particular city grew hot.*

The first direct action campaign led by an MNS collective gave us confidence in this network feature. In 1971, Pakistan's dictator, Yaya Khan, was wreaking what amounted to genocide on the

---

* I describe the strengths of such a "power grid" in "How to Create a Multilevel Movement for Climate Justice," *Waging Nonviolence*, October 23, 2021, https://wagingnonviolence. org/2012/10/how-to-create-a-multi-level-movement-for-climate-justice/.

country's eastern region, supported by US arms, although that fact was denied by President Richard Nixon. An MNS collective teamed up with Sultana Alam, a Bengali woman living in Philadelphia, to launch a blockade in US port cities where weapons were being loaded for shipment. Using canoes and sailboats to capture mass media attention in their attempts to block freighters, the MNS campaign persuaded the national longshoremen's union to refuse to load weapons anywhere in the United States.*

This victory—showing a small group making a difference against genocidal violence happening half a world away—taught something about strategy, especially leveraging power through alliance with workers and others. It also boosted the credibility of the brand-new Movement for a New Society, validating the expectation that members of other collectives should heed the call for assistance from a collective that needed them at a strategic moment.

Later in 1971, the same collective, the "MNS Overseas Impact Nonviolent Revolutionary Group," launched a campaign at the Naval Ammunition Depot Earle near Leonardo, a North Jersey military port town. Their goal was to build anti–Vietnam war sentiment by trying to stop arms shipments to US armed forces in Vietnam. The group began by trying to stop the trains that brought the weapons to the military depot by sitting on the tracks.

US Marines joined local police in attacking our blockade tactics, so reinforcements were needed. The drama of the action induced many to join, and the group escalated by adding a naval component: People were urged to bring canoes and other small craft and go into the sea and try to stop the munitions ships from leaving port. By April, the collective had twenty-six canoes lined

---

* The exciting story is told by a leader in that campaign, Richard K. Taylor, in *Blockade!: A Guide to Nonviolent Intervention* (Maryknoll, NY: Orbis Books, 1977). See also my account, "Opening Ourselves to the Realities of Class," *Waging Nonviolence*, September 4, 2012, https://wagingnonviolence.org/2012/09/opening-ourselves-to-the-realities-of-class/.

up, with at least two people in each, and the news that a ship named the *USS Nitro* was on its way to the base.

The collective leading the campaign called crunch. I was a member of the MNS outreach collective in Philly, and we met promptly to decide how to respond to the call. The group agreed that I should volunteer, and in two days I was with volunteers from other collectives on our way to Leonardo.

Our car stopped before the entrance to the New Jersey Turnpike to pick up a hitchhiker, and we introduced ourselves to each other. He said he was in the military, a Navy Seabee who was assigned to work in Leonardo.

"What kind of work?" I asked.

"There's supposed to be some kind of demonstration by peace people up there," he said, "and my unit is supposed to go help arrest them if they mess with the ship."

"Interesting work," I said with a smile. "Have you done that kind of work before?"

"Yeah," he replied. "Last year I was based in Puerto Rico, and my unit got called to go arrest some Quakers who were protesting on a beach in Culebra."

The others in the car burst into laughter, while I explained to our hitchhiker why we were laughing. We had a great conversation about his experience and the nature of the two events before we dropped him off at his destination.

"Hey," I said, "here's my phone number. I'd like to know where you go next, so I know where I'm supposed to be!"

When we reached the MNS base on the beach at Leonardo, we were quickly put to work by our fellow members who weren't in jail. I soon found myself in a canoe with a new activist, paddling furiously to get in front of a munitions ship that was heading out to sea. We were stopped before we got there; a police boat pulled us out of the way. In the courtroom, the arresting officer testified emotionally about risking his own life to save us from our likely deaths in a collision with a ship already picking up speed.

Although my canoe partner and I were sentenced to a week's jail time, others replaced us, and the blockade campaign continued for months, contributing to the growth of the antiwar movement. Some US military personnel were inspired by the campaign to refuse continued participation in the war.

≋ ≋ ≋

The Philadelphia development of the Movement for a New Society was going well, but I was eager to see it become a truly national/transnational network. In the early seventies, Berit and I took our children to summer conferences, where she and I took turns playing with the children while the other convened meetings with activists to talk about the emerging MNS network.

In our travels, we noticed the eagerness of many activists to join groups that were intentionally committed to learning. Many believed that the sixties movements underachieved because they weren't committed enough to learning from their own experience and that of others. What Berit and I heard matched the experience of Bill Moyer and the Macroanalysis Collective in Philly, which found their curriculum for macroanalysis seminars to be in high demand as study groups proliferated around the country.

Long before systems scientist Peter Senge's pioneering work in the 1990s proposed "learning organizations,"* we created a style for activists that centered the value of learning. (In researching organizational effectiveness, Senge found that many continued to make the same mistakes because they didn't take the time to evaluate and change what didn't work.) As more MNS people

---

* Peter M. Senge, *The Fifth Discipline: The Art and Practice of the Learning Organization* (New York: Doubleday/Currency, 1990).

compared notes on mistakes in their previous activist experience and experimented with new approaches, a flow of short manuals began that described "what worked."

These pamphlets sought an outlet, so a new collective formed in Philadelphia called New Society Publishers. Its best seller was what we affectionately referred to as "the monster manual:" *Resource Manual for a Living Revolution.** New Society Publishers ended up outliving MNS and remains active almost five decades later in British Columbia, publishing books for activists and do-it-yourselfers.**

The research and writing that previously had gone into a booklet called "Revolution: A Quaker Prescription for a Sick Society" was picked up by Bill Moyer, Dick Taylor, Sue Carroll, and me. Over a couple of years, we worked the manuscript into a book titled *Moving Toward a New Society*, published by New Society Publishers and, in turn, adopted by MNS as its agreed-upon theory of change.***

It was an ambitious book. We were keenly aware that the progressive publishing world was obsessed with analysis—of trends, structures, underlying causes, the meaning of the latest bad news. While analysis is essential, we argued that just as important to movements are a vision of what we're aiming for and a strategy for getting there. To prove that it could be done, we divided our book into three equal parts: analysis, vision, and strategy. Importantly, the vision section shows how an economy could work in harmony with the planet's long-run needs, and the strategy section includes a dialogue on the pros and cons of

---

* Virginia Coover, Ellen Deacon, Charles Esser, and Christopher Moore, *Resource Manual for a Living Revolution* (Philadelphia: New Society Publishers, 1977).

** New Society Publishers, PO Box 189, Gabriola Island, BC, Canada, V0R 1X0 or info@newsociety.com.

*** Susanne Gowan, George Lakey, William Moyer, Richard Taylor, *Moving Toward a New Society* (Philadelphia: New Society Publishers, 1976). Toward the end of the writing, Susanne Gowan replaced Susan Edwards (Sue Carroll).

working within the political party system to try to bring major change to the United States.

ϗ ϗ ϗ

After three years of MNS organization-building, I wanted to get back into hands-on campaigning. In 1973, I traveled to Germantown, Ohio, to the founding conference for a new peace campaign, organized by the American Friends Service Committee and the group that became known as Clergy and Laity Concerned about Vietnam (CALC).

In its high-profile mobilization of interfaith leaders against the war, CALC was watching with horror the destruction of Indochina by US B-52 bombers.* Now a new, "improved" monster of destruction was being invented by the military-industrial complex: the B-1 bomber. It would be supersonic, and it could be used in future Vietnam-type wars—although its sponsors said it was designed to deter the Soviets.

The prototype being built was expected to cost more than its weight in gold. A proposal was due to come before Congress in 1976 to build fifty B-1 bombers. CALC wanted to partner with the American Friends Service Committee; by campaigning together they hoped they might have enough lead time to defeat the bomber. The AFSC was interested, but only if the campaign could also educate Americans about the role of the military-industrial complex.

I warmed to the campaign because it might provide a win and also make more Americans aware of the blood-soaked profits

---

* According to the *New York Times*, "America dropped three times more ordnance over Vietnam, Laos and Cambodia than all sides did during World War II." Ariel Garfinkel, "The Vietnam War Is Over. The Bombs Remain," *New York Times*, March 20, 2018, https://www. nytimes.com/2018/03/20/opinion/vietnam-war-agent-orange-bombs.html. B-52s played a major role in that nightmare.

generated by the revolving door between corporations and the Pentagon. The proposal was open to nonviolent direct action, but I thought it was still weak strategically because it lacked a vision of an alternative; "you can't beat somebody with nobody," I've heard politicians say. Similarly, our country is stuck with the military-industrial complex's latest offer of jobs until there's a civilian alternative that meets human needs.

The B-1 proponents skillfully distributed contracts to build the system to manufacturers in key Congressional districts around the United States. This would mean the creation of high-wage jobs in those areas, which was an incentive for the affected members of Congress to vote for the system. I argued in the Germantown conference that to increase our chance of winning, we needed to propose an alternative: a peaceful source of good jobs.

At first, I was alone, a familiar spot for me in my life. I often start there, then others join me later. Maybe that's because of my rebel nature, and also because I've spent so much time studying how successful social movements win. At this conference, however, I wasn't gaining traction.

It was a fierce fight. On breaks, I went to my room, punched and screamed into a pillow, and cried. At one point while we were arguing, one young comrade got so mad I thought he was going to punch me.

I did what I hated to do: made my proposed addition a condition of my participation in the campaign. I was openly acknowledging my reality: I wasn't going to give three years of my life to a campaign I was fairly certain was going to lose without adding the vision of an alternative to the mix.

Finally, a few organizers with influence said they saw strategic merit in my point; then others joined, and the leaders of the effort agreed that it would become a "Campaign Against the B-1 Bomber and for Peace Conversion." I was made a member of the campaign's steering committee, and we went back to our various cities, hoping a spirit of comradeship would arise as we worked together.

Happily, I found MNS people in Philly who wanted to join the new campaign, so we applied for collective status from the network. The next step for me personally was to persuade the Friends Peace Committee to put me back on staff, this time as coordinator of the regional Quaker participation in the new campaign. My family needed the income, and the resources and credibility of Friends Peace Committee would also help our MNS collective do stronger Philly-area organizing.

≈ ≈ ≈

As the campaign moved ahead, I found myself wanting six-year-old Peter to try his hand at activism, but our bomber campaign wouldn't be the right place to start. Some members of Movement for a New Society were helping out in the growing consumer boycotts of grapes and lettuce that had been called by the United Farm Workers (UFW), in California, and they told me they were going to start picketing at our neighborhood supermarket.

I explained to Peter that the aim of the boycott was to improve the lives of children like himself. He immediately volunteered for the picket line. After standing with the rest of us holding his sign while people went in and out of the store, he got a little bored. He handed the sign to me and moved up the sidewalk about fifteen feet from the supermarket door to meet people who were coming to shop. He walked up to somebody and said, "Don't go in there and buy that scabbage lettuce!" I guess Peter had heard us talking about "scabs"—strikebreakers who were being hired by employers.

I saw the shopper hesitate while looking at my boy. With a look of puzzlement on her face, she then continued walking toward the door. Peter, cute as anything, with a head full of curls and a determined look, backed up in front of her as she kept walking, saying in his biggest voice: "Don't you buy that scabbage lettuce!"

She kept walking, and Peter kept backing up in front of her until he backed right through the doorway and into the store. He disappeared from sight for a minute, then came out of the store and walked down the sidewalk to find another shopper to confront. He did the same thing again, walking backward in front of them while saying with a loud little boy's voice, "Don't you buy that scabbage lettuce!"

The third time he did it, he didn't come right out, and I started to think I'd better go in to see what was happening inside. But hardly a minute later, the store manager came outside, pulling Peter by the hand. The manager looked mad.

"Whose boy is this?" he demanded.

I raised my hand proudly: "He's mine."

The UFW won the boycott, increased wages and benefits for its workers, and gained recognition as a union. Years later, when I ended up leading some nonviolent workshops with Cesar Chavez, founder and director of the UFW, I couldn't resist telling him the "scabbage" story. I'll never forget his appreciative grin.

ﻥ ﻥ ﻥ

My favorite tactic in our three years of campaigning against the new bomber was one we tried out in Philly's Life Center community. Our research estimated how much money would be drawn through federal taxes from our neighborhood's share of the B-1's cost: nine million dollars. We visited a variety of organizations in our neighborhood—civic groups, religious groups, parent-teacher associations, Girl Scout troops—and asked them: "Can you think of something our neighborhood needs more than our piece of the B-1 bomber system?"

That opened a discussion of the bomber, its unprecedented costs, and its likely uses. Each organization agreed that our neighborhood could use the nine million dollars much more effectively, then most signed on as cosponsors of a community fair to which they would bring their idea of how to spend the nine million dollars. They could have booths for selling refreshments and other items, as well as solicit volunteers and share how their group's work boosted the neighborhood. One neighbor suggested we call it the "Fair Shake Festival," because "our neighborhood deserves a fair shake."

An awkward moment came at one of the planning meetings, when one of the organizational representatives said, "I want to say what bothers me about George Lakey. He talks about the B-1 bomber, but I suspect that what he really wants is to do away with the Pentagon entirely."

Instead of being red-baited, I was being pacifist-baited. And . . . she was correct! How should I respond?

Happily, another neighbor spoke up. "I don't think it's our business to figure out what George thinks about other issues that aren't on the table. We know he's a good, responsible man helping us organize an event that will be good for the neighborhood. Let's just let the rest of it be."

The fair was well attended, with more than thirty organizations participating, there were pony rides, colorful booths, and delicious food. Our local congressperson came and joined a milkshake booth selling "fair shakes," heartily dipping out the ice cream. By the end of the afternoon, he'd promised to vote against the B-1.

On a national level, our organizers found emphasizing peace conversion made it easier to approach labor unions for support, given the jobs that the United Auto Workers and other unions would get from B-1 contracts. Our research had shown that the same amount of money dedicated to civilian projects, including much-needed mass transportation, would create many more jobs.

When, in 1977, the B-1 prototype was done and tested and Washington had to face the contract decision, the campaign reached its apex. It was close, but lobbying from labor made the difference: President Jimmy Carter cancelled the B-1.* It was fun to see the faces of our tired but happy campaigners.

For me, the win reinforced two practices that were becoming my principles in a theory for change: 1. it's worth fighting for sound strategy; and 2. tackle a campaign you can win to gain satisfaction and higher morale for the struggle ahead.

At the same time as our collective was working on the B-1 and peace conversion, another collective was working to stop the spread of nuclear power. Bill Moyer was at the helm, and it was fun to compare notes with him, especially on such different campaigns. The antinuclear movement got much of its energy from people who didn't want a nuclear power plant "in their backyard." Those were largely people with no campaign experience, and Bill found himself increasingly relied upon for national strategy guidance.

There was no way advocates for safer power could win simply through research, education, and lobbying. A grassroots movement using nonviolent direct action was essential, but who had that skill set? Some activists had organizing skills but were too reliant on mainstream institutions that were out of sync with the rebel energy that needed to be welcomed in successful campaigning. Further, nearly all those new to social movements lacked direct-action skills or a stable theory of change.

Encouraged by Bill, most Movement for a New Society trainers were drawn into the struggle. The antinuke movement mostly attracted white people, who had learned little if anything from

---

* The B-1 was revived by President Ronald Reagan as part of his revving up of the arms race in the early 1980s. The peace movement was overwhelmed by his crusading against "the evil empire." Reagan's claims of Soviet threat were bogus; the ailing economy of the Soviet Union was unable to mount an increased threat. Reagan was actually picking American pockets to increase profits to the US arms industry.

the extraordinary use of nonviolent action by Black people in the sixties. (Racism makes it very hard for white people to learn from Black people; Bill was a stunning exception.) Antinuke activists needed all the training they could get.

Bill was right. The partial nuclear meltdown at Three Mile Island in Pennsylvania, in March 1979, sealed the deal. The early goal of the nuclear power industry was a thousand reactors, and today the US has less than a tenth of that number,* an extraordinary victory for the movement. Some observers said the movement won because of the meltdown, but Bill reminded us that a more dangerous meltdown near Detroit happened more than a decade before and didn't hurt the industry at all.** The difference between the two meltdowns was the 1970s direct-action campaigns around the country, which raised the popular consciousness and jacked up the price of building new plants.***

The movement was up against a formidable array of political and economic powers: the federal government, both military and civilian, along with state governments. Electrical utilities and giant manufacturers wanted nuclear energy, as did mining companies, banks, insurance companies, building contractors, and construction unions. Considering the opposition it faced, the anti–nuclear power movement was arguably the most successful in US environmental history. Yet, few environmentalists talk about it today. I've often been puzzled that some large national environmental organizations didn't learn more from the movement's astonishing

---

* "Nuclear Power in the United States," Wikimedia Foundation, last edited June 30, 2022, https://en.wikipedia.org/wiki/Nuclear_power_in_the_United_States.
** John G. Fuller, *We Almost Lost Detroit*, (New York: Reader's Digest Press, 1975). The Enrico Fermi Generating Station was located on the banks of Lake Erie.
*** Bill Moyer was one of the most brilliant strategists I ever met, and—as with other activists from the working class I knew—it was partly because of his attention to history and practice rather than any preoccupation with morality. He's turned to most often for his "Movement Action Plan," described in his book *Doing Democracy: The MAP Model for Organizing Social Movements* (Gabriola Island, BC: New Society Publishers, 2001).

success—and trumpet it far and wide—beginning in the 1980s, when climate change was not yet on people's minds.* Is it because the movement was so grassroots and direct-action oriented, and the larger organizations didn't lead it?

---

* For some of the most important learnings to apply immediately, see Will Lawrence, "4 Lessons for Climate Organizers from the Antinuclear Movement," *Waging Nonviolence*, June 2, 2016, https://wagingnonviolence.org/2016/06/4-lessons-for-climate-organizers-from-the-anti-nuclear-movement/.

19

a container for liberation

The transition from A Quaker Action Group to Movement for a New Society turned out to be much deeper, psychologically and spiritually, than I realized when I was facilitating it. I was preoccupied with the nuts and bolts of reorganizing a national campaigning group into a decentralized, networked, multilayered, larger, and more dense organization. I didn't realize that in the process, MNS was becoming a container for liberation.

I also didn't realize how much I personally needed it. My year in Britain had been exciting, but mainly drew on, as well as fine-tuned, skills I'd already had. It didn't grow my inner self. The following summer in Norway gave me a much-needed chance to catch my breath and reconnect deeply with my family. Little Peter still seemed emotionally like a half-starved baby bird. I figured once we were back in our own house in Philly, he'd relax into a sense of security, but I didn't reckon on how the new baby Berit was carrying would inevitably need priority attention. I didn't at all see how my masculine training prevented my being fully present for the growing needs of my family; I was too drawn to the challenge of changing AQAG into a deeply innovative revolutionary network helping to make good on the promise of the sixties.

The transition created a more rigorous and complicated organization with higher expectations of its members. MNS evolved a culture that freed people not only for movement innovation but for realization of our own higher selves. "Live the revolution now!" we sang. The younger members had a clearer idea than I did what that might mean. Our organizational design and culture were sufficiently unique to attract two well-known sociologists—Elise Boulding and A. Paul Hare—to come study us.* In addition to supporting people in the obvious ways, like reducing living expenses and establishing shared childcare, MNS was supporting exploration of inner lives that mainstream culture had oppressed. Women's groups formed for this exploration, as did men's groups.

I was highly uncomfortable in the first meeting of a men's group. Some of the other men seemed to be, too, but none of us admitted it. We just somehow didn't get around to meeting again. My close friend Chuck Esser suggested we try again with a different combination of men, and I agreed to show up. It went somewhat better; we actually joked a bit and relieved some of the nervousness. We continued to meet and, partly because Chuck gave more leadership, I began to let down my guard against sharing inner feelings. I even admitted that I had a guard to let down. As the weekly men's meetings continued, I found myself becoming less guarded with Berit, and one night in bed—when all the children were safely asleep—I surprised myself and her by crying with the sheer relief of the peace I was feeling.

℘ ℘ ℘

AQAG cofounder Ross Flanagan—who had played such a prophetic role in focusing Quaker protest against the Vietnam war on the medical aid issue—invited me to try a new peer counseling

---

* Elise's specializations were conflict resolution and family dynamics, but as a Quaker she was also interested in how the Quaker influence was showing up in how we lived and worked together. A. Paul Hare was a leader of Harvard's group dynamics laboratory. Paul was so attracted to our experiment that he moved into one of our collective households.

technique he said might suit me. We had some sessions in which he taught me some theory about the value of releasing feelings in a safe place, and we tried it out, exchanging the role of talker and listener.

With Ross I cried easily and, to my surprise, found that I'd been walking around with what seemed to be an ocean of tears held behind strong walls. I was surprised by this new permission for men to feel our whole gamut of feelings: sadness and anger and longing and fear. I remembered the teenaged robot that confronted my drama and music teachers on the stage during my high school production of *Our Town* and found myself laughing and laughing (while at the same time noticing there was nothing funny about it). Then, suddenly, I felt a strong, tender compassion for that boy who'd already learned to lock himself up in his effort to be "a real man."

The cultural turbulence initiated by the women's movement challenged all kinds of assumptions that had been enforced by the patriarchy, and one of them was enforced monogamy. Some couples within MNS began to ask themselves how much their resistance to opening their relationships to the possibility of sharing intimacy was mainly about psychological insecurity and a mistaken belief that love itself was a "scarce commodity."

When I fell in love with a man in my men's group, the question became real, personal, and painful for Berit and me. We both received thoughtful support from community members closest to us as we navigated the stormy waters. Thanks to them, to our willingness to face painful emotions, and to the reality of how deeply we loved each other, we came through to a peaceful place of openness. We now both accepted that each of us could love others without that threatening our primary relationship, which was with each other.

The feminist wave pervading MNS insisted that "the personal is political, and the political, personal." This now put me in a jam.

Within MNS, most people knew I was lovers with a man. But in terms of the broader public, I was still in the closet. And it was now 1973—several years after the 1969 Stonewall rebellion for gay liberation.*

Compounding my dilemma was my Quakerism, with its emphasis on integrity. I was becoming known among Quakers nationally, and my positive image included being a family man with a talented wife, three beautiful children, and the unstated assumption that I was straight. In those days, if Friends knew the truth about me, my image for many would be quite different, and negative. My Quaker community was fundamental to me and, at the same time, I increasingly felt I was living a lie.

An opportunity came that would change all that. Berit and I were invited to be plenary speakers at the 1974 Friends General Conference Gathering in Ithaca, New York. It would be a chance to come out to a thousand Quakers, all at once!

The very thought started me sweating.

We quickly accepted the invitation to speak on the assigned topic, "Community," and then started to have peer counseling sessions with friends willing to listen and support. We first needed clarity on whether I should come out as bisexual. We didn't object in principle to compartmentalization; it's not always wise to make the private, public. We agreed that individuals do need space from prying eyes (the neighbors' or the state's) to risk, to experiment, to create, to learn. So, there is value in compartmentalization. But there might also be a time to report on an experiment, to share the outcome of a risk—especially if making something public helps free others who are oppressed. Weeks and then months went by as Berit and I turned these questions over in our minds. Increasingly,

---

* An even earlier protest, in 1965 at Philadelphia's Independence Hall, demanded freedom for LGBT people. George Lakey, "What White Allies Can Learn from Allies in the Gay Rights Struggle," *Waging Nonviolence*, July 4, 2015, https://wagingnonviolence.org/2015/07/white-allies-can-learn-allies-gay-rights-struggle/.

I sensed that she would agree, if I could achieve clarity myself as to what we should say.

I remembered the previous year's national network meeting of Movement for a New Society. On the second day, a woman stood up at announcements time to invite women who loved other women to meet together that evening. I instinctively cringed—even here, in a supportive community. To me making love was about joyful connection, but public discussion was something else: a free fall into the scary void, as far from joyful connection as you could get. Would I spoil my experience of loving another man by exposing it to homophobic loathing?

And yet, the reality is that I hate gay oppression and grieve for those it has killed, maimed, and stunted. Even now, as I write this memoir, the violence continues. In 2021, in a middle school hallway, a thirteen-year-old was slammed to the floor and beaten after the attacker said, in public, "I'm going to knock the gay out of him"; LGBTQ folks are four times more likely to experience violent attack than others.* The number of anti-LGBTQ hate groups in the United States has been soaring.** In 1973, when I was struggling with the question of coming out, antiqueer violence was so pervasive that an accurate count of incidents wasn't possible; the media reported attacks on us with baseball bats and deaths by stabbing and shooting.

My life's purpose is to work for justice, peace, liberation. Of all

---

* Joshua Espinoza, "Video Shows Homophobic Attack on Florida Middle School Student," *Complex*, May 26, 2021, https://www.complex.com/life/video-shows-homophobic-attack-florida-teen-school-hallway. A study from the UCLA School of Law using 2017 data found that LGBT people are four times more likely to experience violent victimization compared with non-LGBT people: "LGBT People Nearly Four Times More Likely than Non-LGBT People to Be Victims of Violent Crime," press release, UCLA School of Law Williams Institute, October 2, 2020, https://williamsinstitute.law.ucla.edu/press/ncvs-lgbt-violence-press-release/.

** In 2019, anti-LGBTQ hate groups were the fastest-growing sector among hate groups, according to a 2020 report from the Southern Poverty Law Center: Julie Moreau, "Anti-LGBTQ Hate Groups on the Rise in U.S.,R Warns," NBC News, March 30, 2020, https://www.nbcnews.com/feature/nbc-out/anti-lgbtq-hate-groups-rise-u-s-report-warns-n1171956.

things, how could I give a pass to this oppression, a burden that has been personal and intimate in my life?

Of course, I could speak out against homophobia without revealing the stakes for me, but that would be cooperating with the nature of the oppression itself; one of the pillars of queer oppression is invisibility. At college, Burt and I could quietly make love every night in Klinger Hall, and the structure remained unchallenged, along with the woundings and the killings that the structure generated. Heterosexism needs hegemony; it can't stand the contradiction that visible, proud queer loving creates. Given that, how long could I stand on the sidelines of a fight that was mine in a special way? The universe had handed me the perfect opportunity, with Berit, a courageous ally, at my side. It might be one of the most terrifying moments of my life, but yes, I saw, I need to act.

Making the decision freed me to feel more of my walled-off fear, and I spent the spring of 1974 alternately preparing the speech with Berit and sitting with various friends, imagining giving the speech while shaking and oozing cold sweat from every pore. "Okay, George," one of them would say, smiling in a relaxed and encouraging way. "When you imagine looking out into the audience of a thousand Quakers, how do you feel?"

"Terrible!" I'd reply, and start shaking.

"What might happen?"

"I don't *know!*" I'd yell, and shake more violently as the sweat dripped. The counselor would beam confidence at me; she knew I was just fine, even if I wasn't so sure at the moment.

"George, you're right on track. Stay right there another moment if you can."

"But I'm so *scared!*" I'd say, my teeth chattering like castanets.

The big moment came. Ithaca College's fieldhouse was filled, and you could almost hear a happy sigh as we appeared with three-year-old Ingrid. Christina and Peter were in another building, in the children's program; Ingrid would in a few moments be taken care of by the friends who occupied the center of the front row, ready to beam reassuringly at us when we went up on the platform. Those who had listened to some more teeth-chattering earlier in the day gave us their most confident smiles.

Berit spoke first. I sat near her, marveling as I often did at her poise and clarity as she outlined some of our learnings at the Philly Life Center about community. Even as a young teenager in her Norwegian hometown of Skien, she had been in demand for poetry reading and song performance. As a speaker, she didn't smile as often as I did, and that made the smiles all the more effective. (It also didn't hurt that she was so much prettier.) One of her skills was making her points sound as though they were common sense; her freshness of expression and pointed stories kept people's interest while she journeyed toward points that sounded flat-out true.

After Berit sat, I felt for a second like quitting while we were ahead. All I had to do was omit the last two paragraphs of my talk, and we would continue to be favored by these dear Friends, many of them gray-headed, folk-dancing, peace-pursuing, silence-loving, book-review-reading, quietly chuckling, eyes-shining Quakers.

Well, my dad taught me that follow-through is everything.

As I neared the end of my talk, I tackled the value of trust in building community. "Trust," I said, "can be built deliberately through a process that's simple, although not easy. We can build trust by taking a risk. If the ceiling doesn't fall in, if the ground doesn't open up and swallow us, trust grows.

"One kind of risk taken in community is self-disclosure. For example, I could take a risk here, right now, by disclosing something about myself that most of you don't know. I could tell you something true about me: that I think of myself as gay or bisexual. I can love men sexually as well as women."

That's where I lost it. Although I moved my eyes over the entire audience after saying that, I couldn't stay present enough to see what the reactions were. Later, I learned that some were turning to each other with incredulous looks, while others were clamping their jaws tight. A few, thankfully, began to weep with joy that the unsayable was being said.

After a final summarizing sentence about community that no one paid attention to, including me, I returned to my chair. The gathering went into its customary period of silence, as my stomach began to ache. Then Berit and I descended the steps to form the typical speakers' receiving line; whoever wanted to could come forward and greet us.

I prayed to become present as Friends pressed to see us. Several men rigidly held their bodies under control as they told me how much they detested what I had said; I thought one of them might hit me. Other people fell into my arms with tearful gratitude. One older Quaker woman said, "George, I'll have to think about all this for a long time, but I do take you seriously and I will pray about it."

As the line to speak to us diminished, our front-row friends came forward with Ingrid. "We're running away with you," they chorused, and we surrendered gladly.

Ten minutes later, we were occupying the rear section of Ithaca's best ice cream parlor, ordering outrageous confections and exchanging one-liners. The manager didn't seem to mind how loud and giddy we were, since we were spending lavishly on his prize sundaes.

"I wonder how *Friends Journal* will cover this news," my friend Ellen Deacon said.

"The *Journal's* a monthly," Ross Flanagan commented. "I wonder what the rumor mill will do." Later, we learned that within a week, Tokyo Quakers were discussing the night's revelation.

"Here's the thing to try," Ellen interjected, "orange sherbet coated with chocolate syrup."

Ingrid was passed around from lap to lap, sampling the flavors. As the party wound down, she came to me, hands and face sticky, and fell asleep in my lap.

For some reason, Berit and I hadn't talked about what the next morning might be like. As we brought our three children to breakfast, the massive college cafeteria went silent. The crowd realized what it had done and began to buzz again, clinking knives and forks. I was afraid to look around, and busied myself with getting the oatmeal into assorted young Lakey mouths. The stomachache returned.

Suddenly I was aware of a tall presence next to me. I looked up to see E. Raymond Wilson standing in his customary gray suit and tie, saying something to us. Gray-haired, blue-eyed Ray was one of the most respected Quakers in the United States, known for his integrity and judicious mind. Reared on an Iowa farm, he cofounded and directed for many years the Friends Committee for National Legislation, the Quaker lobbying arm in Washington, DC. I'd known him for a decade through peace campaigns and never thought of him as an ally in the strategy debates that movement leaders go through.

Now he was saying something to Berit and me, but I couldn't quite make it out. Berit nodded and smiled, and I realized he was talking about breakfasts, and children, and how it was looking to be a good day for playing outside. He stayed long enough for everyone in the cafeteria to see E. Raymond Wilson having a warm and friendly conversation with the Lakeys. In his low-key way, he was asserting a solidarity that all could see.

Then he returned to his seat.*

---

* The Quaker magazine *Friends Journal* invited me, in 1975, to write a major article about the philosophical assumptions leading to my coming out: George Lakey, "Speaking of Sex . . . A Fictional Conversation," *Friends Journal*, July 1/15, 1975, https://www.friendsjournal.org/wp-content/uploads/emember/downloads/1975/HC12-50582.pdf.

ℵ ℵ ℵ

Movement for a New Society became a seedbed for small groups that wanted to innovate. Groups that formed to support liberation sometimes called a community meeting for the purpose of a "speak-out." Attendees filled chairs and the floor while the initiating group stood facing them and spoke simply, strongly, and movingly their truths—sometimes making requests for changed behavior in the community.

A speak-out was the opposite of denouncing and then shunning someone. MNS understood that *everyone* is brought up with oppressive attitudes and behaviors and sometimes acts them out; instead of cutting ties, we chose to confront these issues directly in a way that could lead to change and stronger, closer bonds in the future.

The work of becoming conflict-friendly to support the resolution of differences, instead of simply denouncing each other, proved essential. We found often that a fight waged well moved us forward like nothing else could. The sexual politics of the 1970s gave us multiple opportunities for such fights.

In 1975, I cofounded a new collective of men to train others to be stronger allies of women and children. The result was Men Against Patriarchy. As a resource to men in the Philadelphia area, the group led workshops and weekend retreats, as well as publishing nationally articles and pamphlets.*

We were coached by Bruce Kokopeli, a young man who directed

---

* For example, "Understanding and Fighting Sexism: A Call to Men," by Peter Blood, Alan Tuttle, and George Lakey, reprinted over a decade later in a college textbook: Margaret L. Andersen and Patricia Hill Collins, *Race, Class, and Gender: An Anthology,* 2nd ed. (Belmont, MA: Wadsworth Publishing Company, 1995). The article was drawn from Men Against Patriarchy's pamphlet "Off Their Backs and on Our Own Two Feet" (Philadelphia: New Society Publishers, 1983). The pamphlet was a collective product including the thinking of Michael/Firefly Siptroth, Doug Trout, and Kenn Arning, and it reflected the Movement for a New Society's emphasis on going beyond complaint about how things are to suggesting a vision of how they could be.

the Men's Resource Center in Seattle. Bruce joined MNS and wrote with me an article that was republished numerous times, including in a college textbook and also in a feminist anthology in which we were the only male authors. We called the article "More Power Than We Want: Masculine Sexuality and Violence."*

In those days, most groups on the left decided to show some tolerance toward their LGBTQ members, but the queer caucus within MNS was ambitious; we wanted to build gay liberation into the core theory of our network. Gerre Goodman, Judy Lashof, Erika Thorne, and I wrote a book together on LGBTQ theory called *No Turning Back*, which drew connections with other forms of oppression and presented a vision of what a sexually free society might look like.** We circulated the draft to MNS members before the national meeting of the network so that members had time to read it and consider whether it could become policy for the organization.

I figured this would be an edgy step for the national network to take. Sure enough, an atmosphere of discomfort pervaded the room when it came time for that agenda item. A number of conflict-avoiding comments were made, increasing the discomfort. Then someone said, "The trouble with publishing this is that then so many gay people would join us that we'd lose our breadth of membership."

Silence filled the room, while LGBTQ group members sat stunned. Suddenly a heterosexual ally said: "That statement was homophobic!"

Almost as one, the queer caucus rose and stomped out of the

---

* Bruce Kokopeli and George Lakey, "More Power Than We Want: Masculine Sexuality and Violence," first appeared in *WIN* 29 (July 1876), 4–8. It was later republished in Andersen and Collins, *Race, Class, and Gender: An Anthology*, 2nd ed., and in Pam McAllister, ed., *Reweaving the Web of Life: Feminism and Nonviolence* (Philadelphia: New Society Publishers, 1982).

** Gerre Goodman, George Lakey, Judy Lashof, and Erika Thorne, *No Turning Back: Lesbian and Gay Liberation of the '80s* (Philadelphia: New Society Publishers, 1983).

room. The cofacilitators suggested that everyone form buzz groups wherever they were to process what was happening for them personally. An hour of intense work took place, in the larger room and also in the small room where the caucus gathered. In both rooms, members confronted their fears, hurt, and anger.

The people in the queer caucus suddenly reappeared at the entrance to the main room, dressed up in miscellaneous hats and scarves and whatever could be found, marching and singing to the tune of "Auld Lang Syne," "We're here because we're queer because we're here because we're queer!"

A shift had happened in both rooms. When the queer caucus reached the center of the room, it was surrounded by the others with laughter and spontaneous dancing. Finally, the cofacilitators of the meeting calmed us down to continue our business. The short discussion that followed quickly reached a consensus that the book should be published as emerging Movement for a New Society theory.

I'm not sure we could have reached consensus without the sharply stated polarization and the conflict that forced everyone to move to a deeper level. I was grateful that we didn't have political correctness getting in the way of people voicing their real fears; it was the fighting that supported the transformation. Going through the conflict itself forged the unity that made Movement for a New Society a nonviolent army that had impact far beyond our size.

Furthermore, the book reflected the emphasis in Movement for a New Society that showed up in much of our intellectual work: effective movements need more than an analysis of what's wrong, they also need a vision of what would work better and a strategy for getting from here to there. We shortened the key words—analysis, vision, and strategy—to simply A/V/S, and urged the movements against war, poverty, and racial oppression to "do their homework" and present to society a visionary alternative to the status quo.

≈ ≈ ≈

Back in Philly's Life Center community of MNS, liberation work continued. Women were raising the temperature in their confrontation with the men. Yes, the men were changing, they acknowledged, but too slowly. I took their message to heart, and what it meant for my family life was increasingly clear. Berit wanted a role reversal so she could get back into the larger world, with a full-time job that would develop her professional career. I could become the at-home person, doing the primary parenting that she'd been doing for a decade.

Ideologically, I agreed, but I hesitated because becoming primary parent looked like a tremendous leap. In 1975, I leapt, aware of an advantage that typical American nuclear families don't have: our group-living approach gave me some childcare assistance from the others in our house. Happily, it was a big house, enough to contain our family plus five adults.* In adulthood Ingrid remembered that, as a youngster, it was like having aunties and uncles under the same roof. Still, Berit's and my role switch would mean my taking broad responsibility for nurturing and for the difficult boundary-setting aspect of parenting.

Fortunately, we had warm, though infrequent, backup in my parents, who lived two hours away and couldn't be as active as they would have liked with their grandchildren. I loved hearing from Christina after she'd spent a weekend in Bangor, especially about her going fishing with my dad. She proudly showed photos of them holding fish they'd caught in a nearby trout stream.

With the increased freedom, Berit became training director for Women Organized Against Rape, a stimulating and cutting-edge—not to mention emotionally stressful—job. WOAR was one of the first groups in the country to advocate for an end

---

* They were John Braxton and Marcy Morgan, Gail Pressburg, and Stephanie Judson and Chris Moore: friends, comrades, and housemates all rolled into one.

to sexist treatment by police, accompany women who had been raped to court proceedings, hold trainings on rape prevention, assist women in leaving abusive relationships, and host martial arts–based workshops on self-defense.

Berit brought painful stories home with her to share at the end of the day, and I learned more about what loving support required. One night I stayed awake until morning holding her while she, on the phone, talked a client out of committing suicide.

Becoming the primary parent scared me; I felt that I was over my head. Christina was ten, Peter six, and Ingrid four. They were lively children and very different from one another. Like Berit, they would need more emotional support from me than I'd been giving. This was emerging as the hardest challenge in my life. I hadn't been brought up for it, and I knew little about its more nuanced side. I knew not to lean on Berit, with her emotionally demanding job, but to seek support from Life Center men who were developing their own nurturing skills. Fortunately, they were available. That gave me some reason to hope.

In the next couple years, Christina and Peter would indeed challenge me in ways that my upbringing had left me unprepared for. Christina awakened to her racial difference from Berit and me: her birth father was Black, and she struggled with what that meant for her own identity. Acting that out included, in the safety of her bedroom, screaming at Berit and me for being "white honkies who stole me from my people." Of course we'd been living in racially integrated neighborhoods, reading our kids children's books about Black people, greeting warmly the Black friends they brought home, taking them to racial justice demonstrations, and doing the other obvious things antiracist parents do. But still, the issue remained a thorny one to navigate.

We went into family therapy. This was 1976, and the civil rights movement had stalled; I had little hope that the momentum of the sixties struggle against racism would resume any time soon. Ours

was one of the many families, Black and mixed, that were casualties of the stuckness. Christina took deeper and deeper forays
into the part of Philadelphia that seemed to her most emphatically Black, mixing with the young and despairing people she met
there, who expressed their despair through violence against themselves and one other. Her rebel spirit was met again and again not
by true rebellion but by nihilism that left lives shattered.

We never became accustomed to picking her up at police sta-
tions or meeting her at the emergency room. Once, her younger
sister, Ingrid, wanted to come with us to the hospital, where Christina had been taken after being hurt badly in a fight. When we
came to the doorway of Christina's hospital room, Ingrid was the
first to enter. She took one look at her sister's face, which looked
like a smashed plum, and continued across the room to the toilet,
where she vomited.

Eventually, Christina was admitted as an inpatient at the Philadelphia Child Guidance Clinic, where she picked up some of the
pieces from her successful early childhood and made a fresh start.

Christina hadn't succeeded in what I saw as her attempt to
recruit her younger brother, Peter, to be part of the Black caucus
in the family. He was as confused about identity as she was certain; his earlier history as a blond-haired, light-skinned boy left
him sometimes claiming to be Puerto Rican. On Saint Patrick's
Day, he wore a button that said, "Kiss me, I'm Irish."

I was in over my head, but not willing to quit.

I expected the legacy of my birth family would show up in my
own feelings and behavior in the family Berit and I had made.
Part of the issue for me with Peter was my own troubled relationship with my dad. Who knew how far back that trouble
could be traced? At the funeral of my dad's father, I could see
from Dad's face how fraught that relationship had been. Later, I
asked careful questions. He kept coming back to the many beatings he'd received, and once casually mentioned that his dad knew

the addage "spare the rod and spoil the child" because he'd gotten plenty of beatings from his own dad, my dad's grandfather. My dad acknowledged that the father-son history that he knew was one of ambivalence—love and hate.

Maybe this father-son dynamic was an inheritance I could resolve to end in my generation. Stopping the generational transmission of what Dr. Joy DeGruy called Post-Traumatic Slave Syndrome was beyond me, but perhaps my own ancestors' pathology could be tackled. When I began peer counseling, I worked on my father issues nearly exclusively for a year. I deeply wanted not to pass that legacy on to my son.

I gained hope from the many times when, visiting my folks, little Peter would crawl into my dad's lap as Dad was watching football or baseball, watch for a bit, then fall asleep. That, my dad could allow. Sometimes I'd take a look to check in, and my hard-working dad had fallen asleep, too, holding my son. My tears came for not only the sweetness of that sight but also regret for the period when I was little and my dad had been drafted into the army, unavailable to hold me while I drifted off. When he came back, he wasn't as available as he had been, for reasons I couldn't understand.

While seeking and not finding clarity for parenting Christina, I renewed my determination at least to heal the father-son fracture I'd inherited. Peter was never the sunny, happy child Christina had been. Could my love bring some healing for us?

א א א

The chair of the Peace Science department at the University of Pennsylvania found out that I occasionally travelled to another part of the country to speak to peace studies classes, and got in touch with me with a tone of good-natured indignation: Why wasn't I teaching in his department at Penn, at my doorstep in West Philly?

I hesitated, because of my parenting commitment, but then agreed to teach one class as an experiment—on the condition that the class would meet once a week for three hours instead of being spaced out over multiple sessions.

That began a seven-year stint at Penn. By popular demand, I soon offered two sections of the course per semester, then three— and still everyone who wanted to get in couldn't, since I limited the seats to thirty-five in each section, in order to support methods of community-building that intensified the depth of the learning. I taught the class in the rooftop lounge of a high-rise dorm with floor-to-ceiling windows, symbolic of the expansion I expected, and got, from the students.

White students were surprised to find a number of Black students in the class, since Penn at the time was overwhelmingly white; my course was diversity friendly, and that in itself was a stretch for many white students. My experimental pedagogy borrowed from what we were learning about in Movement for a New Society.*

I found the teaching was easy and stimulating, and because I did it while the children were in school, it didn't get in the way of my parenting.

Haverford and Swarthmore College students heard about the course and, since their schools had a tuition agreement with Penn, they began taking the train into the city to take the course. Haverford students then clamored for me to get on the train and teach at their campus, which I did twice, again needing to lottery the course, since I continued to insist on limiting the number of students.

As I taught in the seventies, I unconsciously reached into myself for a dimension I'd never brought to teaching before in a consistent way. This dimension felt different, but I had no words

---

* I've described some of our breakthrough successes in my book *Facilitating Group Learning: Strategies for Success with Diverse Learners* (Oakland, CA: PM Press, 2020).

for it until my Haverford students named it. They spontaneously began to call me "Mother," which I didn't comment on explicitly but accepted as an affirmation. Encouraged by the personal growth work we were doing in MNS, I asked myself where my mother-energy was coming from. My personal growth work was focused on the complexities of my boyhood with Dad, and I realized I was overlooking how strongly I was also formed by my mother's warmth, and her amazing confidence in me.

Once I opened the door, the memories came flooding in: the hours spent as a teenager with her rubbing or scratching my back, while I poured out my worries and disappointments; my peeking through the stage curtain before a show to see where my mother was sitting in the audience; my watching her clip articles from the *Bangor Daily News,* reporting on this or that activity I was part of; our walks to and from church for choir practice, while she listened to my enthusiasms and rants; her encouragement of my friendship with Gary, while my dad furrowed his brow whenever the subject came up; her delight when I went off to sleepaway camp for the first time and her eagerness to hear all about it when I returned. Warmth and confidence—in the midst of adolescent agonies of doubt and overwhelm.

That's part of what I was sharing at Haverford and Penn, as well as in over a thousand workshops since: setting hard tasks and maintaining rigorous standards for the participants, pushing and pushing them to expand, and at the same time exuding warmth and confidence. My dad loved me but was frightened for me, and expressed it as harsh judgment and anxiety. My mother prayed for me, and knew this scared teenager would turn out all right.

As a teacher and facilitator, I extended her attitude toward my students and workshop participants. It's no wonder they respond.

20

1976 brings joy in the struggle

It was July 4, 1976. The high temperature and humidity weren't the only reason we were hot. North Philadelphia, once occupied by British Redcoats, was now occupied by taxpayer-paid police snipers who we could see posted on the roofs of the houses.

Thousands of us were crowded into the narrow streets. The low-income Black neighborhood of row houses and dollar stores was the assembly point for our July 4 parade, because ours was the grassroots alternative to the elite-led celebration in Center City. Now we were massed, waiting for our civil-rights lawyer to negotiate the snipers away. We worried that, when the parade started, provocateurs working undercover with the police might start an incident within the march, giving the snipers an excuse to start shooting. If that happened, all hell would break loose.

Our attorney was explaining to representatives of Mayor Frank Rizzo—a former police chief nationally infamous for his fascist inclinations—that the parade leaders refused to march until the snipers were withdrawn.*

Alan Tuttle and I were tossing jokes back and forth as usual, but without making much of a dent in our anxiety. Alan had come to the Life Center after graduating from Friends World College, where

---

* Frank Rizzo was notorious among progressives as the city's police commissioner but in 1972 became the city's mayor nevertheless. Our attorney, David Kairys, used his brilliant negotiating skills to get us out of more than one tight spot.

his studies included stints in India and Japan. Raised in a Quaker farming family in upstate New York, Alan was now searching for a way to put his education to work through organizing and action. He liked Movement for a New Society's concept of combining action with community and personal growth. He was helping out with the local campaign that I was leading at the time against the funding of the B-1 bomber, partly because the campaign also promoted peace conversion and involved labor unions.

If I had to move away from the crowd for an organizing task, it was easy to find Alan again. He was tall, broad-shouldered, and redhaired, with even features and a cleft in his chin. His muscular body and the gait of someone who grew up doing farm chores projected a reassuring solidity in the midst of the day's volatile crowd. I'd need his solidity even more later, when my life was up for grabs.

The steady drone of police helicopters overhead didn't reduce the tension. If we didn't start the parade soon, impatience in the crowd could mess us up. The fact that the coalition had proclaimed our intention to be nonviolent didn't guarantee everyone would act wisely.

Alan and I kept our banter going as negotiations with Rizzo continued. My work was done, except for bringing a cool head to the hot day; I'd been part of the activists' Bicentennial committee that planned the march. In that role, I'd taken my first stand as a gay man in the rough-and-tumble world of coalition politics. By this time, especially in activist contexts, I often called myself "gay" because it was edgier—same-sex love being what most of all drove homophobes crazy. Also, there was a growing phenomenon of "married gay men" and "gay dads" who might be lovers with the mothers of their children. Labels, then as now, are often simplifications of complex personal realities.

Our Bicentennial coalition consisted of Old Left and New Left, along with groups possessing no clearly defined politics. We had unity on our central message: give up imperialism and rejoin the revolutionary impulse of 1776. I looked into Alan's green-brown eyes and remembered how important his support had been in my pushing the coalition. I'd been nervous. I had argued that there was a new and necessary plank for the liberation platform, and that the lesbians and bisexuals and gays who for years had worked invisibly in social movements deserved to be claimed by the coalition.

The night before the key meeting, Alan and I rehearsed the points I would make. I found myself growing angry at the coalition members whose homophobia might block my motion, and angry at myself for being so scared about their reaction. The angrier I got, the more Alan encouraged me to vent. Soon I was pounding the mattress and yelling–until it occurred to me that they might say, "Good idea, George, let's do it." At that point I started to laugh and told Alan about this new thought.

"No," he protested, "you activists aren't supposed to agree yet! Give George a harder time first!" We both collapsed on the bed in hilarity.

The next evening was anticlimactic. I made my proposal and argued for it with a confident voice; the response was completely positive and came from a range of leaders, and the motion carried.

"Look, George, those snipers are pulling back!" Alan pointed, and now we saw police giving way on roof after roof. The helicopters also backed off, still hovering within sight but no longer so menacing. The parade, at last, began to move, and with it the swell of a chant: "The people, united, will never be defeated!"

Alan and I each threw an arm around the other's shoulder, despite the heat, and fell into line. As we moved through the streets with their close-packed houses, people came out to join us. Colorful banners bobbed and weaved; guitars and trumpets and a drumming brigade kept a beat that was ignored when individuals zigzagged through the lines to greet old friends.

Blobs of melting tar on the street didn't seem to matter so much when someone struck up the old civil rights song, "We're on Our Way to Freedom Land" Our growing thousands were, in our barely organized way, calling for another Independence Day—independence, this time not from the British Empire, but from the American empire.

Dark clouds had been rolling in for some time, with no lessening of the heat. "Now we know the meaning of a brick-lined oven," someone quipped as we sweated through the streets of redbrick row houses.

Suddenly we crossed Ridge Avenue into Fairmount Park. We surged into the greenery, toward a large open area resonant with the sound of dozens of steel drums. Hips started to sway in rhythm. Those in the front lines moved fully into dance. Just as most of us had crossed into the park, the storm broke. Screams of joy broke out as men pulled off T-shirts, youngsters tore across the fields in ragged lines, and dancers increased in numbers and passion.

Alan and I laughed and danced with the rest, snipers forgotten, eyes locking with shouts of love. For now, we were safe. The blessed rain was cooling our skins and baptizing our community—a July 4 to remember. We didn't mind that the rally speakers were being rained out.

≈ ≈ ≈

One morning at breakfast, five-year-old Ingrid seemed intent on eating her cereal, then suddenly addressed me and Alan, who had slept over with me the previous night. "Daddy, you and Alan are lovers, right?"

"Yes," I replied.

"Then," Ingrid continued, "why don't we call you a mommy and daddy?"

I smiled at Berit and turned to Ingrid. "Because you already have a mommy and a daddy, sweetie, and that's Berit and me.

We're your very own special people. Alan likes to play with you and cares about you, so maybe you could call him . . . 'uncle,'" I finished awkwardly.

Alan grinned at my discomfort. "You can call me uncle if you want, Ingrid, but I like it when you call me Alan. The main thing is that we're all friends and you get a lot of love."

Ingrid grinned back at Alan, and asked, "Can you fix my bike after breakfast?" We all laughed.

"So *that's* the bottom line," Berit observed dryly.

A month later, Ingrid's best friend, Evy, was eating dinner at our house. After the silent grace, Ingrid spoke up with what seemed to be the continuation of an argument she was having with Evy. "Daddy, isn't it true that men can make love with men and women can make love with women?"

"Yes, that's true," I said.

"You see?" Ingrid turned to Evy. "Men don't even need women to make love."

Evy hastened to cover her tracks. "I already knew *that*," she said.

Ingrid turned back to me with a puzzled expression. "How do men make love?"

I started to answer while adults around the table, trying to look casual, dug into their food. I didn't go on very long because Ingrid's curiosity was soon satisfied, and she launched into another topic.

Alan was eager for me to meet his parents on their upstate New York farm. They knew about me through Quaker circles, but our paths had never crossed. Alan hadn't in so many words told them everything about our friendship, but he told me he figured his hints were enough.

Alan's dad met us at the train station and gave me a warm welcome. I asked for stories about the period when he taught at the Quaker school in Ramallah, Palestine, and we arrived at the farm in no time. The farmhouse was old and comfortable; bright fabrics from various countries enlivened the wooden walls. Alan's mom had tea and a snack waiting, and stories continued until bedtime.

"Alan," his mom said brightly, "as you know, your sister has left for school, so her room is empty, and I changed the sheets so George can sleep there."

"Thanks, Mom," said Alan with a smile, "but George will sleep in the upstairs bedroom with me."

"Oh, no, that won't be necessary," she said anxiously. "Your bed is really too small for comfort."

"That's okay, Mom," he said. "There's really enough room for both of us."

I noticed Alan's father looking on with interest; he had the slightest of smiles on his face. He probably knew this was coming and had decided to stay out of it.

"I'm sure your sister won't mind, and George will be so much more comfortable," Alan's mother continued, aware she was running out of arguments.

"I appreciate it, Mom, but I've decided. George will be upstairs with me. Sleep tight." And with a goodnight kiss for his mother, Alan led me up the steep wooden stairs.

The next morning I awoke before Alan, dressed, and came downstairs to the smell of coffee. Alan's father was alone, standing by the stove scrambling some eggs. "I guess we're the early birds, huh?" he said. He looked at me, a twinkle in his eye. "And how's the other half doing?"

We both laughed, sharing the significance of the wording of his question. Like so many Quakers, he didn't mind the laugh turning into a quiet pause.

"I'm glad you came to visit us, George, and so is Alan's mom, really."

We nodded to each other, knowing that the oppressive weight of centuries can sometimes, at the right moment, be negotiated around the little things.

getting the goods on cancer

Alan and I joked as we lay in bed together. It wasn't an unusual event, except this time we were in a hospital room in South Philly.

The nurse walked into my room. "All right, you guys," she said, looking pointedly at Alan and pretending exasperation. "You're the last visitor left, and now you really have to go. New Year's Eve is no exception!"

Alan laughed and hopped out of bed. "Celebration isn't what it used to be," he quipped. Then, knowing he was hours past visiting time: "Thanks for your patience."

The young nurse laughed, then looked out of the window as another set of firecrackers went off outside. She turned back to Alan. "Your friend chose an odd time to come in here for diagnostic tests."

It was the last night of 1976. I'd been in and out of the hospital for months, trying to figure out why I was so anemic. I knew my bowels were leaking blood, but what was the cause?

The months following the first hospitalization had been a busy round of family and medical appointments. I was primarily parenting but also teaching a course at Penn. The only thing the doctors could say for sure was that, with my blood levels, I should be reclining on sofas instead of continuing as a worker bee. Even the homeopathic folks—I took alternative medicine seriously— didn't succeed in making a diagnosis.

Winter became spring of 1977, my body weakened while the mystery remained unsolved. Alan and my other friends grew closer, taking turns going to the doctors with me and giving me emotional and spiritual support. Berit expanded her care of the family while continuing her demanding rape crisis work.

Finally, my body forced the issue. The blood leakage became a torrent: I began to hemorrhage early on a June morning. My close friend Chuck Esser had slept over with me that night; he rushed me to the emergency room, where blood transfusion began immediately. Chuck told me later that I was delirious until the new blood took effect; I kept repeating that I had to get out of the hospital bed and do the carpool so the children would get to school.

When I was back in my right mind, I learned that I needed exploratory surgery. Solving the mystery had turned urgent. The doctor told me I would need a couple of days for transfusing more fresh blood and getting some strength back, then I would go under the knife.

The few days went quickly. Berit and I spent quality time thinking about our children and the future. Alan and Chuck got friends to come to the hospital to do peer counseling with me, so I could enter the operating room in the best possible frame of mind.

I argued with my anesthesiologist about whether to go unconscious during surgery. I wanted a spinal anesthetic so I could stay awake while minimizing the pain. That's my philosophical attitude: in favor of conscious awareness. We agreed to a compromise: start with a spinal and resort to general anesthesiology only if needed. As it turned out, I ended up unconscious.

When I returned to my hospital bed after surgery, the surgeon came to see me. He said he'd sliced my belly wide open in order to do a thorough search. Chuck was visiting me at the time, and the surgeon asked him to step outside.

Chuck came back into my room when the surgeon left. He

told me later I was deathly pale with my eyes wide with fright. I told him, "It's cancer."

The next time the surgeon came to dress my wound, we talked. The lymphoma was extensive, he said; it involved both bowels and also the bladder. He took what he could and left the rest. Probably they would do both radiation and chemotherapy, he said.

He wouldn't meet my eyes as he spoke.

My medical student friend David Nicklin, who as a Haverford undergraduate had taken my peace studies course, did research on diffuse histiocytic lymphoma. He explained the likely reason why the medical specialists who were visiting me weren't meeting my eyes: my chances of survival were slim.

I was a stranger to fear of this size and had never experienced anything close to this much physical pain. Yet, I didn't think I would die. The challenge was the heaviest in my life so far, but somehow I didn't expect it to overwhelm me.

About four days after surgery, I learned from the medical staff that the painkiller they were giving me was slowing down the healing. I took myself off the drug, and learned more about me. From my journal:

> *Of course there must be worse pain than what I experienced, but I know that Sunday after surgery, when I stopped accepting Demerol and fought from 5:30 a.m. to 7:00 or so in the evening (until relief came)—that was pretty extreme. Time was so frozen in my head—there wasn't a sense that the hurting is only temporary and later I'd feel better. Now seemed the only time in the world that there was or could be, and it was awful.*

When my friend Ellen Deacon came to visit, she saw immediately the hell I was in. "Oh, Ellen," I gasped, my head turning from side to side, "I can't tell you what this is like."

"Well, George," she said with a smile and a relaxed voice, "I can see you're getting pretty intimate with Pain. Have you been properly introduced yet?"

Seeing me roll my eyes, she continued, "Well, after all, if you two are getting that intimate, you should at least be introduced."

Even though I was groaning, I could see she was going somewhere with this. Ellen was tall, with long, very curly red hair and an air of authority. She was a music educator as well as a member of our Movement for a New Society network. I trusted her a lot.

I surrendered. "Okay, okay, Ellen."

"I'll conduct the introduction," she explained, "and you'll speak both for yourself and for your pain. How about starting by telling Pain your name, and that you don't usually have Pain visiting, and how you feel about it."

Ellen soon had me voicing a dialogue between me and Pain, during which Pain told me—and found me skeptical—that it was actually on my side and wanted to be my friend. By the end of the dialogue, I learned to regard the pain as my companion, sharing with me in the process of healing. And, of course, the hurting diminished, since pain is mental as well as physical. I didn't go back to the pain medication.

When Ellen's dad walked in a couple days later, however, he didn't find a man with a positive attitude. I was still very scared of dying and full of "Why me?" complaints: the very essence of victimhood. Earl Deacon saw my condition and matter-of-factly explained that some years ago he'd beaten a cancer that was supposed to do him in. He said when his daughter told me about me, he felt moved to come visit. I got curious and asked him about his experience, and he slowly worked his way around to the punch line: "I took responsibility for my illness and asked myself how I had helped to make the cancer grow."

My attitude slammed into reverse. "No way," I said.

To me the cancer was an alien killer, intruding from outer space, wholly other. I was a helpless victim who had been going about my life seeking to do good. No way could I have any responsibility for this demon in my body.

Earl was relaxed and patient with my resistance. When he left, my work started, because I couldn't help asking myself: "What if I were to take Earl's view—not that it could be objectively true, mind you—but what if I were to hold the attitude that I had some responsibility for the growth of my cancer? It would mean that, having been powerful enough to grow it, I'm also powerful enough to shrink it, maybe even to make it disappear!"

Power interests me.

I got interested.

Could I adopt an attitude I didn't entirely believe in philosophically? Why not? Had I lived my life with a 100 percent consistent worldview? Does anyone, except perhaps some legendary guru in a Himalayan cave? Now, I felt, was the time to reach for the methods that support life. (My Methodist upbringing again.) One method might be an inner search that could reveal a part of me that would invite a cancer. It wasn't so strange for me to take responsibility; I do it a lot in my life.

This wasn't about self-blame. Self-responsibility is a very different kind of notion; it's about power, whereas blame is the cultivation of powerlessness.

Before surgery I had agreed with my friends that it would be excellent to have someone with me twenty-four hours a day, starting when I came out of the operating room. They raised the money to pay for a private room for six days and created a schedule so people could volunteer for shifts. The musicians in the community often chose day shifts, so they could bring their instruments and serenade me without disrupting people down the hall.

When visitors finished their shifts, they wrote in the log that hung on my bed, recounting the events and my condition, so the person taking the next shift could pick up quickly on how things were going. Here's a sample from the log:

> *George's body is healing well. He's experiencing quite a lot of pain. I think it's good to gently encourage him to be aware of things happening around him. When he's not sleeping, talk about real things happening in your life, in the room, out-doors—not from your need but just to be real and human with George. When he's resting, gently sit beside him. Touching him is always on target (while reading to yourself or resting or thinking about George).*

I asked Alan to make a wall poster that would remind me of times when I was unambiguously a lover of life. Another friend hung on the wall a giant picture of a wooded stream. Chuck held my hand after I first dared look at my belly while the surgeon dressed my large wound. When the surgeon left, Chuck gazed at me with clear, warm eyes while I trembled and stormed at what felt, in one way, like an extreme violation of my body.

As my weeks-long hospital stay neared its end, Ross Flanagan called up. He'd been spending the year in New Paltz at the State University of New York, sharing with criminologists the success of the Life Center's neighborhood safety program that he and Lillian Willoughby had led. Ross wanted to know if I had a nurse for when I returned home. It hadn't crossed my mind. Ross said Berit had plenty to do without having to do day-to-day nursing of someone in my shape, especially with her as worried as she was. He volunteered to break away from the university to come back to Philly for a month to nurse me.

All my friends were saying to me, in different ways, that it was right to take time, to mobilize all resources—inner and outer—for the struggle against cancer. "It's another campaign," some said; "this time it's not against the Pentagon or the patriarchy, but it's just as worth lavishing your energy and talent on. And we'll help."

≈ ≈ ≈

Having a life-threatening disease offers an incentive to confront illusions about oneself, just as citizens in an empire in decline can benefit from giving up their own ways of pretending. At thirty-nine I believed myself to be entirely self-invented. The illusion had blossomed in my boyhood. I identified with the heroes of the weekly radio serials that interrupted my homework: Superman, Captain Midnight, the Shadow, the Lone Ranger. Each was essentially alone, yet making the difference. (True, the Lone Ranger had Tonto, his Indigenous sidekick, but the racism of the day prevented Tonto from being a person in his own right.) Those radio icons assured me that my lonely path could support a worthwhile, even heroic, life. The Movement for a New Society was developing a theory and practice intended to contradict the individualism of its members—but even though intellectually I had given up the Lone Ranger ideal long ago, he held on in my unconscious.

My cancer experience was a massive contradiction to this illusion. There's a saying that the prospect of death tends to focus the mind. I paid attention as I never had before—and found my community loving me.

Berit organized a support committee, as a kind of strategy group, to help me sort out my options and make sure I wasn't overextending myself. I realized later, though, that in the process we both forgot something vital: the group needed to think also about Berit herself and whether she was getting sufficient support. Berit's job had her confronting the consequences of rape every day. At home, she had three scared children to nurture. And it appeared likely that she would lose her life partner. I failed to consider how stressed she must be as I prioritized my struggle to live.

In the hands of Berit, Alan, Chuck, and so many others, I found the Lone Ranger's mask slipping, the Batman's cape falling, the Man of Steel melting. The loneliness of the heroes of my youth couldn't quite stand up to the loving friends of my midlife crisis. I won't say that the superheroes disappeared, but they weren't so super anymore. My next discovery was as much political as it was personal: installing a superhero model may be a substitute for, and avoidance of, the inner reality of power. Freud suggested that grownups can remain children, prone to seek father figures wherever they go, by turns submitting to them and rebelling against them. He influenced me intellectually, and I figured much of my role as a trainer and organizer was supporting groups to become more sensible than their individual members usually are.

That work still needed doing, but in the laboratory that my cancer provided I found something else going on. The community was pushing me through my inner defenses so I could see the reality of my own shining brightness! Imagine my surprise when—seventeen days after surgery, still in the hospital with tubes coming in and going out, missing my children, and feeling broken, helpless, and useless—I had this revelation, which I recorded in my journal:

Inside me is a cathedral, grand, like St. Mary Redcliffe Church in Bristol, a gothic gem. Inside me is exquisite color, shining on walls, on floor, and most brilliantly seen when the glass is directly apprehended. Great peals of the organ resound in the cavernous stone recesses (I am vast inside) and also the merriest music available, like that favorite Bach cantata we sang in the choir.

Inside, tapers are lit, dramas occur, continuities are maintained, fresh words are uttered for new days, doors swing open, sunshine comes in. I am clean and healthy and wholesome, and love is everywhere, completely without apology.

In the following weeks, I decided on the main feature of my campaign for wellness: not to put all my strategic eggs in one basket but, instead, to replicate Movement for a New Society by being multidimensional.

My gastrointestinal specialist strongly recommended chemotherapy, and my support group was divided. My primary care physician went with me to visit the oncologist Michael Karpf. I explained to Dr. Karpf my reluctance because of how hard the chemicals are on the immune system.

"True," he replied, "but what has your immune system done for you lately?"

I had to chuckle; I didn't expect a witty chemotherapist.

"If you decide to go with me," Dr. Karpf continued, "I must tell you that I will be very aggressive because of your diagnosis. I will bring your white blood cell count down so low in the middle of each cycle that you are more likely to die from a cold than from the cancer. I'll give you my personal phone number, and if you catch cold, you'll call me and I'll meet you at the emergency ward."

That sobered me, and also increased my interest in working with this straight-talking man.

I next visited a leading homeopathy clinic to see what its director would recommend. He began by giving me the expected rap against chemo and the superiority of alternative treatment that, he acknowledged, was gentler and took more time. I then explained the nature of my fast-growing disease.

"If I were you," he said, "I'd do the chemo."

I already had a healthy diet, so I built on that by taking B, C, and E vitamins and giving up sugar. I did my daily yoga, and walked and increased my play with my children. I also increased hugs, snuggling time, and massage. I doubled my time at the piano and surrounded myself with music. To further reduce my anxiety—and to work through old emotional wounds that might

be related to my disease—I tripled my use of reevaluation counseling, a kind of peer support. To boost my immune system even
more and support it against the attack of the chemicals, I turned
to a guided visualization technique for meditating three times
each day.

Early in the chemotherapy, when I went for another round
of treatments, I told my doctor about the other modalities I
was using. Dr. Karpf dismissed them all, especially the vitamins,
which he considered a scam. "Only my chemicals can heal you,
George," he said.

After repeated attempts to share with Dr. Karpf, I got tired
of his dismissive attitude and stopped telling him. In the meantime, I got closer with the head nurse at the oncology unit of the
Hospital of the University of Pennsylvania, and found she was
strongly interested in my holistic approach.

I've known many people who resist counseling or other means
of exploring what lies below their conscious minds. I can relate; I
don't really want to meet my inner demons. On the other hand,
Ellen's father told me it was the path to power.

Also underlining the psychological work, ironically, was information from my chemotherapist. Dr. Karpf told me that one
reason he was so aggressive was that my particular disease sometimes went into remission and then returned with a vengeance.
"Our best chance," he said, "is to get it the first time around."

In addition to occasional vivid dreams, I sometimes woke in
nameless, wordless terror. Several friends slept with their phones
next to their beds for just such occasions. One night I called Keith
Miller, and he decided to come over rather than hang out with
me on the phone. Keith was a schoolteacher with co-counseling
skills. As a member of Movement for a New Society, he organized
our neighborhood's first co-op. I appreciated Keith being working
class and bringing the directness and irreverent sense of humor
that often goes with that upbringing.

Keith kicked off his shoes and crawled into my bed. "What's up, George?" he asked as he reached for my hand.

I started to tell him about the feelings that woke me up and, encouraged by his relaxed smile and interested eyes, soon transitioned into feeling the feelings instead of talking about them. I sweated the cold sweat that goes with heavy fear and suddenly saw before me the edge of a cliff. "I can't look over, Keith, I can't look over the cliff!"

Keith gave me the look of someone who believes I can do anything I want to, so I did it: I looked into the void. Every part of me shook; my teeth sounded like castanets; my eyes went wide with terror. I stifled the occasional scream, not wanting to wake the children, and pulled my hair. Drops of cold sweat trickled from my armpits. I lost track of time, but finally the shaking subsided, and I cried in Keith's arms. "I will never be loved," I told him. "I will always be alone."

Keith smiled. "Well, George, that could be a reason to give up."

Abruptly, I giggled. The distance between my despair and my present reality was so vast as to be comical. But who would know, if I hadn't looked at—or felt—the usually hidden bleakness of my despair?

To my surprise, I located deep inside me a wish to die. It was hidden from me by my physical bounciness, my enthusiasm for political work, my zest for intellectual challenge, the pleasures of music and drama and romance, my love for my family and friends. These attributes shaped my persona, and obviously someone like me can't just throw in the towel. Better, far better, to grow a cancer, and be treated with honor on the way out.

That's one way to do a midlife crisis.

Even now I don't quite know how to name my despair. It had to do with love, and idolatry, and living again what can never be relived. It had to do with disappointment, deadly anger, holding back, hiding my power, and also hiding my need.

Where was that inner me who for so many years emphatically chose life? When I was in my late teens, I had a rich interior life and trusted my intuition. I dedicated my life to working for a just and peaceful world, however little the world might appreciate my decision. I was a nonconformist, but not often scorned, and my friends loved me. On the really important things, I counted on me.

In my twenties, I took steps that broadened me and increased my understanding, but somehow decreased my confidence in my intuition. I got married and lived in another country where the cultural cues were new and different. I adopted a fairly conventional lifestyle and tried to bury my love for other men. My upward professional mobility accelerated; in my effort to grow more sensitive professional middle-class antennae, I undermined my solid sense of the fundamental, working-class-formed me. In graduate school, I got the message that the only things that are true are things that can be supported by footnotes.

This experience of cancer might be an opportunity to choose life by choosing *me*—that young, working-class me, who trusted himself and his intuition.

Amazingly, the cancer was a blessing; it was big enough to put me back in touch with my essence. My community's high-intensity love surrounded me; some of it had to get in and reach stale corners of self-doubt. I found myself relying on my intuition, even on medical questions, when only I had enough of the whole picture to decide. I learned that I could really count on myself to make the big judgments when I needed to.

Finally, the physical pain was something I had to bear alone. Although their support was incredibly important, I couldn't share that with even my dearest friends.

צ צ צ

While still in the hospital after surgery, I attended a chapel service friends organized for me. The singing was beautiful, including the old gospel song "Healing River" and the new Catholic song "Joy Is Like the Rain." Friends recalled times, often humorous, when my commitment to life shone through. I listened and cried. We prayed. At the end, I stood in the middle of the circle and everyone touched me. Someone asked how I was healing. I said, "Beautifully."

The same question was voiced again. I said, strongly, "Like an oak!"

The group said, "So be it!"

In my journal, scattered through the pages, I later wrote in capital letters, "SO BE IT!"

I attended a retreat for spiritual healing at Powell House, a Quaker conference center in New York state. I loved how matter-of-fact those Friends were about healing. My stereotype of healers had been self-important people talking in hushed tones—a stereotype that was quickly dashed to pieces. I was prayed for, and I felt warmth where the cancer was. One Friend who practiced "laying on of hands" with me noticed the warmth in her hands when they reached the site of my tumor and asked, "Is that where it is?"

I was buoyed by the hope and expectancy, and stayed on at Powell House a few days after the conference to continue to dwell at my center without the distractions of home life. On my walks, I noticed that deer continued their grazing while I walked by near them.

I visited evangelical healing services in suburban Philadelphia and was boggled by what I heard and saw there. Trained to be a skeptical sociologist, I was not prepared for the healings that seemed to occur in front of my eyes. Again, I was reassured by the lack of hocus-pocus among the healers there. The main minister seemed both confident and lighthearted, and went at healing almost with the air of a garage mechanic starting in on a damaged car. I was deeply moved by the power in the place: a church jam-packed with people on a rainy Friday night, supremely confident that Jesus was healing and loving, among them at that very moment.

My fortieth birthday party that fall was a jamboree. Trollheim, my house in the Life Center community, was stuffed with jubilant people. The three floors of the house were divided into activity areas: in one room, singing and playing folk songs; in another, dancing wildly; in another, giving foot massages and talking quietly; in the kitchen, cooking crepes; on the porch, making ice cream. People were tactful about avoiding taking photos of me; I looked like, well, someone fighting cancer.

My younger daughter, Ingrid, was six years old at the time. She remembers wandering around the house and being puzzled to see joy in the more public spaces while, in the corners, people were holding each other and crying. What she didn't understand at the time was that some had come from a long distance, believing it was the last time they would see me alive.

At one point, small groups went off to corners of the house to prepare skits on various aspects of me: daddy, Quaker, gay man, teacher, activist. They then gathered on the first floor to present the skits to each other and to me. The skits were hilarious and sometimes moving. There was silence, people holding hands, and tearful eyes as we sang softly together about love and strength and the dear gift of life. At that moment, I hoped everyone would know deeply that we all deserve such fierce and tender comrades, and that it is worth the struggle.

‽ ‽ ‽

After nine months of treatment, Dr. Karpf was satisfied that I was cancer-free. I went to the nursing director to tell her the good news. We chatted for a while; then she said, "I don't know if I should tell you this, but when you stopped reporting to Dr. Karpf about the other work you've been doing on your cancer, he started coming around to me after each treatment to find out what you told me. He was intensely interested; he just couldn't show you that."

Later, I learned from my primary care doctor that Dr. Karpf had called my recovery "a miracle."

22

Christina's miracle

The years immediately after healing from cancer in 1978 were largely quiet for me on the activism front. Doctors told me that, if my kind of disease didn't kill me the first time, it was prone to return within a couple of years and often succeeded on its second try. I needed to prioritize my holistic approach to wellness, as well as attending to our three children. Berit became director of Women Organized Against Rape. I managed to continue to teach my course at Penn, and sometimes Haverford College and Swarthmore.

While part of me was listening for the other shoe to drop—a return of the cancer—it would have helped me to know some of the things that waited for me in my future: joining the first mass civil disobedience to confront the US Supreme Court's homophobia, learning to lead multicultural training workshops in Asia, training the mine workers' union for a successful strike, protecting human rights lawyers in Sri Lanka from assassination, launching a new climate-justice campaigning organization, and much more. (Obviously, the cancer didn't return!)

However, despite our best efforts, our two teenagers were not doing well. The optimism that was generally in the air when we adopted Christina and Peter cross-racially had evaporated; we were now hearing multiple stories from other parents in painful struggle. As a whole family we were in therapy; at one point,

Peter was admitted to an inpatient program for children and adolescents.

Looking back, we realized that when we made our adoption decisions in the 1960s, Berit and I failed to see how deeply and early racism impacts people's lives. As I write this book, half a century later, Americans are still reckoning with the depth and complexity of racism's poison, despite the antiracist efforts that have been undertaken in that half century. Many educated people, white and Black, have resisted seeing how tightly racial injustice is interwoven with economic injustice, and imagined that a racist culture could be transformed with measures like affirmative action without changing society as a whole.

The heaviness of racism continued to dog our family and was showing up through dangerous acting out, even while we reached for resources to—in the words of Rev. Jesse Jackson—keep hope alive. Then, in 1981, when Christina was sixteen, we feared that we'd lost her forever.

ℵ ℵ ℵ

"How much did she take?" My voice was scared, urgent, as I held the cool washcloth on my daughter's forehead. Streams of sweat were coming off Christina's face as she moaned and writhed on her bedroom floor, her white blouse already wet. I heard Berit's steps returning from the bathroom. "She took everything! Aspirin, flu medicine, a whole bottle of Tylenol." She grabbed Christina's jacket from the bedroom closet. We half pulled, half lifted her to her feet and awkwardly walked her down the stairs. Christina was no longer the little girl I could bounce on my shoulders. Her groans became cries of protest. "Just let me be. It hurts!" Then she screamed, "Let go of me!" We continued to help her down the stairs. I noticed she wasn't physically resisting. Part of her must have realized the emergency room wasn't a bad idea.

The ER at the children's hospital was crowded, but the staff moved when we used the words "suicide attempt." A medical team quickly inserted a stomach tube, and the flushing began.

For the first time since leaving the house, Berit and I looked fully at each other, searching for strength. Berit's jaw was set with determination; she was going to get through this. My stomach was in knots. I looked at Christina's flushed face; sweat plastered her dark curly hair to her temples. "Did she really do it this time?" I asked myself. My field of vision shrank. All I could see was my daughter, and Berit, and the medical people in their green scrubs as they checked vital signs and drew blood. I heard a roaring in my ears.

"George—the doctor." Berit touched my arm. I came back from my trance and paid attention. "The lab will do the blood-work immediately," the resident was saying. "I doubt that we got the Tylenol out of her stomach—it goes into the bloodstream so quickly. Your daughter will go now to the ICU, and we'll tell you as soon as we know something." Orderlies wheeled out the exhausted and barely awake Christina. We followed and were told to sit in the family lounge across from her room. Berit picked up a magazine out of habit; that's what people do in waiting rooms. I kneaded my neck and let out a sigh. Our vigil began.

Christina had been throwing herself away for a couple of years now, and nothing we did convinced her to stop. We went from therapist to therapist, experimented with alternative methods of parenting, listened to conflicting advice of friends, and searched our souls. Our life was a roller coaster of tearful reconciliations followed by new crises. There was no end in sight, until this fateful night. In the last two years, I'd spent countless hours going after my daughter, venturing into seedy bars and dark alleys, hoping to find her and bring her home. Tonight, she might have put herself beyond reach, even beyond searching.

"We have the test results." A resident we hadn't seen before stood at the doorway of the lounge. We were alone, so he came in. "We pumped a lot of stuff out of her stomach, but the Tylenol did enter her bloodstream. We checked with the national poison control center. Your daughter has twice the lethal dose in her system." He paused to let that sink in. "We can expect her organs to fail within two days at most. She's obviously not a candidate for an organ transplant because of her mental condition."

He paused again. "It's your job as parents to decide whether to tell her about her prognosis." He remained standing, looking at each of our numb faces. His voice softened. "Call me when you have questions." I nodded to him as he left. Neither Berit nor I spoke for what seemed hours.

"We must tell her." Berit broke the silence. "But I can't do it." Tears formed in the corners of her blue eyes, swelled, ran down her wan cheeks. "I just can't tell her that," she repeated. "You have to do it." I envied Berit and her tears as an enormous weight settled on my chest. I stared at the floor, shaking my head from side to side. While some parents might debate whether to tell their young one the harsh reality, we both had a principled loyalty to truth, especially when it comes to life or death. She knew I would tell Christina in the best way possible.

"We'll do what we know how to do, right?" I looked into Berit's eyes, now streaming. "Pray, and ask people to help?"

She sighed, and nodded, and blew her nose. "Now go, George." As I entered her room, Christina was in bed watching reruns of a soap opera called *General Hospital*. She'd showered and had some toast and ginger ale; ironically, she looked like her healthy, pretty self once again.

I didn't beat around the bush. I told her what the doctor had said: I told her that, as far as he knew, she would pass away sometime on Friday. I told her that I respect medical people, but I don't believe they always know everything, because there's more that supports life than tissues and blood and what you can see under a microscope. I told her that Berit and I would call Quakers and other friends and start prayer services in the hospital chapel, and we'd call relatives and friends in other countries and ask for prayer circles to join us. I told her that we were cheering 100 percent for her to live, but that I didn't think that would be enough unless she chose life for herself. I told her that if she made that choice, then she had a chance.

I stopped. She continued to gaze at the television set, showing no indication that she'd heard. "If you want to," I went on, "you can come down to the chapel and join us—maybe just to see if we're there." I stopped again. Her body seemed to relax, but I couldn't be sure. "I love you, Christina," I whispered, and squeezed her hand.

"Okay, Dad," she said; it was her usual way of saying goodbye.

Wednesday and Thursday I remember only as a blur. We took Peter out of his boarding school so he could be with his big sister in what might be her final days. Our housemates came through with food and childcare and extra hugs. Our Friends Meeting sprang into action, as well as our activist community. We heard about prayer circles in living rooms in England, Norway, and Holland. At one point, Christina appeared in a wheelchair at our service in the hospital chapel, "just to check on you," as she put it.

On Thursday night, the medical people were puzzled: "We're not yet seeing signs of organ failure." Late on Friday morning, a doctor found us in the lounge. "We've done a thorough check of your daughter," he said, "and there's no reason why we can't discharge her. She seems just fine. You need to schedule psychiatric follow-up before you go."

He paused, tilting his head. "But we don't need a medical follow-up." We stared at him, dazed in our exhaustion. The doctor smiled. "Yes, she's all right. You can take your daughter home now."

A few weeks later, after Meeting for Worship, Berit and I were standing together chatting with friends during coffee hour. A gray-haired woman who had spent the past month traveling came over to us. "Well, Berit and George, I followed from a distance the crisis with your daughter. I want to tell you I was carrying you in my heart." We smiled our appreciation.

"You know," she continued, "that was really quite a miracle."

Berit's smile broadened. "I'm not sure I intellectually believe in miracles. But we still have George here, after the cancer that was supposed to take him away. And now Christina. Whether or not I believe in miracles, I guess our family counts on them."

23

campaigning for Jobs with Peace

"Daddy, last night I had that terrible dream again."

I looked at my eleven-year-old with surprise. It was 1982. Ingrid and I were the first ones to the breakfast table this morning, and I was reading the morning paper. Our round wooden table usually accommodated three or four of our household members by now, busily chowing down on eggs and toast or granola.

"Tell me about your dream," I said to Ingrid. She was usually full of bounce and smiles even in the morning, but at the moment she held a grave expression on her face.

"I dreamt that there were big bombers coming over our house. They made a lot of noise, so I thought I woke up, but I really didn't. Because it was a dream," she explained.

"Uh-huh," I said. "Then what happened?"

"A big explosion went off down the street, and somebody yelled, 'A nukular bomb!' and then I don't know what happened." She paused. "But it was scary."

"It sure is," I agreed. "Gee, you'd think with all that noise I would have heard it, too."

"Oh, Daddy!" Ingrid laughed. "Don't be silly. You can't hear somebody else's dreams!"

I got up and put another slice of bread in the toaster while reflecting on the impact of President Ronald Reagan's fearmongering election campaign. Claiming that the United States would fall behind in the nuclear arms race was hokum, but Reagan, a B-list actor, had previously had a career selling himself on TV for General Electric. I wondered if he had any sense that what he was doing was continuing to bomb the resilience of American culture?

"Ingrid, you're not the only person having dreams about this stuff. You've heard the grown-ups talking about the danger of nuclear war, and a lot of people are worried about it. Your mother and I are working on our country's leaders to reduce the danger—I want you to know that. And I have an idea about something you can do toward fixing it."

Ingrid eagerly leaned forward.

I told her about the group of college students that I was coaching to organize a neighborhood diversity fair down the street, at Clark Park. She'd already met them because I brought my Haverford College peace studies class on a "field trip" to my house to show them a sample of our Movement for a New Society lifestyle, and in our living room Ingrid had responded to their questions about a child's view of our community. At semester's end, one of my students enlisted some of his Haverford College friends for the diversity fair's organizing team.

The fair's goal was to provide a venue for neighborhood groups to come together to show off to each other, especially the minority groups among which hostility simmered. The Hmong residents promised to bring their crafts and dances, African American groups promised soul food and drumming, Cambodians agreed to teach games and share music, and other groups promised a flea market and pony rides. Our city council representative agreed to come and give out free ice cream cones for all.

The police department was nervous about bringing these groups together and, at first, insisted on a strong uniformed presence. We talked them out of that by promising to train peacekeepers who would circulate throughout the fair; the police ended up sending plainclothes officers instead.

And so it was that Ingrid and her best friend, Evy Deming, also eleven, found themselves at the "Speak Out Corner." For weeks, they had been rehearsing their speeches against nuclear arms, and now—while the Haverford students were speaking and gathering a crowd—Evy and Ingrid were arguing about who would go first. Both had gotten stage fright and wanted the other to start.

"How about this?" I suggested. "Both of you stand up together, and then, Ingrid, you start, and Evy, you take your turn while you're both up there together."

This proved acceptable. A visibly nervous Ingrid, freckles made even more visible by the summer sun, launched into her speech. The line I remember was, "I don't want any more scary dreams," which got the crowd's fervent applause. And the outcome of the fair that I remember best, even though exhausted student organizers and happy neighbors alike agreed it was a successful event, was that Ingrid stopped having her nightmares.

Funny thing, how taking action reduces anxiety.

ぇ ぇ ぇ

The Nuclear Freeze Campaign was growing nationally and being considered in Philly. I, however, was eager to work on economic justice in some way; I wanted to demonstrate to my dad that his son really was on his side, despite my sometimes going down paths that bewildered him.

I heard about a new campaign called Jobs with Peace. It proposed an alternative to the cutbacks in federal aid to housing, education, transportation and the like—cutbacks that started under President Carter but increased under Reagan in order to pay for new high-priced weapons. The campaign emphasized that more jobs are created by civilian spending than by military spending, thus wedding the two issues of economic well-being and peace.

A carload of us from the West Philly Movement for a New Society drove to Boston to meet leaders of Jobs with Peace. Young German activist Antje Mattheus was in the car. A tall, lanky woman with blue eyes and light-brown curly hair, Antje loved dancing, arguing about politics, and wrestling with guys to prove that women are strong. She frequently won these wrestling matches.

Antje had come to the United States eight years earlier as a volunteer with Action Reconciliation Service for Peace, a German pacifist group that helped young people serve in countries that had been at war with Nazi Germany, as a kind of people-to-people reparation program. Antje's specific assignment was to work with the United Farm Workers' national campaign for economic justice for farm workers. Based in Philadelphia, she gravitated to our community and, instead of returning to Germany at the end of her Action Reconciliation service, stayed on with Movement for a New Society. She was ready for a new campaign and was intrigued by Jobs with Peace.

In Boston, we spent most of our time with Frank Clemente, who was the national coordinator of Jobs with Peace. Quick with a smile and even quicker with a political analysis, Frank explained that the goal of the Jobs with Peace Campaign was to shift federal spending priorities to meeting social needs while producing more jobs. In both Milwaukee and Boston, in the general election in those cities a majority voted yes in the referendum on Jobs with Peace; in Boston it was 66 percent. The reasoning appealed to white working-class people, as well as people of color—and also to progressive members of the professional middle class. When Frank said some unions around the country were getting interested, I thought about my dad.

On the highway back to Philly, we talked nonstop and agreed to explore a Philadelphia campaign. Philly would be the biggest city so far for Jobs with Peace, which was a bit intimidating. But we could gain acceptance as a collective within the network of Movement for a New Society. The broader support structure of the organization would be reassuring. Antje said she'd help staff the campaign on a volunteer basis until we raised some money, and so did several others.

I talked it over with Berit. She had recently become director of the Fellowship Commission, a nonprofit agency that promoted human rights and equality among the diverse population groups in our city. Berit said she could support the family herself until Jobs with Peace could afford to pay me, so I could volunteer while the children were in school.

ʊ ʊ ʊ

In June 1982, half a million people marched to the United Nations to protest the nuclear arms race. I took Ingrid and Evy, along with a Nancy Drew book, which I read to them on the bus to New York and back. Philadelphia's contribution in numbers to the march was substantial, the result of an unusual degree of cooperation among progressive labor, liberals, and traditional peace activists. Joe Miller, a longtime Philly activist who catalyzed the local participation, wanted to build on the momentum and create an ongoing peace coalition in our region. I persuaded Joe and his closest associates that Philly could do just that by tying into the embryonic national Jobs with Peace Campaign.

What we didn't reckon on was chairs being thrown.

The framing of the Jobs with Peace Campaign invited a diverse coalition, because using a substantial part of the Pentagon's budget for meeting human needs would benefit everyone—especially those now in poverty. A strong coalition is a temporary alliance of organizations and groups who work together for a common goal. Unfortunately, coalitions composed of various peace groups in Philadelphia had a tradition of looseness that strained the definition of "coalition." The Philly peace version was an association of individuals, most of whom didn't represent anyone! There was usually no formal membership of groups in the coalition, and no accountability.

I'd been active in a number of such "coalitions" over the years, and they drove me crazy. A few people, even total strangers, could come to a meeting at any time and derail a carefully built consensus through eloquence or manipulation or both. It was also a setup for the FBI or anyone who wanted to undermine us. Such coalitions were usually scorned by mass-based organizations with real clout and credibility, organizations like labor unions that needed accountability instead of chaos.

Despite the disadvantages of that style of "coalition," there were many people who liked it because filling up a room with a lot of individuals felt wonderfully reassuring, like "a real movement." It also gave some people more influence than they would otherwise get, including eloquent speakers, or youths or Black people who implied they were speaking for a whole constituency even if they weren't. I knew that a few such people would argue strongly for the traditional style of peace "coalition," and I would meet real resistance to pushing for the more accountable, organizational model.

In an attempt to head off that fight, I'd gone to the house of a couple from a group that typically showed up in coalition meetings and wasted the time of others making ideological points that weren't even on the agenda. I knew they wouldn't like the idea of a more structured and accountable kind of framework. I dialogued with them for hours in their kitchen, trying to get an agreement before our big meeting. I failed.

The stakes were high for me, personally. As an active parent, I was done with four-hour evening meetings of bleary-eyed people exhausted by digressions and flights of rhetoric. To me, it was a choice between democracy and mobocracy. If individuals in the "peace coalition" were reluctant to form an organizationally based coalition, I intended to tell them the latter was a requirement for those of us prepared to build Jobs with Peace organization by organization. I warned Antje and others in our community that there would likely be a fight on this point. We decided I should put my own cred on the line to tip the scales.

The crucial evening came, and I made my argument for an accountable coalition of organizations. As expected, the counter-argument came forward—especially from the sectarian parents I'd tried unsuccessfully to head off. They brought their children to the meeting that night to give the impression that they represented an actual group.

After some back and forth, I took a stand: either create an executive committee of organizational representatives to make decisions, or I wouldn't participate. The first chair was thrown in the back of the room, while I was headed for my seat, which was located near the front. I sat down as the father started yelling from the back row about tyranny and that he wouldn't stand for any meetings that weren't open to all. Several more chairs followed, thudding against the floor of the Quaker building.

Facing everyone, I simply extended my arms to the side as a silent entreaty to the room. The parents looked around at a room of shocked faces and realized they'd gone too far.

With a signal to the children, they walked out, and the Jobs with Peace Campaign was born.

Later, when I was debriefing the meeting with Antje, she asked me, "George, where does your capacity come from to confront people and, well, let people bang against you?"

"My dad," was the answer that came immediately. "Well, maybe in his case it was mostly anger instead of strategy, and for me it's both. Sometimes I have a stubborn confidence that I'm right and should make an emphatic stand and take their reaction in stride. As you know, the main thing to avoid is escalation from my side."

ಸಿ ಸಿ ಸಿ

Now that the sectarian North Philly activist group had failed to get its way, the door was open for a strong and consistent presence for North Philly in our campaign. With its continuing poverty and other effects of racism including violence, North Philly has long been a part of my world, dating back to the time I spent practice teaching in the Reynolds School during my last year of college. The place reminds me of an American economic elite that stubbornly resists justice, and the neighborhood inspires me with heroes who just won't give up.

The hero I got to know best was Father Paul Washington. He was rector of the Church of the Advocate, an Episcopal church built to be a cathedral when North Philly was prosperous. Decades of disinvestment left a congregation too poor to support the church financially. The Episcopal diocese, to its credit, subsidized the church and Paul's ministry.

Everyone wanted Paul for their project, so I was delighted when he agreed to become president of the campaign. He wanted as much as I did a citywide coalition to join the national effort to take money from the defense budget and put it into civilian jobs: housing, education, transportation, infrastructure, and the like. Paul was eager to connect the issues of peace and economic justice, and North Philly badly needed jobs with peace.

When we met, he'd already hosted a national Black Power convention in his church and been an informal chaplain to many grassroots rebel groups. His bishop spent a lot of time defending him against right-wing and even centrist Episcopalians who were indignant that the diocese supported Paul. Their anger reached new heights when Paul's church hosted an act of ecclesiastical disobedience against the national church: the ordaining of a dozen Episcopal women as priests.

Paul's career was something like that of his spiritual cousin

Nelson Mandela. He consistently held a vision of the big picture that maintained the moral high ground, and his many critics often found themselves looking small by comparison. Paul ended up winning one of our region's highest honors, the Philadelphia Award, although the city fathers had to worry that he might not appear for the ceremony—he might be detained while picketing that day for Palestinian rights at the Israeli consulate.

I loved Paul for his warmth, showing a pastor's patience with the individuals in trouble who endlessly sought him out for counsel and support. I learned most from his use of vision, the way he used his big picture not only to guide his judgments but also to support himself in the midst of the steady erosion of North Philly. He and his partner, Christine, lived there and went through the sixties riots, the decline in jobs, the increase in drugs, prostitution, and crime as demoralization set in for so many.

Like another of his spiritual cousins, Martin Luther King, Paul was alive to the suffering in Vietnam, Central America, and other places where the United States supported death and oppression. He knew despair, and he knew a place still deeper: God's abundant love and the resource of vision.

When Paul agreed to become president of the Jobs with Peace campaign, he said his church could take our campaign under its fiscal umbrella. Whenever our campaign hit an obstacle, he was likely to crack a joke, remind us that we could find a way forward, and lift up once again a vision that called us to our best selves.

When the church treasurer, Rosalie Stephens, died, I went to her funeral. Paul conducted the funeral with the dramatic narrative characteristic of the high church tradition. As a proper cathedral should, the Church of the Advocate had a crypt beneath the sanctuary where honored members were buried. At the climactic moment, the church's floor opened and Rosalie's casket descended, accompanied by a tremendous burst of organ music and the choir singing Handel's "Hallelujah Chorus." I was already crying, but the suddenness of the sight—and the joyful musical shout that is the "Hallelujah Chorus"—had me gasping for breath. This breaking in of Spirit, I realized once again, is one way to keep hope alive.

ᘔ ᘔ ᘔ

Jobs with Peace continued to gain strength. Henry Nicholas, a prominent Black labor leader, headed one of the most progressive of our unions, the Hospital Workers Union 1199. He agreed to let us use space in his building for our office for a token rental fee.

Movement for a New Society member John Goldberg, who went to Boston on that earlier road trip, had already been making experimental visits to neighborhood associations to see how residents responded to Jobs with Peace. He found a neighborhood group in North Philly whose name for itself was "Forgotten Blocks." He couldn't stop talking about it. "George, the streets looked like London after World War II German bombing attacks! I wanted to cry. How could this happen in the wealthiest country in the world?"

With both Paul Washington and Henry Nicholas on board, I was ready to hire a couple of Black organizers—Wayne Jacobs and Jerry Hill—to work with John, who was white. Our initial budget was small; John was willing, for the time being, to be unpaid, along with other Movement for a New Society collective members on our unpaid staff, and do silk screening in the basement of his Life Center house to make a living.

Other members of our team were hard at work developing our basic Jobs with Peace pamphlet, based on research they did on how many more workers our city could afford to pay to renew housing, extend public transportation, teach, and take care of people if we had the wealth now drained from us to support the

Pentagon. Our training coordinator, Antje, was setting up workshops in organizing skills for volunteers.

Our first big goal was developing enough activity to impact the city council and get the Jobs with Peace referendum question on the ballot for the big city election of 1983, asking Philadelphians whether they would prefer money to be taken out of the Pentagon budget and put toward meeting civilian needs. I was confident that contributions to our campaign would flow once the question was on the ballot.

Paul went with me to see David Cohen, the most progressive member of the city council. David was excited to hear about Jobs with Peace, liked our research, and obviously thought the world of Paul. He cautioned us about the city council, however. "No way will they put a referendum question on the ballot without you first convincing them of your muscle in producing turnout. They don't want to encourage a lot of ballot questions that are just advertisements for some point of view—it needs to be real."

To accomplish that, we were building a multiracial, multiclass coalition, assisted by a leader from the United Electrical Workers. But some of the startup energy for Jobs with Peace was, of course, coming from Movement for a New Society, which was a largely white and professional middle-class group. I was aware that class tensions got in the way of some environmental coalitions and would probably come up in ours.*

Fortunately, the Philly chapter of Movement for a New Society had recently been working seriously on its class dynamics. Pamela Haines and others who launched our class work were not impressed by a tradition among some Marxist groups of trying to empower people by starting with theory and ideology. Instead, they called us all together for an evening and formed small groups

---

* Fred Rose details these in his helpful book, *Coalitions Across the Class Divide: Lessons from the Labor, Peace, and Environmental Movements* (Ithaca, NY: Cornell University Press, 2000).

to share some of the features of our lives when we were children: Did we go to camp in the summer? Sleepaway camp? Did our families take vacations? Abroad? Were our parents sometimes unemployed? On welfare? Did we own or rent? What were our tables like at dinnertime—crystal goblets or jelly glasses?

As the evening progressed, we sorted ourselves out. The facilitators had us use colors rather than names to designate classes, reducing the emotional charge and keeping us focused on experience rather than on academic debating points. By the end of the evening, the scales had fallen from many eyes, while others were newly confused.

"My parents didn't tell me we were poor."

"My mother and father came from really different backgrounds, and I don't know what I am."

"My parents said we were middle class, but now I realize we were owning class—what was that about?"

Spinning off from that evening workshop were affinity groups, peopled by members who wanted to explore more. I'll never forget the first meeting of the working-class caucus. I was stunned by how many of us were present. "The reputation of Movement for a New Society in the larger movement is that we're a bunch of middle-class activists," a participant said, "and I thought so, too. But what about this?" He gestured to the room of people.

It took a lot of chewing to get our mouths around all this: our own not-knowing, the sense some had that they were different from the middle- and owning-class comrades that they lived with paired with the lack of a way of figuring it out, the strangeness of coming together in a room by ourselves and also the comfort in it.

At the monthly meetings of Philly's Movement for a New Society, the class affinity groups began to report on what they were doing, sandwiched in between items like reports from direct-action campaigns, neighborhood organizing, and the food co-op. The middle-class group seesawed between confusion ("How shall we define class, anyway?") to moments of tremendous clarity ("We're the ones who've been brought up to manage things and teach people stuff!"). The owning-class group reported that it was struggling with guilt over the amount of privilege its members had grown up with—realizing that guilt doesn't actually help anyone but still having to admit they felt it. And we working-class people reported that we felt freer with each other than we did in the larger group, and realized that we must be putting some energy into fitting into a Movement for a New Society organizational culture instead of being our spontaneous selves.

The more that people listened to others in their affinity group, the more they realized that there is a kind of "culture of classes"— norms and values that go along with the rungs their families occupied on the economic ladder. They realized that as children, they were given messages about what's right and wrong, and that these messages were laden with class expectations. "Too loud!" is what middle-class (and especially owning-class) parents said about working-class people. "Stuck-up and impractical," working-class parents said about the other classes. All these discoveries resonated strongly with me, as an upwardly mobile working-class guy.

And so, even with these comrades from Movement for a New Society who risked jail and more with each other in direct action, there were subtle ways that we judged and separated ourselves from each other based on class. Who knew? We radicals, who wanted to believe that ideas are everything, got a crash course in the cultural programming of class differences.

That work we did within Movement for a New Society paid off for those of us now in the Jobs with Peace coalition. I knew to expect the subtle anxieties that came up, the need a homeless person had for extra support when sitting across the table from the millionaire, and vice versa. I became practiced at listening to a union organizer complain to me after a meeting about the woman who didn't like the fact that her comment was ignored when, later, a man said the same thing and it was acted on. "What's her problem?" he said with irritation. "She got what she wanted!" I knew by then that working-class people are usually brought up caring most about task, not process, because—in our work life—it's the product, or the result, that counts.

And of course, my shoulders were cried upon by middle-class women who felt dismissed when they wanted to add a concern about nutrition to the agenda—like the inclusion of a vegetarian option for the upcoming fundraising dinner—and saw some working-class guys rolling their eyes. (This was the eighties.) Middle-class people rarely know what a sacrifice evening meetings can be for people who started their hardworking day at 7:00 a.m.. The last thing tired people want is "unnecessary" agenda items.

The frequent collision of class cultures, with zero awareness from strong egos about acting out class scripts, was sometimes funny to me and sometimes exasperating. The plus side was that when we took the time to fight with each other, and each took the time to learn what was really at stake for the other, we were actually in the process of liberating ourselves from the rigidities of our class upbringing.*

An early payoff, as we formed Jobs with Peace, was the struggle over how organizational representatives would make decisions together on the campaign's board: majority vote or consensus? At first, the debate was ideological: What was most "democratic?" On that level, we stalemated.

I noted that the labor union representatives were most comfort-

---

* Several members of Movement for a New Society went on to initiate new inquiries and materials to help Americans penetrate the mysteries of class; see Betsy Leondar-Wright's book, *Missing Class: Strengthening Social Movement Groups by Seeing Class Cultures* (Ithaca, NY: Cornell University Press, 2014); see also a national nonprofit for training and action: Class Action, https://classism.org. Waging Nonviolence published eight of my articles on social class in 2012, plus "Unions have been down before, history shows how they can come back" *Waging Nonviolence,* June 29, 2018 https://wagingnonviolence.org/2018/06/unions-have-been-down-before-history-shows-how-they-can-come-back.

able with the traditional top-down meeting approach of Robert's Rules of Order, while activists from the professional middle class preferred consensus. So, I urged advocates for the two views to go beyond preferences to the level of *needs*. The labor reps explained that accountability is usually built into union organizations, such that they need to clearly explain to the union how the coalition's decisions were made. The unions didn't mind if their point of view lost sometimes, but it was important, in such cases, that their reps were recorded as opposed. Those who preferred consensus explained that their constituencies didn't mind delaying a decision to maximize the chance of finding a creative way forward. Each side began to hear the other, and through the dialogue we came to an agreement in Jobs with Peace that we would ordinarily struggle to reach consensus—and when we didn't get there, and it was a matter of urgency, we would vote, and an 80 percent majority would carry the day.

The debate proved to be a bonding experience for our coalition. The union people found that "know-it-all" middle-class people can actually listen, and the activists found that "rigidly hierarchical" working-class people sometimes are working with a different set of responsibilities. I was ecstatic: we were learning about class, from the inside out, and gaining more unity at the same time.

To gain the credibility we needed to impress the city council, we organized a Jobs with Peace Week. We created so many events in so many neighborhoods in that week that city council felt it. Our Black organizers, Wayne Jacobs and Jerry Hill, did a fantastic job, as did John Goldberg. When labor leaders and influential Black preachers made phone calls to city council members, and some of those members in turn sponsored the legislation, our Jobs with Peace question went on the ballot, asking voters whether they wanted some Pentagon funding to be shifted to jobs that met human needs.

I had no experience in running referendum campaigns in an election. My political experience was in direct action, what community organizers called "street heat." Just how do you plan a referendum campaign for a city of two million people?

Antje suggested we ask Paul Tully to help us. Tully was a big, arm-waving, middle-aged man from an Irish working-class neighborhood in Philly who liked managing campaigns for Democrats like the Kennedys and Walter Mondale. He agreed to take time out from high-level Democratic politics, and I set up a day-long workshop. Antje had briefed him on who we were. He began his workshop with a smile and a personal note.

"Electoral politics gets priority attention from the mainstream mass media," he said, "and we're grateful and are always looking for more." He smiled again and shrugged his shoulders. "But the media don't tell people how dependent my people are on what you movement activists do. What you do is dig into issues that arouse concern, and with your actions you figure out how to frame those issues, how to arouse people to the point where they're willing to fight for the issues because they really matter.

"My candidates have to run on a platform, right? They need to figure out what issues to get on the right side of, the side that will enable them to attract votes on election day. So, what we campaign managers do is scan what you activists are doing, what you find matters to people enough that they come to that church basement and get involved. And then, looking at the issues you identify, we pick what seems best for our candidate to run on."

He paused, looked around, smiled again. "What you folks do is the beginning of the process of change. You set the terms. You get things started. Then we come along and grab your best stuff and turn it into media coverage and votes for our candidate.

"So, right now, at the beginning of the workshop, I just wanted to be straight with you. I know the mass media won't give you this information, because they like the glamor of my campaigns. So, I need to tell you frankly: the fact is, *you're* the prime movers."

Paul's workshop was helpful, and we were quick learners. We fielded a great many volunteers, backed by an effective staff: there were endless meetings in church basements and recreation centers all over the city.

꙲ ꙲ ꙲

"We need a number!" I told everyone, knowing that the clarity offered by a challenging goal inspires people to work hard. "What's our goal? By what percentage do we want to win?"

In the Jobs with Peace referenda in other states, the "yes" votes tended to be in the 60 percent range. Our members dreamed and argued, and the board decided: 75 percent! John made a poster with a huge "75 Percent" and put it on the ceiling above his head so he would see it last thing at night and first thing in the morning. Staff and volunteers, on meeting each other, smiled and said, "Seventy-five, right?"

Our other field staffers, Wayne Jacobs and Jerry Hill, joined John Goldberg in going beyond the people they already knew: "Let no ward go untouched!" Some veteran politicians had suggested we not bother with some of the white, working-class wards that often polled conservative and focus instead on running up our totals in progressive places like Center City and northwest Philly. I pushed back, saying it would be a bigger win if we got at least a majority in all the wards. Some eye rolling was detected.

As the election date neared, I was asked to meet with leading city Democrats and the man they were running for mayor, W. Wilson Goode. As the meeting started, nearly everyone but me lit a cigarette, and I thought, "Right—there really is a smoke-filled room!"

Their agenda: Would I have a problem if Wilson Goode endorsed the Jobs with Peace referendum question?

That was easy: "No problem." Their next question was whether I'd like Democratic Party personnel at polling places to hand out Jobs with Peace leaflets as people arrived to vote. That "yes" was just as easy.

Our gang was beyond excited the day before the election. Not everything had gone as smoothly as the meeting with the head honchos of the Democratic Party, but we impressed ourselves with the outreach we'd done. The next day, we'd be running around to polling places to encourage those handing out our literature. "Remember," we said to each other at the end of the day, "75 percent!"

We couldn't stop smiling about the result: a 76 percent "yes" vote in the largest city that had so far held a Jobs with Peace referendum. And we carried every ward.

≈ ≈ ≈

Credibility beyond the activist margin can be sweet. We got a call from the one of the largest unions in the state, the American Federation of State, County and Municipal Employees. Would I come to the state capitol of Harrisburg and meet with them and other labor leaders? Pennsylvania law didn't allow for statewide referenda, but they offered to finance our running Jobs with Peace campaigns in multiple other counties in the state in the 1984 national election, and the state AFL-CIO would back us up.

Julius Uehlein, the president of the Pennsylvania state AFL-CIO, got used to my sticking my head into his office a couple of days each week and asking brightly, "Whatcha got for me today, Julius?"

He generally had another open door for me in some county or other, or Harrisburg itself. He was so helpful that I suggested that Jobs with Peace hold a big dinner in his honor in Philly, which we would also use as a fundraiser. He readily agreed, but it turned out to be a mistake on both our parts. He called me and said that he sadly had to back out of the award dinner and, more sadly, had to take the AFL-CIO out of its relationship with Jobs with Peace. He said that Lane Kirkland, the head of the national AFL-CIO, had gotten wind of our work together and that it violated a rule that only the national could deal with international policy matters. Kirkland was a right-wing Democrat, suspicious of all things related to peace. Fortunately, the loss of their sponsorship didn't affect our partnership with other major unions.

The Jobs with Peace referenda did well in the November 1984 election in the Pennsylvania counties Jobs with Peace won, with at least 60 percent voting yes. President Reagan also gained reelection, which struck many observers as a contradiction. Fortunately, in Berks County, our organizers did exit polling on election day. The pollsters asked a sample of voters who they voted for in the presidential race and also how they voted on the Jobs with Peace question. For the voters who said they voted for Reagan and also for our campaign, the pollsters asked why. The most frequent response went like this: "President Reagan is a great man and a great leader, but he doesn't know everything and he's got it wrong about this arms race thing. We've got to set him straight on that."

It taught me the danger of making assumptions about why people vote for right-wing candidates. Voters' political thinking about issues may be more complex—and interesting—than their vote for a candidate indicates.*

א א א

---

* In an article I wrote for *Waging Nonviolence*, I point to dangerous assumptions about the politics of working-class people, including the labor movement—for example, the AFL-CIO being the first mass representative organization in the United States to come out against the Iraq war, and the first (in 2011) to call for rapid US military withdrawal from Afghanistan: George Lakey, "What Militarists Don't Want You to Know about the Labor Movement," *Waging Nonviolence*, November 4, 2014, https://wagingnonviolence.org/2013/11/militarists-dont-want-know-labor-movement/.

The ambiguities of voter behavior, and their sometimes strong attraction to something visionary, stirred the memory of our 1970s B-1 bomber campaign, which we won during President Carter's administration, thanks to labor joining our efforts. The win was temporary, but even that couldn't have happened if we'd counted on simply our opposition to the bomber —instead of offering a positive program in its stead. Now that Jobs with Peace was a presence, both in Philly and statewide, why not return to the program proposed by the B-1 bomber campaign: economic conversion?

After all, the dependency of people on jobs created by the military-industrial complex gives politicians an excuse to ignore the results of referenda and continue to tilt the budget toward the military. We could make a start on changing this by giving citizens the capacity to plan for civilian use of military facilities and the skills of military workers. If there were viable alternative-use plans for sites now devoted to the military, people would be in a stronger position to insist that their elected federal officials earmark the budget for the alternative, civilian use instead of the military use.

In the next year, we developed state-level legislation that would provide for "alternative use committees" at the local level in areas that depended on military contracts. That would usually be weapons manufacturing, but it also might be an area that had an army post or air force base that was important to the local economy. An alternative use committee would be comprised of citizens and economists who would research civilian uses for a facility and its workers should a contract be lost or an air base be closed.

Even common-sense policies, however, usually require a struggle in a capitalist country biased against whatever doesn't narrowly benefit the economic elite. We set up a state strategy committee to lead this struggle, composed of legislative directors for major unions and representatives of Catholic and Protestant churches. They said the state senate would be the problem, since it was majority Republican and would want to be in tune with President Reagan. Through our growing statewide network, we persuaded two Republican state senators to sponsor our alternative-use legislation; the positive voting totals in the Jobs with Peace referenda made that possible. In the Democratic house, we found a leading Democratic state legislator eager to sponsor it.

The senate's majority leader immediately bottled up the bill in committee, and there was nothing the senate rules allowed us to do about it. Our strategy committee all looked to me, and I asked if anyone had tried a direct-action campaign inside the capitol itself. Some looked startled, but I noticed a couple of interested smiles. It wasn't hard to convince them to try it. In addition, I sent Erwin Rose, an especially shrewd Penn student of mine, to the home district of Majority Leader Robert Jubelirer to rouse some pressure on him in Altoona.

Each Wednesday, the campaign took the central hall of the elegant state capitol building to hold a news conference, after which those of us prepared to risk arrest headed up to the senate majority leader's office. We proceeded to block his office for a couple hours, then adjourn while we organized the next week's event. We had a clergy day, mothers' day, grandmothers' day, and so on.

My favorite was children's day, when I held the news conference with a grandbaby in my arms. Ingrid was one of the speakers, along with my fellow *Phoenix* crew member John Braxton's son Eric. The children had brought toys along, and the area in front of the majority leader's office was full of teddy bears, toy trains, and the like. Jubelirer came along and had a challenging time trying to make his way into his office without stepping on either babies or toys!

We learned that, indeed, this was the first time that a civil disobedience campaign had been held inside the Capitol building, and media coverage was excellent.

Escalation in a direct-action campaign is often a good idea, so when we obtained evidence that the state's chamber of commerce was actively lobbying against us, John Goldberg set up a picket line outside their headquarters. That was another first, we were told, which amazed me since I figured the organization lobbied against many good causes.

Jubilerer relented and allowed the bill to come to a vote. The bill failed—by one vote. One of the cosponsors of our bill—a man I had, rightly, distrusted—went to the bathroom at voting time.

I was deeply disappointed. The labor leaders in our coalition consoled me with stories of the many times they had also lost in close calls, but still it hurt. The bill was obviously designed to benefit the economy of Pennsylvania. "To them, that wasn't the point," Dave McCann from the social workers' union told me. "The point for corporate owners was they'd be losing a bit of control, and that matters more for them."

In the meantime, our coalition in Philly had continued to grow. One remarkable addition was the National Union of the Homeless. At one point, homeless leaders were in the same Jobs with Peace meeting as one of the richest men in Philadelphia.

Using the mandate we claimed from the successful Jobs with Peace referendum in 1983, we had taken on the Philadelphia Navy Yard, one of the oldest navy shipbuilders in the country. About eleven thousand people worked there, and my reading of the evidence convinced me that the navy yard would soon be on the list for closure. Unfortunately, the unions at the navy yard were in denial, as were the US senators from Pennsylvania and New Jersey.

Some unusually successful fundraising enabled us to hire a former union president from the Boston navy yard to move to Philadelphia and direct an industrial development entity we organized for conversion, the League Island Development Corporation. (League Island was the historic name of the navy yard site.) Our research yielded increasingly persuasive civilian uses for the navy yard's excellent facilities and workers' skills, including state-of-the-art environmental and energy uses. Again, we portrayed our work as simple common sense: just in case the navy does close the yard, shouldn't we be ready with a Plan B that saves all those jobs and skills and puts to work such a valuable facility?

Philadelphia has a private/public economic planning agency through which our economic elite weighs in on policy issues, the Philadelphia Industrial Development Corporation. The agency weighed in and vetoed the city's consideration of our Plan B.

I'd been hoping my prediction that the navy would close the yard would be incorrect. However, the navy did what I said they would do—in 1995 closed down the yard for shipbuilding, scattering the workforce and delivering a major blow to Philadelphia's economy.

In my life, I had often innovated and then found others joining in. I'd steered Pennsylvania's Jobs with Peace coalition into taking on peace conversion on the chance that we weren't too far ahead of history. As it turned out, we were too far ahead—there was no way that the economic elite was going to allow such an economically rational process as having a Plan B. For them, their control—in Philly, as well as on a state level—was apparently more important than practicality. Why let citizens think they can help steer economic decision-making? Another likely consideration was that the profits guaranteed them by military spending could hardly be duplicated by the economic realities of the market.

Our experience with economic conversion also illustrated the much-discussed point made by French writer André Gorz in his *Strategy for Labor*: there is a difference between a "reformist reform" and a "revolutionary reform." The latter is harder to get because it involves a power shift, and therefore requires larger, coercive force—at times, even a general strike, depending on how strongly positioned the adversary is.*

---

* André Gorz, *Strategy for Labor: A Radical Proposal* (Boston: Beacon Press, 1967).

I'd thought that both of our measures, on state and local levels, landed somewhere short of a revolutionary reform, because in neither case were we proposing a citizen-based authority with the power to implement an alternative, civilian use for the navy yard or other military facility. All the more interesting, then, that the economic elite felt so threatened as to prevent even having a backup plan on the shelf, just in case.

It was one of many times in my long career in social change that I suspected that the economic elite estimates the power of average citizens as potentially larger than we ourselves see it. What if they're right? If so, then the many activists who spend their lives on the defensive, reacting to the latest unjust move by the elite, might instead stand upright and initiate more vision-led campaigns that strategically mobilize more power than we were able to do in the eighties in Jobs with Peace.

24

family stresses lead to major change

I've heard that airplanes fly on course only part of the time; they get from point A to point B because they make very frequent course corrections. I imagine there are people who live their lives that way, making subtle course corrections on a regular basis, but others of us (seekers of drama, perhaps?) make a big deal out of correcting our course.

My cancer crisis in 1976–77 offered a chance for course correction, and I grabbed it. Strongly supported by my community, I then made friends with my despair and chose life. A decade later, I once again faced strong headwinds, with both unhappy teenagers and the continuing ascendancy of the political right. The combination of inner work and external support enabled me to meet my days, but I still felt off course.

Ever since he'd gotten inpatient treatment at age eleven, Peter had been doing better, but then he found ways to access drugs. He stole from us to pay for them. Berit and I stayed up through one harrowing night to support him through a bad LSD trip.

Peter was spinning out of control. He was thrown out of school, so we found another—and he was expelled from that one, despite heroic work by the school counselor. Then we started him in a third school, with the same outcome. Intense family therapy sessions didn't seem to be helping him at all.

Finally, the only school in the Philadelphia region that would accept him insisted that I sit next to him all day to control him. It was in that period that I felt the most desperate, spending all day next to a boy whose only interest seemed to be to come up with new ways to make trouble. After a tedious day, I drove him home, praying that the evening wouldn't be as hard as usual.

It usually was.

Peter seemed to enjoy turning our struggles physical, once dashing into traffic at rush hour to dance among the speeding cars and laughingly dare me to come and save him. I did. That incident was one of the times when I let my temper fly and hit him, hard.

I'd been hit hard quite a few times as a child, which was in part an explanation, but no excuse. Given my stand against violence, I felt horrible about my actions. Violence is a behavior I'd rejected even for my self-protection, much less in order to coerce another person into behaving differently. But here I was, committing it.

I didn't expect my violence to do any good. I didn't know anything else that would, either. I knew I was frustrated, venting by taking it out on him—and then emotionally beating myself up afterwards.

Our family therapist had already called in an associate to join her, and even then nothing they came up with made a difference. Berit's and my despair found new depths. Finally, the pair of them recommended an inpatient therapeutic community for teenagers who were acting out, located in a rural spot in Maine. Compassionate friends quickly raised the needed money to supplement what we had, and the center agreed to accept him a couple of days hence.

Peter slipped away in the night and, with a neighborhood friend, rode a bus for hours to a town in Northern Pennsylvania. Local police there caught them in a break-in and called us. After Berit explained that we would pick him up on the way to an institution in Maine, the police agreed not to charge him.

We set off to pick up our boy. When the police handed him over to us, they could see how frightened and resistant he was, so they put handcuffs on him. He was wiry and strong. I sat in the back seat holding him to prevent his leaping out of the car while Berit drove. Even then, in his desperation, he squirmed to move his feet in position to kick her head, jeopardizing us all.

My job was to hold him for several hours until we could reach friends in Connecticut who could give us a break. During the drive, he tried to bite me as I held him away from Berit's head. Our friends fortunately had tranquilizers on hand and put them in Peter's tea, so he calmed down for the rest of the drive to Maine.

We arrived at the center safely; I'd never seen our boy look more frightened. We said goodbye, then sat in the parking lot, held each other, and wept as time seemed to disappear.

After a year and a half at the center, Peter returned to us having learned to follow most societal rules, but he was still dogged by drug addiction. We got along better. He was able to hold a job and for the most part live independently.

Things wouldn't stay this way with Peter, but I was happy for the normalcy we did experience and learned to live with my sorrow that I couldn't be his savior.

Our teenagers' acting out had been extremely hard on Berit's and my relationship. In those years of family therapy, an issue that became increasingly obvious was the difficulty Berit and I had getting our parenting styles on the same page. It wasn't a difference of philosophies; we both wanted to follow the coaching of the therapists but found we simply couldn't work as a team in following through. We added couples counseling to our increasingly desperate search for the change we all needed.

We both worked hard with our couples counselor but didn't find a breakthrough. In 1985, we agreed that we should split, after twenty-six years of marriage. We then spent months more with our therapist working to retain a solid friendship between the two of us, even though we were letting go of being lovers and coparents.

Our counselor was visibly surprised at my response when he asked where the two of us would live. I said I wanted to continue in the house with the children. The counselor was sure I'd be eager to move to the Gayborhood and leave the house and children to Berit, but I wanted to give close-up parenting another go. Berit agreed to move to an apartment only a few blocks away, giving her easy access to the children. We continued to share the car, and Berit continued to be part of the support structure for the children—then, in later years, for the grandchildren and great-grandchildren, even after she moved to Washington, DC to become an organizational consultant for boards of nonprofit organizations. Happily, in retirement, she came back to the Philly suburbs, hosting family occasions and staying close to our family's changes and growth.

Berit's and my agreement that I could stay in the house hugely influenced the course my life would take. I found myself caring for Christina's daughter Crystal for more years than I had cared for her mom, and she still lives with me as I write this memoir. I also took on Christina's son, Christopher, beginning when he was eight years old. Then I played the dad role for Crystal's son Yasin, my great-grandson. I knew that I wasn't the only person in their eighties still taking care of children—it's more common in Philly's Black community.

A few months after Berit moved out of the house, back in 1985, our old friend Lillian Willoughby visited. Ingrid and I had lunch with her on the deck on a beautiful, warm day. Lillian asked Ingrid, in a concerned tone of voice, how she was doing with the split of her parents and was surprised by the response.

"Oh, it's good for me," she said. "Mommy's happier, Daddy's happier, and I can visit Mommy whenever I want."

Ingrid correctly read me as far less stressed, even though I would remain hugely involved in the ups and downs of, for example, the well-being of Christina and her new baby. Through the counseling, my capacity had grown. My support community was still there. And it turned out that more support was on its way.

≈ ≈ ≈

People were putting on their coats, cracking jokes, and moving toward the front door of our Movement for a New Society common meeting place. Near the door was a set of mailboxes into which mail was sorted for various collectives and individuals, but the most recent batch of mail hadn't yet been sorted. While I was putting on my coat, I tried to paw through the letters and envelopes. Jokingly, putting a bit of exasperated drama into my voice, I asked loudly, "My mail, my mail—where is my mail?"

"Here I am!" Michael Beer chirped loudly in the hubbub behind me.

When I first saw Michael, at a gathering of queer Quakers, we seemed a very unlikely pair of lovers. He was decades younger than I. He was athletic, flirty, and cute; I was clumsy, oblivious, and a merely pleasant-looking middle-aged dad. He did catch my eye, but then, Michael caught everyone's eye. His looks and playfulness made him the life of any party. "Too young for me," I told myself, and returned to enjoying the company of old friends.

"Come on, dance with me!" I looked up, and there was Michael with his arms outstretched, wriggling his body to the fast music. On impulse, I stepped into the crowd of dancers. Michael grabbed me and began to whirl me around, in perfect rhythm but with no pattern I could see. All I could do was hang on and stare at his unusually large mouth, stretched into a goofy grin, other dancers swirling around me in a blur. Suddenly I was laughing and laughing; he looked as though that had been his goal.

Some months later, I was packing for a trip one morning

while Michael, who wasn't going along this time, sat on the bed watching. "George," he said, "who's going to make sure you'll have some fun?"

When I told him my fiftieth birthday was coming up in November 1987, and it would be a chance to create a birthday party and fundraiser for the Jobs with Peace campaign, he insisted he would be a great person to organize it. And he was. We raised a lot of money and had a lot of fun. He was also sleeping over so often that my children and housemates accepted him as part of the family. He played basketball with Peter in the back yard and sang with Ingrid.

I had indeed found additional support.

25

confronting a homophobic Supreme Court

In 1986, the issue of gay oppression came to a head at the US Supreme Court. Many were furious because the court ruled in *Bowers v. Hardwick* that, in the state of Georgia, the police had the right to go into people's houses and arrest same-sex couples in bed together.

In October 1987, we conducted the first mass civil disobedience at the Supreme Court in the nation's history—six hundred of us were arrested.* I went to DC with friends from Movement for a New Society, but the turnout for the event was so tremendous that I became separated from them.

For years, MNS had been urging movements to build affinity groups into their confrontational actions. The idea was that individuals would arrive at a demonstration already with a small group—or quickly form one—that consisted of approximately four to fourteen others, thereby enabling them to act together in mutual support. So, when I arrived at the Supreme Court protest, I went looking for, and was happy to find, an affinity group I could join. We quickly introduced ourselves to each other, sharing our expectations and worries. I reminded myself to be ready to think fast and keep a good eye on everyone in my group.

---

* Lena Williams, "600 in Gay Demonstration Arrested at Supreme Court," *New York Times*, October 14, 1987, https://www.nytimes.com/1987/10/14/us/600-in-gay-demonstration-arrested-at-supreme-court.html.

The sense of humor that many of us LGBTQ people are proud of showed up in the action. When we filled the plaza in front of the Supreme Court building and sat down, police were sent into position. They were wearing pink gloves as a hygienic measure, because of the growing threat of AIDS. Someone started a chant, and soon we were all happily joining in: "Your gloves don't match your shoes! Your gloves don't match your shoes!"

All the police I saw seemed determined to keep a stiff upper lip, but I like to think some were smiling inside.

The arrests started at the other end of the plaza from us, and I noticed a young man sitting across from me in our circle becoming restless. I urged us all to hold hands, which we did, but he looked more and more panicked. The police made the arrests affinity group by affinity group, and as they got closer to my group, the young man lost it. He turned beet red; the whites of his eyes were shining with fright. He began to hoot loudly: "Hoot! Hoot! Hoot!"

I'd never seen that particular expression of panic before, but he was obviously beyond his self-control. He needed our help. Fortunately, others in our affinity group saw he was in danger of being badly beaten by the police—there's nothing like fear meeting fear. Several of us protected him with our bodies while talking to him as reassuringly as we could. Others explained loudly and firmly to the police that we were taking care of him and that he would be okay if they would let us do our part.

Our guy kept hooting, but at least he wasn't flailing, and he accepted our body-to-body shielding operation. The police backed off for a minute to decide what to do. They then carefully arrested us in a way that enabled our shield to stay intact around our guy, and together we moved into the waiting police bus. Once on the bus, with the police outside guarding, our guy relaxed and reentered his right mind in time for processing.

I realized later that the day was a win-win-win: we protected someone from severe injury, showed the police that we could take care of ourselves, and kept the focus on the basic reason we were there. A big win for the value of affinity groups, and one more step in the progress against homophobia.

෴ ෴ ෴

"Take care of yourself so you can take care of others" was a guideline in Lifespring, a personal growth seminar that had made a difference for me in the early eighties. Since my college days, I'd been interested in humanistic psychology as a resource—not only for people plagued with serious mental health issues but also for "normal people" like me who stress themselves by taking a lot on their shoulders. I knew there was an interaction between what I could carry externally and the old burdens carried internally. The combination sometimes got in the way.

When my friend Viki Laura List told me early in 1986 about the new resource in town, Insight Seminars, she said she thought highly enough of it that she'd like to buy a couple of the seminars and offer them for free to social activists. First, though, she'd like my opinion.

I trusted Viki's judgment and went to the hotel on the first night of the five-day seminar with curiosity. The facilitator announced a "buddy system" for mutual support, and said the way we should discover our buddy was to stand up and eyeball the one hundred or so people present. On first contact we'd see who our buddy would be. Johnny Lapham and I were the tallest in the seminar; even though we were at opposite ends of the crowd, we instantly saw and acknowledged each other. Although we weren't paying attention to looks as we sought a buddy, I didn't mind that he was classically "tall, dark, and handsome."

Johnny was a terrific buddy. He listened to me thoughtfully, observed the seminar with acuity, and shared his own struggles with vulnerability. He was twenty years younger than me, but we were both in transition and equally focused on sorting out our lives in the context of progressive politics. By the end of the seminar, we were friends as well as buddies, and decided we'd make a point of getting together again. Johnny was an activist and joined me in giving high marks to the seminar, so I called Viki and gave our recommendation, offering to help enroll activists for it.

Our next time together was on Johnny's turf in Boston, which gave me a chance to see his artwork. He was exploring hands, through painting and sculpture and sometimes both. I liked the dynamism of his art and his way with color. We spent hours walking at Walden Pond and discovered that rarity for tall people: someone else with a long stride. Johnny's wavy dark hair had a springiness to it, so when we ran down a hillside, his hair bounced. I was attracted to him but I figured he was straight.

Johnny soon returned the visit, and we walked miles in Philly and explored the art galleries. I learned that he liked Broadway musicals and had been part of Little Flags, a Boston political theater that mounted their own leftist musicals. When Johnny visited Philly, I gathered friends to sing with him around the piano.

Johnny was on the steering committee of the National Organization of Men Against Sexism, and since I had been doing that work a decade earlier with our MNS collective Men Against Patriarchy, I went with him to the national gathering that summer. I enjoyed watching Johnny retain his sense of humor even when surrounded by a few participants who were sticking grimly to political correctness. Fortunately, dozens of radical fairies also came to the gathering; their dancing, pranks, and out-front sensuality made it easier for Johnny and me to resist the Puritanism of those who seemed more motivated by guilt than by hunger for freedom from the patriarchy.

"There's something I've been meaning to tell you about me,"

Johnny said one day, on another of our long walks. "It's not easy to talk about."

I waited, honestly having no idea what he had on his mind but hoping it wasn't too horrible. Johnny stopped at the turning of the path.

"I was born into a family that owns a chunk of a corporation," he said. "I'm actually a wealthy man."

My astonishment almost prevented me from seeing Johnny's suddenly crumpled posture, his broad shoulders sagging, eyes anxiously looking at me from beneath heavy eyebrows. Johnny usually wore thrift-store clothes (then fashionable among many activists), packed a lunch to eat on the train from Boston to Philly, lived in a cooperative house that had an air of benign neglect, and drove an old car. Johnny, a millionaire?

"You could have fooled me," I said, then laughed. "You did fool me. Why didn't you mention it before?"

"I knew your working-class background, and I was worried about that and your politics getting in the way between us—that it would mess up the way you saw me."

I laughed again at my cluelessness. "But, Johnny, where's your arrogance? I mean, not to stereotype or anything, but I've met plenty of know-it-all owning-class people. You're not one of them!"

He smiled ruefully and stared at the path. "I have plenty of arrogant thoughts," he said, "but I just don't express them. I know how alienating they are."

I started to walk again, then stopped and wrapped my arms around him. "I love you, Johnny, and I forgive you for being rich! And I'm glad you told me, so you can stop pretending, and I don't see how it will mess us up, because I feel like we're politically on the same side."

"One reason I wanted to tell you was just to let you know that the day might come when my money can help you out, and you only need to ask."

That stopped me. I knew from studies that, statistically, the rich are the least generous with their money (and the working class the most generous), so coming face to face with a rich person opening the door like that was, well, a moment.

I walked again until I returned to my comfort zone of sturdy independence. "Thanks, Johnny. I'll try to remember that."

We hugged again and quickly changed the subject.

≈   ≈   ≈

By Christmas 1987, my family had hosted almost two decades of annual Messiah sing-ins. Each year, my house filled with singers accompanied by strings, winds, and piano; we took turns conducting and singing solos and, by dint of sheer persistence (and much laughter), made our way through the entire three-hour oratorio. We didn't realize that our annual celebration of that oratorio would continue without a break until we reached the fifty-year mark, after which the COVID pandemic broke our record. By the time we reached half a century of enthusiastic music-making, our growth forced us to move downtown to our Quaker Meeting-house.

My lover Michael came to the house early on the big day to help Ingrid and me set up chairs for the event. "George, I hear that Johnny is coming to sing with us," Michael said.

"Yes. I suggested that with his baritone voice he could have fun singing 'The Trumpet Shall Sound,'" I said. "Are you going to sing one of the tenor solos?"

"Why not?" Michael said with the goofy grin that usually accompanied his intention to take a risk. Michael loved the oratorio as much as I did.

"By the way," he said, stepping closer so Ingrid wouldn't overhear, "I think that tonight's the night you and Johnny are going to make love."

"No way," I said. "We don't have that kind of friendship. What gives you that idea?"

Michael's blue eyes twinkled. "You know me–I can smell sex a mile away. I could be wrong. But I'd bet on it, if my Quaker parents hadn't taught me not to gamble."

Handel's oratorio has many times been sung better, but perhaps never more enthusiastically than we sang it that evening. Michael took a turn conducting for the first time, Johnny enjoyed his solo, Ingrid hit the high notes, and we had fifty tired and happy people at the end of the evening.

Michael winked at me as he left and, reluctant as I was to admit it to him the next day, he turned out to be right. Happily, Michael wasn't the type to be jealous, nor was Johnny. They live with a worldview tuned to abundance and don't seem to view love as a scarce commodity to be controlled and limited. Amazing!

I knew I'd need all the love and music and prayer I could get to be useful as President Reagan's administration set up our country for graver challenges to come: increased poverty and declining educational opportunity as the military budget claimed more of our resources to try, in vain, to handle the threats to the empire. How could I maximize my contribution as changes showed up within the movements and more innovations, plus more training, were needed to meet the moment?

26

training coal miners for a win

The 1960s were, for me, mostly about study, doing actions, and training, while in the seventies and eighties my focus was on organizing new efforts: Movement for a New Society, the B-1 bomber campaign, and Jobs with Peace, with some teaching on the side.

In the mid-eighties, Movement for a New Society began to sag. It had let go of its requirement that membership needed to be through participation in a team of some kind, which reduced the power of collectivity. Its training approach failed to remain fresh, and the training programs petered out. Also, the network was no longer doing significant research and development for wider movements, because it had lost its own internal capacity to learn and innovate as an organization. This was related to another trend: in some members' zeal for making their egalitarian values real, too many had resorted to what I called "levelling," undervaluing creative and experienced leadership.*

Along with Antje Mattheus, a member of Movement for a New Society's Jobs with Peace collective, I tried to lead a "renewal movement," but it failed. Since I had been the main person who catalyzed Movement for a New Society in the first place, I felt responsible to assist the group in laying itself down. It took years

---

* Andrew Cornell, *Oppose and Propose! Lessons from Movement for a New Society* (Oakland, CA: AK Press, 2011).

to reach an agreement. Wearied by the stalemate, a weekend gathering of the network including members from a dozen cities finally reached a reluctant consensus.

Letting go of Movement for a New Society was big. Our work had ranged widely and made a difference in activists' individual lives and in multiple social movements, especially the anti–nuclear power and feminist movements. We had even blocked a foreign policy initiative when Nixon and Kissinger wanted the United States to supply weapons to dictator Yaya Khan of Pakistan. We'd made training a normal feature of progressive social movements and spun off lasting initiatives.

For me, Movement for a New Society had been the fulcrum of my political life for almost two decades. Its collectives were at the heart of campaigns I'd helped build: the campaigns against the B-1 bomber and for peace conversion, as well as Jobs with Peace. They were among the examples that validated the group's approach, doing exactly what our theory of change said was needed. An activist entrepreneur like me who starts things can do a better job, and grow personally as well, if I do it as part of a collective.

I could think of no way to fully thank the comrades and community of Movement for a New Society, except to continue in the life-centered way to which we tried to stay true.

ℵ ℵ ℵ

In early 1989, the United Mine Workers of America (UMWA) called to ask for my help in training for their next big coal strike. Through Jobs with Peace, labor unions had heard about my training skills.

Coal miners have had a record of especially tough fights. In 1921, when the miners tried to unionize in Appalachia, they were confronted by thousands of armed men supported by US army planes and bombs, in what is now famously known as the Battle of Blair Mountain.

Both of my grandfathers were slate miners their entire working lives, as were all my uncles for at least part of their lives. At several points in my dad's life, he worked in a slate mine, and my younger brother, Bob, worked there for a summer between his junior and senior years in high school. I would have myself, if the mines had been hiring in the summers, when I was available. I took factory jobs instead, feeling very left out of the family tradition.

I decided to dedicate this training opportunity to my seventy-five-year-old dad. Certainly, the mine workers were facing a challenge. The coal companies had agreed among themselves, before their upcoming round of contract talks with the union, that one of their number would refuse to come to terms. The Pittston Coal Company would dare UMWA to strike Pittston, so the coal industry could test the strength of the workers and see if the companies could retake the offensive in their never-ending war with workers.

Realistic about the stakes, the UMWA leadership decided to work at Pittston without a contract for a year—usually a big no-no to them—to give the union time to get ready. The leadership knew it had to up its game, which meant eliminating or at least reducing the casual violence by workers that in the past had weakened them. All the union members were sent VHS recordings of the Academy Award–winning film *Gandhi,* which they were to watch with their families. The union wanted a vigorous nonviolence training program, and they wanted to know if I would train the union's field staff so the staff members, in turn, could train the workers.

I met with six executive staff for the interview, around the table in the union's board room. Across from me on the wall was a large photo portrait of the late John L. Lewis staring down at me, eyebrows every bit as bushy as his reputation. I remembered my dad's reverence for John L. Lewis, for forty years president of the UMWA and founder of the Congress of Industrial Organizations, the more militant wing of the AFL-CIO.

Midway through the interview, we got sidetracked by one of the men picking up an argument they had been having: whether in the course of the struggle it might make sense to occupy one of the mines. One faction believed it would send a shock wave through the labor movement, which had not seen major occupations since the 1930s, and would therefore garner additional support. The other faction said the legal consequences would bankrupt the union.

After listening for a while, I interrupted by suggesting they consider what had happened in the coal mines of Soviet Siberia. There, when the miners struck in a couple of the mines, the bureaucrats in Siberia were shocked and didn't know what to do. They asked for instructions from their higher-ups, who in turn asked their higher-ups, passing the buck all the way to Moscow. By the time the question reached Moscow, the entire coalfield was on strike, and it was too late to try to repress the strike with violence. Moscow acceded to the miners' demands.

I noticed the people at the table leaning in. One suggested, "We could choose a mine that crosses state lines, so that two governors would need to be consulted before forceful action could be taken, and that would give us time." Another added, "Maybe we could seize a mine, knowing we'd stay only a couple of days, then come out and declare victory before they even get around to arresting us!"

The meeting ended with our agreement that I would colead the training with a colleague, who turned out to be another experienced trainer, Nancy Heskett. The weekend included intense role-plays with equally intense debriefs; Nancy and I were working with forty staffers who knew the stakes were high.

During a break, I chatted with the director of the field staff, who told me, "George, I went into the mines as a teenager and I want to be honest with you: workers my age enjoyed the violence that went along with a strike. Think of being underground most of the daylight hours when you're that age—you look forward to the chance to get strike pay and be above ground harassing the scabs and fucking up whatever machinery you can. The violence was a relief, man." He smiled with the memory and took another swallow of coffee. "Those were the days. But as much as I prefer the way we did a strike then, I know it doesn't work anymore. So, go ahead. Teach us this nonviolence stuff. We need to win."

When the strike was called, it was multidimensional and extended. While there was some throwback violence around the edges, the workers maintained a remarkable degree of discipline, reinforced by women from the mining towns joining picket lines and participating in the fight in other ways. Women, I knew, don't have masculine conditioning for violence and are more likely to do what works.

In the end, the union did use the tactic learned from my Siberia story: they occupied a mine as a short-run tactic. When, after a few days of occupation, a flatbed truck pulled up to the mine entrance in the evening with union leadership and a band, plus celebrities, the media arrived in full force. Floodlights played on the truck, illuminating the music and speeches. During the event, the miners occupying the mine stole out quietly, circled around the back of the truck, then emerged suddenly into the floodlights declaring, "We won!"

And the union did, in fact, win. I called the UMWA headquarters and asked a key official about the role of the mine occupation. "No doubt," he said, "the occupation was one of the factors that tipped the scales!" For me, it was a reminder that trainers—and everyone else—can be more useful for strategy when we do our homework on what it is that other movements have done that helped them to win.

א א א

Johnny and I were eating in a café in my neighborhood. Sometimes it was easier to talk intimately amid the background clatter of a restaurant than at my house, where interruptions could be frequent. It was 1989, I was fifty-two years old, and this conversation would be a game-changer for the decades to follow.

Johnny first caught me up some on his latest work as an artist. After a while, he commented, "You're not as full of stories about Jobs with Peace as usual, George."

I looked at my food, then up at his warm brown eyes. Johnny was ready for anything I was ready to tell him. *I'm a lucky man*, I thought.

"I need to take a good look at how I'm doing at Jobs with Peace. I've run out of creativity—but the coalition is still politically important!" I took another drink of coffee. "To be honest, Johnny, I'm ready to be done with this," I said. "You know, it's just not like me to be carrying a project for as long as seven years."

Johnny smiled, probably with recognition. He also moves from project to project, although I suppose artists are more often expected to do that than organizers are.

"Who's your successor going to be?"

I leaned forward, smiling. "You know that woman I've been telling you about, Barbara Smith—the Black teacher who came to us and showed amazing talent as a campaigner? I made her deputy director and have been mentoring her; she's terrific."

"How about your president, Rev. Washington?" Johnny asked.

"He's a rock!" I said. "He'll especially want to support Barbara because she could become the first Black leader of a peace organization in Pennsylvania."

It was Johnny's turn to lean forward. "And what about you, George?" he asked. "What will be next for you?"

"Well, various things occur to me. I've always wanted to work for Greenpeace; maybe I should explore that." In my 1973 book, *Toward a Living Revolution*, I'd argued that the environmental issue is crucial, but so far I hadn't done much about it. I paused. "What I really need is some time off to rest and regenerate—a kind of sabbatical—but of course that's not possible. Another option might be to work here in Philly with Quakers; and then there's the men's antisexist movement, which is flagging and could use some sustained attention."

"George, go back to that one you dismissed—something about 'rest.' Why is that impossible?"

I looked again at Johnny. His smile had broadened, as it does when he teases me, or when he wants me to level with him. "C'mon, what about that 'rest' option?"

"Johnny, you know as well as I do that being a movement activist isn't the same as if I'd chosen a career as a professor—there's no institutional back-up; there's not a way to get a sabbatical, even though, heaven knows, there's more danger of burnout among activists than professors."

"Right," Johnny said, "I know all that, but maybe there's more going on than that. Maybe your working-class background keeps you from seeing a new possibility. I heard you say you really need the sabbatical. Maybe I could help you make it happen."

"You know me too well!" I mock-yelled into the noise of the restaurant. "All right, if I weren't to let my scarcity mentality block my creativity, what would I imagine?"

"You'd imagine me and other friends setting up a committee to fundraise and make a sabbatical happen for you."

I couldn't hold Johnny's gaze, and I felt the tears begin to form. I reached across the table, and Johnny quietly smiled and took both my hands, his eyes shining, knowing that in this moment his wealth and social position could help him cross the class divide to help a working-class man get a deeply needed year to rest, reflect and refocus.

In personality charts we sometimes use to help organizations in our trainings, I identify as a visionary, an innovator.* Up until

---

* In the handout "Team Types," Training for Change uses the metaphor of the four compass directions, with the "visionary/innovator" role occupying the east direction: "Team Types," Training for Change, accessed July 5, 2022, https://www.trainingforchange.org/training_ tools/team-types/.

age fifty-two, I'd been able to bring my full zest and creativity to a priority project for a short period of time: two years at Friends Peace Committee, three years to A Quaker Action Group, four years to the Martin Luther King School, four years to Movement for a New Society, three years to the B-1 bomber campaign. The Jobs with Peace Campaign kept me seven years because we shifted to the vision work on local and state levels.

But now I was deeply tired, not least because parenting in such a complicated family was also so demanding. My optimism about vision on both personal and political fronts was getting raggedy. A sabbatical would be a chance for badly needed rest and a return to the bubbling spring of innovation within me, the mix of spiritual vision and adventure that inspires in me a bold commitment.

Johnny was able to raise enough money for fourteen months off—enough for plenty of rest and prayer, personal-growth seminars and music, and who knew what brand-new adventures? It was a sure bet that out of that process would come the next major phase of my life.

responding to tragedy in Sri Lanka and at home

My longtime mentor George Willoughby had a suggestion for me. "So, the point of a sabbatical is to free you up to do something different, right?"

We were drinking coffee on my front porch. It was just a few blocks from the Peace Brigades International office, where George had come from a meeting. For three decades now, George and I had been in and out of each other's lives and projects. Peace Brigades International's mission was to recruit volunteers to go into conflict areas where human rights defenders were at risk and give them protective accompaniment. I called it "nonviolent bodyguarding."*

"Well, you know, I was just in a meeting over at the Peace Brigades office, and it looks like we're going to go ahead with our first project in Asia. The human rights lawyers in Sri Lanka are really up against it. The head of the national bar association just called. Another human rights lawyer got assassinated recently, so now some are looking to leave the country altogether and move to Britain or someplace."

"But George," I asked, "can't they get the government to stop the assassinations?"

---

* "About PBI," Peace Brigades International, accessed July 5, 2022, https://www.peacebrigades.org/en/about-pbi.

He smiled, ruefully. "They figure the government's behind it. The bar association leader went to the country's president and asked for help, and the president shrugged his shoulders and advised him to seek help from local law enforcement. But the lawyer already believes local law enforcement is in on the assassinations."

"What's at stake?"

"The civil war in the south is growing, on top of the civil war in the north between Sinhalese and Tamils. In the south, it's a class war between peasants and owners, and law enforcement believes that students are helping the peasants, so of course they arrest students to torture them for information on other students. But the frantic parents get a human rights lawyer to intervene.

"So human rights lawyers need protective accompaniment from high-visibility individuals, which means from abroad, preferably from the United States or another country that donates foreign aid to the Sri Lankan government."

I could see where this was going.

"George, you want me to go to Sri Lanka on my sabbatical and help keep human rights lawyers alive?"

George smiled, settled back and took another sip, confident I'd get there as quickly as possible.

ᘄ ᘄ ᘄ

Tourists love the ancient capital of Sri Lanka. Kandy has beautiful batiks, handsome temples, a quiet lake alongside a green that features an elephant giving rides, and strolling saffron-robed monks carrying their trademark black umbrellas.

Peaceful appearances to the contrary, in 1989, it was also a city caught in a war. I took the train to Kandy from the Peace Brigades base in Colombo, to negotiate with a human rights lawyer our conditions for giving him protective accompaniment. When

I arrived, he was finishing his meeting with a student; the lawyer suggested that the student hang around in another room and then leave with me.

The lawyer was clear that he didn't need me to hang out at his professional office, because it was in a very public and therefore safe place. I would need to sleep at his house and accompany him on certain auto trips; he said he was confident that he knew his points of maximum danger. I explained Peace Brigades's conditions: he needed to give up his gun for the duration of our relationship and rely instead on the nonviolent protection of his unarmed bodyguard. He agreed, seeing accompaniment as more likely to be effective than his gun against a hit squad.

The student joined me as I left, telling me about himself as we walked toward the city center. He said he was underground, an activist in Students for Human Rights, which was an organization the government wanted destroyed. I took my cue from his relaxed gait and found that walking along the quiet residential street with its stately palm trees was a welcome interlude after the interview and the tense prospect of starting this new accompaniment. First, though, I would need to report back to the Peace Brigades team.

"When is the next train to Colombo?" I asked.

"Six o'clock," the student said, "and it will get us there at ten in the evening. But I wonder if I could ask a favor? Ten will be past curfew in Colombo. It's dangerous for me with all the checkpoints. Could I stay with you in a hotel room tonight, here in Kandy, and then we could take the early train tomorrow morning?"

I agreed, thinking that a few hours difference wouldn't matter to the project. I was tired, and an early bedtime would be good for me.

As we checked into a hotel, I reflected more on how unusual, and laden with contradictions, this form of peace work appeared to be. I was aware, for example, that I was using white-skin privilege to keep local people alive to make positive change in their society. My job as an unarmed peacekeeper was to step between the threatened one and the attacker; the reality was that, if a Sri Lankan hit squad arrived in the middle of the night to assassinate someone, they were more likely to be deterred by a white person getting in the way than a person of color.

When the student from the underground and I came to the hotel to get a room, he knew it was better for him to be regarded by the clerk as someone being paid by an older white man for sexual services than for the clerk to wonder if this was a student who might be wanted by the police. If convinced of the latter, the clerk would probably call the police, who would seize and torture the student. This unstated set of assumptions meant the student operating underground could feel safe suggesting we go to the hotel together that night. Staying alive in a police state sometimes relies on impression management, and subtleties matter.

Decades later, I would realize that subtle strategizing of this kind shows the limitations of identity politics, whose rigidities can get in the way of the bold and effective action needed to tackle oppression. A Black student of mine at the Martin Luther King School of Social Change, Phil McLaurin, once explained to me what he called "mother wit": the sense of nuance taught through stories told by older to younger generations of Black people, stories that aid survival.

As we settled into bed, the student said, "I don't know what to do about my father. He is so worried that I will be killed by the police or the army. He says I must go to Switzerland and stay with my big sister and her family. But I refuse, because my work is here, defending democracy and human rights. If everyone who believes as I do leaves the country, there will be nothing here but dictatorship!"

"I understand your dad worrying about you," I said.

"And the thing is, in my culture, a boy does not defy his father. If my father believes strongly that I should go, how can I stay? I feel disloyal to him, like a bad son. I don't know what to do."

The boy punched the pillow in frustration, and I turned to face him. Clearly, what this boy most of all needed was the listening ear of a neutral person, someone who would not urge him to one or another course of action.

The night sounds deepened as the student examined his heart, torn between political calling and personal duty. He wanted to know about my relationship with my father, and with my son. By morning's light, he looked relaxed, his inner conflict resolved for the moment by a recommitment to the movement. I was surprised that I wasn't more tired. It felt right to spend the night attending to father-son, son-father.

~ ~ ~

"I'm home," I called as I walked into the Peace Brigades International project house in Colombo. Bue came quickly from the back of the house, and Quique came bounding down the stairs. Tall, blue-eyed Bue was from England and had previous experience doing protective accompaniment during the civil war in El Salvador. She was the coordinator of our little team. Quique was a medical doctor from Spain with a bushy beard and a ready laugh. He also had experience in Central America; I was the new kid on the block in this accompaniment work.

"Your wife, Berit, called yesterday while you were in Kandy, and left a message for you to call her," Bue said.

In a heartbeat, I knew intuitively: one of my children was dead.

"You can't use our phone in the house for outgoing calls abroad," Quique said, anticipating my question. "We don't have that service yet. You have to make your call from the neighborhood post office."

In Colombo, the street noises are loud, but I couldn't hear them for the pounding of my heart as I walked to the post office. "Who is it?" I kept repeating over and over. "Is it Christina? Is it

Peter?" I willed myself to walk, not run, and told myself there was no way I could know someone had died. It might be something far less drastic. But with each step, the question insisted with the power of a kettledrum: "Who is it?"

After what seemed like forever, I heard Berit answer the phone. "I got your message," I said.

"It's Peter," she said in a hollow voice. "He was found dead yesterday."

The return to the Peace Brigades house was a hodgepodge of heightened visual images: beggars with outstretched palms, a buffalo blocking my path in the alley, the searing sun in a cloudless sky, a vine of pink flowers stretching out of garbage. And, all the while, a shrieking sound inside my head drowned out everything else.

I stumbled into the house for the second time that morning. Bue and Quique were in the living room, silently waiting. "My son is dead," I said, my heart breaking. I fell into their arms and sobbed, huge belly sobs, and the three of us sank to the floor holding each other.

Quique said they could put me on the next plane out, and Bue knew with British certainty that a cup of tea would be the right thing for now. One of them was always beside me as the waves of grief hit my shore, seemingly as inexhaustible as the ocean. Somehow the packing happened, somehow the taxi got us to the airport. I remember the last moments of waiting, where I drew strength from the deep compassion in the faces of my teammates.

I was placed in the central row of the wide-bodied jet bound for Amsterdam. Two seats to the right of me was a white European couple holding a dark Sri Lankan baby. Three seats to the left of me, another white European couple with another dark baby they were adopting. Unable to sleep, I spent the flight watching the new parents touching their little ones, counting the tiny fingers and toes, smelling their heads, pressing them close, remarking to each other on every new discovery. I remembered doing just the same with Peter in 1969 when he was our newly adopted baby.

The couples must have known I was gazing at them, this big white man with tears trickling down his face. I'm forever grateful for their tolerance, not minding my grieving while they continued delighting in their new loves.

A rash appeared all over my body during the flight, and I was itching everywhere. Amsterdam seemed every bit of a hemisphere away. I kept praying, knowing that Jesus was very close, knowing that my teammates were holding me in their hearts.

When we touched the runway in Amsterdam, I remembered that there was a chapel in the airport, and I headed there after confirming my flight to Philadelphia. As the old spiritual states, "There is a balm in Gilead." The empty room was the essence of peace, and I took deep breaths of gratitude. I don't mind crying in a crowded place, but the introvert in me deeply cherishes solitude. As I settled into prayer, the door opened, and a woman walked in, quiet as the angel she turned out to be. She sat behind my left shoulder, and after a pause leaned forward and said, "God can heal it all." The trickle of tears turned into a torrent once again, and the itching eased.

I don't remember much about the transatlantic flight. There were no newly adoptive couples in my row. I was numb with exhaustion, but I doubt that I slept. Questions about Peter's death recurred; later I learned that he was found on the bathroom floor of his apartment. The night before, he'd gone to a party and gotten drunk, as he usually did. Someone gave him morphine. Someone gave him crack cocaine. Perhaps he waited until he got home to take one of those two, but the coroner said both were in his body. His heart just gave out.

≈ ≈ ≈

In the past year, Peter had seemed to be getting a grip on himself. Up until then, I'd been holding myself ready for news, any day, that Peter had overdosed, or crashed in an auto accident, or been knifed in a fight. But lately, I'd begun to think Peter might make it after all.

He was going to a twelve-step group more often, was holding a steady job as a painter in a large apartment complex, had moved into an apartment with a friend. One by one, Peter was reconciling himself to the family members he'd alienated with his lying and stealing. He even remembered Father's Day, with a card to me signed, "Your only son, Peter."

That touched a place in my heart: he got it! In my response to the Father's Day card, I was still the hurt daddy who a few years earlier had accompanied Peter far beyond anything I could have imagined, a kind of bottomless, frantic effort on the chance. . . well, simply on the chance. And later, after I'd stopped my desperate reaching, came that card with his declaration that he was my only son—a unique and intense connection.

Ironically, over that last year, I'd dared to begin hoping he'd be all right. He came to the support meeting Quakers held the night before I left for Sri Lanka, and afterward hung out with a few of my friends, when we grabbed the piano in the Meetinghouse to sing Cole Porter's song "True Love." Our little circle stopped at an ice cream place for sundaes on the way to the subway. During the conversation I heard Peter engaging with the others, talking for the first time, in my hearing, like a man among men.

He was twenty. I'd thought maybe he would be one of those young Black men who actually made it to twenty-one.

ন ন ন

Finally, the plane reached Philadelphia. I was met by Ross Flanagan and Susan Taylor, two very dear friends. They were living near the Philadelphia airport in a Quaker study center, Pendle Hill. "Come with us," they said. "You can stay at Pendle Hill until you've decided what to do next."

I was a wreck, and they could see it. I staggered, couldn't manage my bags, didn't know which way to go in my home airport. They cheerfully led me to their car, and Susan rubbed my shoulders while Ross drove. In no time, I was in the room next to theirs and they were tucking me into bed. "I can't sleep," I said groggily. "Will you sing me lullabies?" Stroking my hair and holding my hand, they sang me to sleep.

The next days were busy. Berit and I planned a viewing, not because she and I especially liked that custom but because Peter's friends might need it—and Peter's older sister, Christina, and younger sister, Ingrid.

"There's only so much you can do to make him look good," the undertaker explained, "when the body dies of poisoning." Our handsome Peter.

My Friends Meeting appointed a committee to arrange the memorial service; we chose a date ten days away, to give people a chance to change their schedules if they wanted to come. Friends and family needed to be kept in the loop.

I spoke on the phone with my younger daughter, Ingrid, who was studying at Oberlin College. "I don't know what to do about coming home," she said. "Of course I'll come before the viewing and memorial service, but maybe I should come right now. It will mean missing the first concert of my a cappella singing group, though."

"It's up to you, Ingrid. Are you getting the support there that you need? You know we'd love you to be here."

"My roomie and other friends are being great, Dad," she said. "The concert is tomorrow night, so I guess I'll stay and do it and then fly home the next day. You're the one who taught me that 'the show must go on.'"

Neither of us mentioned that this would be her first performance I'd miss. We'd talked about it a month earlier, when I told
her about my mission to Sri Lanka. Somehow, I'd always managed
to get to her school concerts and shows. She was used to seeing
me in the front row, laughing loudly at the jokes, even when I was
attending the show for the third night in a row.

After we hung up, I realized I didn't have to miss her performance at all! I could get on a plane the next day and listen to her
sing.

By the time I reached Oberlin's campus, it was a half hour
before the concert. I loitered in an out-of-the-way corner until I
was sure her group was backstage, then I took my seat toward the
rear of the darkened auditorium. I didn't want to test her courage
at going through with the concert knowing I was there; I knew
she would utterly lose it.

I looked at the program, a collection of pop standards and jazz
featuring Nothing but Treble, which got the first smile out of
me all day. I remembered some of the happy times playing with
Ingrid and Peter when they were little, only two years apart. One
of my treasured snapshots shows them in the back of a van leaning
against each other, asleep, surrounded by bottles of milk from the
dairy farm that supplied our co-op. Even as an older teenager,
Peter continued to be proud of Ingrid. His musical preference was
heavy metal, and so he surprised her all the more by showing up at
one of the high school musicals in which she played a leading role.

A tremendous cheer went up as the small group of young
women crossed the stage, and I overheard audience members
saying Ingrid was being very game indeed to sing this concert.
I was bursting with pride as they swung into their first number,
Ingrid as poised as ever.

The fourth song began with a solo by Ingrid, which she introduced with a trace of hesitation. She stopped abruptly, turned to
the audience and said, "Sorry, I started on the wrong pitch." To

my amazement, I heard from the audience at this highly competitive music college, "That's okay, Ingrid." "Take your time, Ingrid." "We love you, Ingrid."

The pitch pipe sounded, and she found her note and jumped into the song on key. The warmth in the room was palpable. I blinked back tears.

The last encore concluded; the audience receded. I waited a few moments, then walked backstage, searching for the green room, where the singers would be surrounded by praise and banter. As I entered the doorway, I saw Ingrid at the far end of the room, a bouquet of roses in her arms. She looked up and yelled, "Daddy!" We ran to each other and met in the middle, tears and laughter mingling in one of the greatest hugs of my life.

Back at home, outside the Quaker Meeting room where hundreds were already gathered for Peter's memorial service, I found my parents, whom I visited upstate but who rarely traveled to Philly anymore. I was so deeply feeling my grief that I had almost no attention for them, or for others. It was as if I was walking on the sidewalk in the midst of a turbulent rainstorm, barely able to make people out as they reached out to me. I couldn't even rise to speak during the meeting, although I could hear others' words of compassion when they stood and shared. Miraculously, Ingrid rose in the silence and sang "You'll Never Walk Alone," which then became our family's theme song for remembering Peter.

I didn't stay in Philly for long; I kept remembering that we had only two members on our Peace Brigades team able to protect vulnerable human rights lawyers working to prevent more deaths. What to my heart was a monstrous violation—that my son should die before me—was in Sri Lanka a mass phenomenon. In that country, there would be plenty of company in which to walk in pain.

༄ ༄ ༄

In Sri Lanka, I soon got back into the swing of things. I was able to work, but I found that frequently, on an errand, I would stop in at a place of worship to grieve. Those places were many: Buddhist temples, Islamic mosques, Christian churches. I found comfort in all of them.

The team sent me to the north to assist the University Teachers for Human Rights (UTHR), a group at great risk. I was taken to the house of the parents of the group's first leader, who was known far and wide simply as Ragini. We had tea on their broad veranda. The sweetness of blossoms filled the air, and the cicadas were doing what cicadas do. A bubble of peace surrounded us, even though armed bands roved the forests not far away.

"Tell me more about Ragini," I asked her parents. I knew their loss was recent. Ragini was a biology professor at the University of Jaffna and almost single-handedly held together the curriculum that prepared future medical students, since a number of her colleagues had gone into exile. She was herself the object of numerous assassination threats, because the UTHR protested violations on all sides.

"Well," began her father, "we did convince her that she should leave the country for her own good, so she went to stay with a relative in England for a month toward the end of term. We were breathing much more easily until we heard she was coming back. She said she had to give her students their final exams, to qualify them for medical school."

He stopped, unwilling to put into words what happened next. Ragini gave the exams and corrected them, and was on her way to the dean's office to turn in the grades when she was gunned down in broad daylight.

We sat together in silence. "We love our daughter." Ragini's mother spoke with a tremor. "She loved us. She was a good girl. When she was with her cousins, she laughed more loudly than any of them." She paused. "She loved us, and now she is gone."

More silence. I suddenly remembered that, as I was leaving Philadelphia to return to Sri Lanka, Michael suggested I bring back some object from a grieving family, a token of the solidarity that transcends culture. "I've admired that plant that grows along this veranda," I said, "the one with dark green leaves and red veins."

"We call it 'bleeding heart,'" Ragini's mother said. "Would you like to take back some bulbs to plant?"

"Yes, I would, because as they grow I'll remember your daughter, and my son, and how hard it can be to be parents, and how life continues no matter what."

"That would be appropriate," Ragini's father said in his dignified way. "Let's do it."

≈ ≈ ≈

When I'd finished my service in Sri Lanka and returned home, I showed the bulbs to Michael before we went to bed. The next morning, we planted them in small pots where I mixed in some of Peter's ashes. The plants took off, growing at a staggering rate.

The plants needed to be transplanted into bigger pots just in time for the annual February gathering of queer Quakers. "Let's transplant these in a prayer circle at the gathering," Michael suggested. "I'll especially invite people who are close to you, and we can play Fauré's *Requiem*, since you like that, and so many gay Quakers knew Peter and your family, so it will be just right."

The plants were beautiful, agreed all who circled up in one of the rooms in the Friends school where the gathering was held. Large empty pots stood ready, alongside potting soil, water, a trowel. We sat in silence together, holding hands, remembering Peter and praying for solace. The Fauré began, and I moved into the center, with Michael at my side. It was hard to see through the tears, but step by step, I took each plant out of its pot, poured the mixture of soil and Peter's ashes into a larger pot, put the plant in and added fresh soil, watered the plant, and held it for a long minute before going on to the next.

The wailing started on its own, from somewhere deep inside me. My family has no tradition of wailing, and I have no recollection of ever being present when someone was doing it. I didn't know if I was doing it, or it was doing me.

Quakers passing our room stopped at the door and bowed their heads, reverently holding the space for that chilling expression of anguish.

Then it was over. The circle converged, holding Michael and me in a giant, sweaty hug, wet eyes everywhere, bodies swaying gently. Someone made a side crack, chuckles started, another wit launched a comment, and laughter shook the circle. We disengaged, blowing noses, wiping eyes, laughing, and making more cracks. "Grieving sure makes me hungry!" someone said. "Where's lunch?"

On our way to the cafeteria, a young man stopped me. "George," he said, "there's something about Peter I'm not sure you know."

"I'll bet there are many things about Peter I don't know!"

"Right, but I want to tell you how he gave me a hand. Last year I was a brand-new father, and I didn't have any confidence at all. I really didn't know how to be with my little boy. Peter decided to coach me, and he spent time with me, showing me how to nurture and love my baby. That was Peter. I wanted you to know that about your son."

28

putting training on the front burner

One of the pleasures of returning to Philadelphia at the end of my Sri Lanka mission was catching up with friends like Barbara Smith, who was now directing Jobs with Peace. Barbara was from a poor Black neighborhood in Philadelphia and had come to the campaign as an administrative secretary with few credentials. She struck me as unusually gifted in many respects: a tall, beautiful Black woman with a strong voice, Barbara could command the room when she chose to and, at other times, knit a disparate group together. She identified with her Seminole as well as African heritage, and was not ashamed of having been raised poor. She loved learning as much as she loved teaching, which had earlier been her career.

Not very long after she arrived at Jobs with Peace, Barbara asked me to mentor her. It was a pleasure. I enjoyed the wisdom she shared as we worked together: "Bridges are underappreciated by those on both sides of the river." "Misbehavior in others may become intolerable, so don't tolerate it—but welcome them back when they're ready."

She loved being forthright. When newly elected president George H.W. Bush visited Philadelphia, his staff wanted a photo op with children, so they arranged for the president to observe an after-school program in Barbara Smith's neighborhood of Mantua. Barbara was teaching in the program that afternoon.

Afterward, as the president's entourage was about to leave, Bush told Barbara, with the cameras rolling, "You're doing an excellent job, Mrs. Smith."

Barbara responded immediately with a smile. "I wish I could say the same for you, Mr. President."

It was typical Barbara, and she told me that story with relish. I laughed, then remarked that she seemed unable to stay away from teaching—even though she was carrying heavy responsibilities at Jobs with Peace.

"Like you did," she smiled.

"Okay, okay!" I laughed. "Even if a teacher likes to organize, we still get a kick out of that thing called learning!"

At my encouragement, Barbara had taken a five-day Insight Seminar. I asked her what she thought of it. "That was all about empowerment, but I didn't expect the human, healing dimension," she told me the day after. Then her Black working-class zeal for equality kicked in. "Yes, I loved it, but who were the people in there with me? I get mad when I think that so many of the people taking Insight are white professionals in corporate management. The people who most need the chance for that training are *my* people!"

"I couldn't agree more," I said. "Working-class people of all races deserve it—especially if they're involved in working for justice." I told her about the thirty-six-day training for facilitators that I'd taken in Santa Monica, also run by Insight Seminars. "What do you think—would there be interest among a diversity of activists to take trainings from us that contained a transformational edge, an equivalent, something like Insight offers?"

Barbara got excited. "We're not learning fast enough just from our own experience. And not *deeply* enough. All our groups should be what the consultants call 'learning organizations.' We should learn to be critical of the 'same-old, same-old' protest style we're used to, not to mention the subtle racism and other dumb stuff, and we should still be supported to love each other.

"George, keep in touch with me. I want to support this and play a role if possible."

I did some interviews of activist organizations and sent around a questionnaire to find out whether the hunch Barbara and I held was correct. Our needs assessment signaled "Go!" Even while leading Jobs with Peace, Barbara cofounded with me a new nonprofit, Training for Change, intending to offer trainings at home and abroad. My Quaker Meeting gave me strong encouragement.

We kicked off with a workshop on nonviolent struggle on Martin Luther King Day in 1991. We deliberately introduced new teaching methods and gained a reputation for innovativeness that made Training for Change the go-to place for other training organizations to upgrade their trainers, including the educational departments of trade unions. Sadly, Barbara fell ill and wasn't able to continue beyond the first years, but her inspiration of the organization continued.*

The result of acquiring and inventing new tools and insights and submitting them to rigorous application was that the Training for Change approach became substantially different from the popular education that many of us relied on in the seventies and eighties. It was so different that we coined a new name: "direct education." I especially liked using that name when leading trainings for labor unions. What rings better to a working-class ear than direct education?

We paid close attention to the feedback we got from participants. An academic prone to note-taking told me after taking the weekend training-of-trainers workshop that he'd listed forty-eight exercises we'd used, so I wasn't surprised when that workshop became our flag-

---

* Articles that describe examples of training and its impact, the first of which includes Barbara Smith: George Lakey, "Training as Action," *Waging Nonviolence*, July 2, 2012, https://wagingnonviolence.org/2012/07/training-as-action/; George Lakey, "8 Skills of a Well-trained Activist," *Waging Nonviolence*, June 11, 2013, https://wagingnonviolence.org/2013/06/8-skills-of-a-well-trained-activist/.

ship training. It turned out that other groups' workshop attendees were more than ready for something fresh that went deeper.

One way Barbara's influence continued to be felt was the concern for diversity. A member of the Mohawk Nation who attended gave us feedback that some techniques we were using were also found in Native American cultures, with different names. He especially liked how we supported a group to grow closer as it moved into the challenging activities.

≈ ≈ ≈

"Call me as soon as possible," the voice mail said. "It's Ron, from ACT UP."

The group was well named, although its critics said it should be called "Act Out." The full name was AIDS Coalition to Unleash Power. New York gay author Larry Kramer helped found the group in 1987, when people were dying from AIDS and the health establishment and politicians were shrugging their shoulders. ACT UP, which included members who were already infected with the virus, confronted authority to demand a response; "Silence = Death" was their slogan.

My high school best friend, Gary, was the first of my circle to catch the virus, in the early eighties. I'd lost track of him even though he lived in Philly; our interests had diverged, and I didn't like his pestering me to join his adventures with drugs. We'd even missed the latest of our annual Christmas visits.

I'll never forget a wintry afternoon in the early eighties when I saw Gary on Broad Street. I had to look twice to be sure it was him. Gaunt and wasted, Gary walked with a cane and looked thirty years older than the last time I'd seen him. Wind gusted down Broad Street, and Gary was about to be swept off his feet. I rushed forward to greet him.

"Gary!" I hugged him, then held him against the wind. "What happened to you?"

In a voice of sheer exhaustion he replied, "I've got AIDS."

My heart sank. "Here's a store," I said, nodding my head toward the men's clothing shop a few steps away. "Let's get inside. Then we can talk."

Sinking into a chair, Gary confessed to having slipped out of his apartment, where a daily attendant took care of him. It was the same Gary I'd always known. Mischievous escape whenever things got boring: that was his hallmark.

After Gary rested awhile in the store, I hailed a cab and took him to his apartment. Gary died not long after, leaving a hole in my life that never got filled.

Saddened by the loss of Gary, I tried to be useful whenever I could to the growing movement demanding priority attention to the epidemic. I especially appreciated the rebel militancy of ACT UP. I called Ron back to find out what his Philly chapter had in mind. This was 1991, and the group was growing as the epidemic remained unaddressed by the federal government.

"Well, the city settled," he began.

I hadn't heard yet. When President George H. W. Bush came to Philly for a fundraising dinner, ACT UP confronted him with a large crowd at the front entrance of the Bellevue Stratford Hotel. Frustrated that Bush was slipped into the back by the Secret Service, and police physically blocked ACT UP from entering, the activists passed around whistles and began to blow them in concert. If the president wouldn't see them, at least he would hear them.

The sound was deafening. The police charged into the crowd wielding billy clubs and blackjacks; blood flew. The media coverage showed the event to be a police riot, an over-the-top violation of the protesters' First Amendment rights. ACT UP sued the city, and the result was a cash settlement for injury to bodies and to rights.

"Well," continued Ron, "it was a successful fundraiser!"

We laughed. It was the kind of gallows humor that gays—and so many oppressed groups—have specialized in.

"The trouble is that with all that blood-letting, I don't know what the future holds, you know, in terms of getting any kind of numbers at demonstrations and getting allies to come."

"I know what you mean," I said. Police repression can build a campaign, as Martin Luther King knew so well, but it can also create a threat of violence that keeps people away.

"So the leadership has decided we need a nonviolence workshop to get our act together and get our confidence back. We'll be preparing a civil disobedience action. Will you lead the workshop?" Ron asked.

I told him the truth: it would be an honor. I'd been in some ACT UP actions, but this would be our first Training for Change workshop with ACT UP.

The church basement where ACT UP met weekly was even more crowded than usual. I took a quick look around as I set the newsprint pad on my easel. I saw more than fifty mostly young people, in jeans and sweatshirts, some leaning against the back wall of the dingy room. The place was pulsing with rebel energy; if it were liquid, I'd need hip boots. I noticed the leaders weren't showing eagerness to introduce me, so I got the picture. The people who wanted this workshop weren't the members; this was the idea of the *leaders*.

I decided to dump the introduction and jump right in.

"Okay," I said, straightening my shoulders and taking the time to make eye contact with all parts of the room. "Let's do a quick go-round, just to check in and see where folks are tonight. I'd like each of you to say one word about the kind of attitude you'd like to take to your next demonstration."

Without hesitation someone shouted, "Fury." The person next to her said, "Outraged." One at a time the others shouted their words: "On the offensive." "Take the streets." "United." "No turning back." "Passionate." "Stare them down." "Escalate."

These folks are not going to be boring, I thought to myself. Time for step two.

"Your leaders asked me to come lead a training about nonviolence. But the thing is, 'nonviolence' is like a lot of concepts: there's an upside and a downside. So before we get started, I'd like us to explore a little bit the pluses and minuses of nonviolence."

Inwardly, I winced a bit at using the term "nonviolence" instead of "nonviolent direct action" or "nonviolent struggle. "Nonviolence" often conveys too little or, conversely, it can be heard as meaning saintliness, or even conflict avoidance. But at this moment, in *this* room, I wanted to get quickly into the exercise itself and not fiddle around with words. At the top of the newsprint, I wrote "NONVIOLENCE," then put my marker beneath the middle of the word and drew a vertical line straight down the page. Then I put a plus sign to the left and a minus sign to the right of the line.

The crowd needed no urging. "'Nonviolence' is letting yourself get walked over!" someone said. With neutral body language, I wrote the comment on the minus side and looked up for the next volunteer.

"Nonviolence looks like cowardice!" I wrote that down, then immediately wrote the next one I heard: "Nonviolence doesn't protect anyone."

The minus side of the sheet was soon filled, and I turned the page of the flip chart, writing a new minus sign at the top right. More negatives came.

While I was writing, I stole a glance at my watch. There was still time, I thought to myself, to get to a movie. I'm usually behind in catching up with films that come to town; tonight I could bag this workshop and relax in a darkened theater!

Then, someone said something unique: "Nonviolence gets us a better media image."

I looked up with my marker in my hand. "Where does that go?" I asked in my most neutral voice, wanting to be sure I'd heard right.

"On the plus side," someone said impatiently. I wrote it on the plus side.

We continued with a few more minuses before another plus showed up: "It's easier to gain allies when we use nonviolence." I wrote the comment in the plus column.

Once the dam broke, more positives flowed, along with a few more negatives. I might not get to that movie after all!

I straightened up to gesture at the array of newsprint now nearly covering the front of the room, containing an almost equal number of pluses and minuses.

"Well," I said, "what do you think? Shall we do this workshop, or not?"

Silence greeted my question. Then a young man leaning against the back wall stepped forward. "I can see where this group is going—I can see it. You want our confrontations to be more nonviolent. I can't buy it, myself, but I don't want to get in the way. If that's what most of you want, you should do it."

I looked around the room. The group was having a moment.

A young woman from the other side of the room rose from her chair. "You know, I've been arguing for more militancy, but I can also see where the group is headed. I won't break solidarity, but I don't think I have it in me to be nonviolent when they arrest me again. So, I'll come to the next demo, but I'll stand across the street and you'll know," she said as her voice broke, "I'm rootin' for ya."

Again, there was silence. I looked around, then asked, "Does this mean we have a workshop?"

"Hell, yeah!" came from the back of the room, along with widespread head-nodding and some looks that said, *Where'd we find this clueless facilitator?*

We had one of the best civil disobedience workshops I've ever facilitated.

A week later, the group was on the Benjamin Franklin Parkway, a broad and beautiful avenue that Philadelphia modeled on the Champs-Élysées in Paris. The darkness of the night was pierced by the rotating red-and-white lights of dozens of police vehicles. A truck had also brought a floodlight, shining down on the intersection where the young people were blocking traffic.

Some of the members in the street were visibly sick; two were using wheelchairs, and one had a walker. The members were channeling the spirit of Dr. King, strong in their grace and dignity. Gandhi himself would have been proud.

Then I noticed two men standing together off to the side, locked in intense conversation. One was my friend Ron; the other seemed to be the police captain in charge. They were probably negotiating about something. I moved closer so I could overhear.

"You know you'll get the media coverage," the police captain was saying. "All right, we'll arrest you the way you want."

Ron didn't say anything. The captain continued. "Look, give me a break. I only have a year until I retire. I'm just tryin' to get out of here alive."

Ron met his eyes. "Well, now *you* know."

I glanced at his comrades in the street.

Ron went on. "Now you know what *we* want—to get out of here alive."

The growing ACT UP movement did play a leading role in shifting the attitude toward AIDS within the medical profession, the health-industrial complex, and government. Countless lives have been saved as a result.

צ צ צ

As the reputation of Training for Change grew beyond the United States, over time we were invited to give workshops on five continents. Inevitable communication glitches, however, sometimes led to unrealistic expectations from the local sponsor.

A Thai nongovernmental organization frequently invited me to lead workshops there. For one of them, the sponsor decided—

without checking with me—to invite groups from Cambodia and Myanmar to join as well, forgetting to specify the learning goals for that workshop.

As a result, each of the three national groups arrived with different learning goals in mind. The Burmese university students wanted to make a revolution, the Cambodian women wanted to rebuild their country after its civil war, and the Thai activists wanted media-oriented campaign strategies. Each time I addressed one group's requests, the others tuned out.

By the end of the second day, I was fuming: *How can I teach effectively with three groups, wanting to learn different things?* I stalked back to my bamboo hut, frustrated. Suddenly I remembered where I was—Thailand, with resources for people in my psychological state!

How would Buddhists look at my condition? I asked myself. *Attached*, came the answer, *attached to results.*

What, then, must I do to become unattached? I asked.

It has to be all right if they don't learn a blessed thing!

I burst into tears, and cried for an hour. Each time my tears subsided, I remembered again: *It has to be all right if they don't learn a blessed thing!* Then I'd go right back into my tears of frustration again.

My emotional rainstorm ended as suddenly as a monsoon's afternoon showers. The sun came out. I taught the remaining three days from a centered and peaceful place. The participants said they learned a lot; they asked for another visit. I learned more about surrender and how ego gets in the way of grace.

For many decades, I've been grateful for the enormous resource that crying is for me. Other emotional expression can also be useful, like allowing my teeth to chatter (discretely) and my body to shake when I'm scared. Releasing my feelings instead of containing them is not only relieving in the moment, as it was in Thailand, but it's also healing in the longer run. I seriously doubt

I would have made it through cancer if the people around me hadn't supported my crying oceans of tears.

The payoff in strength and clarity through emotional release might be what men of my generation were unconsciously seeking by getting drunk. Intoxication never tempted me, because I never saw positive results in the men I knew. I came to realize that full-on, aware crying and other emotional/physical release put a new, critical lens on the rigid training for manhood that was typical for most boys in my day.

Another expectation of "real men" was that we should be willing to work ourselves into the ground, if that's what it took to make our contribution. Fortunately, my family heritage included a father and two grandfathers who knew how to pace themselves, and lived to a ripe old age. I wanted to do the same, and over the years found romantic partners who agreed with me that even a commitment to activism doesn't mean we shouldn't take time to have some fun.

"Let's go to the big Pride March in Washington together in October," Johnny said in the spring of 1993, during another of our visits. He got an easy agreement from me, especially since the march would add pressure to the demand for AIDS action.

The day of the march arrived, dazzling in the bright October sun.

"I should have brought another box of the T-shirts," Johnny said, as he surveyed the massive crowd gathering on the National Mall in Washington. Crowd estimates would put the number at half a million—the largest national march of lesbians, gays, bisexuals, transgender people, and allies in US history.

We didn't take long to sell out Johnny's T-shirts. His design was attractive: the front said "Hi," and the back said "Bi." Young people, especially college students, were our most frequent customers.

"What do you expect?" Johnny said when I pointed this out.

"Young people are less likely to see the world as either/or. If you don't polarize sexual choice, then you can do what comes naturally."

He followed that opinion with a prolonged French kiss, long enough to allow me to let go of the fear that always came up when I was kissed by a man in public. Soon, I was more than enjoying it. We stepped apart, hands clasped. That night, Johnny and I went to a legendary gay piano bar at Dupont Circle. We pushed into the jammed club; the room for dancing was packed. We made our way to a room that had, next to the bar, a concert grand piano. Bit by bit, we moved to a spot next to the pianist, who told us he was about to leave but no replacement had shown up.

It was easy to convince the harried manager that I should replace the pianist. "I'll give you fifteen minutes," she said, "and then I yank you unless you're good."

"Johnny," I reported back, "you have to help me. The setup here is to sing the tunes as well as play them, but I'm terrible at remembering lyrics. How about you stand next to me to lead that part?"

"All right, you guys are on!" the guest pianist said.

Johnny and I scrambled onto the platform that barely held the giant grand. I swung immediately into "Cabaret," and we were off and running. Even Johnny doesn't know the lyrics to all Broadway songs, so he announced an all-request evening. He gave the microphone to the person who requested a song, figuring that person knew the words to his own favorite. Then it was my job to play any song that someone might request. I find it much easier to remember tunes than words, so we soon found ourselves in a community sing-along of a kind that piano bars rarely see.

As the hours rolled on, I forgot the manager's threat, and the house pianist never did show up. By 2:30 in the morning, the requests from our mostly drunk crowd had turned lachrymose, so we turned to "Auld Lang Syne" as a finale, with much sentimental pressing of flesh. As we left the bar, the freshness of the air outside hit us with such force that we roared with laughter. Staggering down the street, we leaned against each other, inebriated not with alcohol (there'd been no time for us to drink!) but with the prolonged high of group spirit.

Johnny and I, seamlessly working the energy to make community—this is one of my favorite ways of making love.

꙳ ꙳ ꙳

The demand that Training for Change was experiencing in the nineties, however, didn't leave me much time for going to demonstrations. For our workshops we were finding, inventing, and using experiential training tools as well as teaching their use to others. I also delighted in recovering earlier practices, including from the civil rights movement's breakthroughs in preparing people for handling violent opposition.*

As our toolbox grew, we learned more about which tools work well in multiple cultures and which are culture-specific. By experimenting over years, we built our confidence that we could work not only with a wide variety of groups separately but also with a mix of cultures within one workshop—so long as the goals were clear and in alignment with what the sponsoring group was requesting.

As the word continued to spread globally, we led workshops in multiple countries. In two of them, Russia and Thailand, we returned annually for a decade so we could leave behind networks of local trainers who could teach still other trainers.

---

* See: George Lakey, "In Times of Rapid Change, Victory Comes to Those who Train for It," *Waging Nonviolence*, June 30, 2020, https://wagingnonviolence.org/2020/06/in-times-of-rapid-change-victory-comes-to-those-who-train-for-it/. Getting a bigger picture of how to prepare for potential violence became very useful when the threat of a right-wing coup emerged later, in 2020; see my article: "How to Face Right-wing Violence While Defending the Election—A Conversation with George Lakey," *Waging Nonviolence*, October 15, 2020, https://wagingnonviolence.org/2020/10/facing-right-wing-violence-while-defending-election-coup-george-lakey/.

Remembering my work in Sri Lanka, I turned to Daniel Hunter, a veteran organizer and trainer who I'd met decades earlier when he was a committed and brilliant teenager looking for a mentor. Daniel and I researched, field-tested, and published a new training curriculum for protective accompaniment for people in violent situations. *

In US workshops, Dr. Judith C. Jones became my most frequent cofacilitator, her sharp eye and ear increasing my awareness of special strengths and needs of Black people like her. Meanwhile, Movement for a New Society alum Antje Mattheus inaugurated a decades-long series of trainings for white people ready to tackle racism.**

I was grateful for our choice to teach our trainers how to handle strong emotions when, on September 11, 2001, terrorists destroyed the World Trade Center and part of the Pentagon. Most Americans were completely unprepared for this shocking backlash against our empire, and the fear was palpable.

Alarm and grieving dominated our country's atmosphere, and

---

* For that work, we gained a two-year grant from the US Institute of Peace to develop training methods for this innovative kind of training. We interviewed other organizations whose workers in the field were at risk of harm, like Doctors Without Borders, and also leaders of United Nations peacekeeping troops. Daniel and I gathered best practices and invented some new training tools while describing those that seemed already to work well, and the result was published by Training for Change. Samples of the tools are on the Training for Change website: https://www.trainingforchange.org/.

** The anti-oppression workshops I was now designing were fundamentally different from those of decades earlier, when I led some workshops in which I was pleased that people were feeling guilty, and afterward felt soiled. (The New England Puritans were all about guilt, and my interest is first in liberation!) I realized eventually that empowerment for tackling oppression requires self-knowledge, plus self-affirmation and confidence we can make a difference while continuing to make mistakes and learn from them. George Lakey, "Get Real about Privilege—Become an Ally," *Waging Nonviolence*, April 9, 2013, https://wagingnonviolence.org/2013/04/get-real-about-privilege-become-an-ally; George Lakey, "What Makes Effective White Allies? Training, Not Shaming," *Waging Nonviolence*, June 1, 2015, https://wagingnonviolence.org/2015/06/what-makes-effective-white-allies-training-not-shaming; George Lakey, "What White Allies Can Learn from Allies in the Gay Rights Struggle," *Waging Nonviolence*, July 4, 2015, https://wagingnonviolence.org/2015/07/white-allies-can-learn-allies-gay-rights-struggle.

the spiritual leaders who initially convened services to assist people to deal with what might have become a wake-up call were soon edged out by political leaders who showed no sign of learning something new from the tragedy.

My eldest granddaughter, Crystal, came back from her college class feeling proud that she had responded to her teacher's angry rant by insisting there was a bigger picture, expressed in the phrase "chickens coming home to roost." I congratulated her, while knowing we were in a small minority—although less so among the Black people she identifies with—who had few illusions about whites' frequent insistence on dominating others.*

During my fifteen years with Training for Change, the training associates and I conducted more than seven hundred workshops for more than fifteen thousand participants. We did seventy-eight training trips to twenty-one countries. We held an annual seventeen-day Training for Change global training institute so that aspiring facilitators from additional countries could learn to use direct education. The new pedagogy reached others in the world of adult learning through the publishing of my book *Facilitating Group Learning*; even some high school teachers found the methods brought new life to their classrooms.

Leading Training for Change for fifteen years doubled my previous record for job longevity. By 2006, I was ready to be done, and the board decided to let the organization "lie fallow," as a farmer might sometimes let a field go uncultivated for a time. After the fallow period, the training associates banded together to revive Training for Change with new energy. Two young, talented

---

* George Lakey, "As the US Empire Declines, What Openings Exist for Progressive Movements?" *Waging Nonviolence*, August 18, 2021, https://wagingnonviolence.org/2021/08/afghanistan-us-empire-decline-good-news/; George Lakey, "Envision or Perish—Why We Must Start Imagining the World We Want to Live In," *Waging Nonviolence*, February 2, 2021, https://wagingnonviolence.org/2021/02/envision-or-perish-why-we-must-start-imagining-the-world-we-want.

people of color I'd been mentoring, Nico Amador and Daniel Hunter, stepped into leadership.

I carefully gave them a lot of space, showing up once a year for graduation at the global training institute. A major emphasis for the new leadership was serving activists of color. Now Training for Change has been serving social movements for three decades and counting.

wins for climate justice and democracy

I was twenty years old when I first worked with Swarthmore students. Still a student myself, I'd been hired by the American Friends Service Committee to lead college-student volunteers through an intensive weekend offering company to patients at Embreeville State Hospital, a progressive psychiatric institution. On Fridays, students from five or so colleges and universities in the Philadelphia area converged at the West Chester train station. I picked them up and took them to an old house on the hospital grounds that had been set aside for our weekends there.

I'd already shopped, and the first task for the students was to prepare a supper of spaghetti and salad. That occupied many hands, while the students began to warm up to each other. We all ate around a big table, giving us more chance to get acquainted. I noticed that most Swarthmore students presented as super-bright, articulate, and focused. Within half an hour, they generally managed tacitly to be placed by the other students among the top rank of the group's "pecking order."

In 2006, I was invited to immerse myself fully in the Swarthmore world by becoming the Eugene M. Lang Visiting Professor for Issues in Social Change. Choosing me was the idea of long-time feminist activist Pat James, who'd known me for decades. At the Lang Center, she assisted students to plug in to meaningful community service.

I was free, having just retired from Training for Change. I managed to talk Swarthmore out of its expectation that I live on campus, since I was then parenting a young grandson who wouldn't have done well there. The half-hour train commute from my house to the campus each day also helped me keep my activist wits about me, with time to ponder new ideas for actions and campaigns.

Much had changed for both Swarthmore and me in a half century, but what had positively impressed me about the "Swatties" remained true still. I was expected to teach only three courses in the year, so I could maximize my informal time with the students and be a better resource for their interest in social justice.

The college did not say, however, that it expected my students to join me in committing civil disobedience. But now I'm leaping ahead.

The Lang professor was expected to be a resource to the students for a year and move on, to be replaced by another person who combined academic credentials with social change impact. I was surprised to be asked to stay a second year. I was more used to the place now and saw more opportunities to innovate—always a sure way to be happy—so I said yes. A bonus to teaching at Swarthmore was that students from nearby Haverford and Bryn Mawr easily found their way to my classes.

At the time, I was unhappy with the US peace movement. Six years had elapsed since the terrorist attack on New York and Washington, and the movement still hadn't championed a clear, nonviolent security alternative to the "war on terror." I tried to persuade peace leadership to create a vision but found little interest. I was disappointed because—as with my prior peace conversion efforts—I was reminded of the old saying, "You can't beat somebody with nobody."

Since I wasn't leading a national peace organization, I couldn't force a change in approach. But at least at Swarthmore I could do *something*, so I offered a course on nonviolent responses to terrorist threats. I was intensely curious about how many students would sign up. To my surprise, they filled the course, and stayed even when I told them how challenging it would be. Each student would choose a country somewhere in the world that was presently threatened by terrorism, I announced. "You'll take the role of a consultant to that country's government and devise a strategy for nonmilitary defense against terrorist attack."

To get them started, I provided eight nonmilitary techniques that have been used by one or more countries to respond to terrorist threats, with some degree of effectiveness. The entire grade in the course would be based on the quality of the "consultant's" paper. In our class sessions, we would delve more deeply into the eight techniques; we'd waste no time criticizing current US military responses to the threat.

It was tough work, and highly stimulating. Most of the students had a ball. Some did brilliant strategizing for the country they chose, after researching that country's assets and liabilities and the nature of the threat it faced. Students especially liked brainstorming synergistic effects—what happens when technique three interacts with techniques two and five, for example. During class time, they freely gave each other ideas that were working for them.

A Pentagon unit of experts on counterterrorism heard about our course and asked me to come to Washington to share what we were doing. In the Pentagon meeting, I described the toolbox of eight techniques we were using and asked for their expert feedback and suggestions. The unit's chief summarized their response by saying that they saw no problem, in principle, with devising a counterterrorism strategy for the United States that would create synergies among the tools we were using.*

---

* The eight nonmilitary tools for countering terrorism are described in my article "8 Ways to Defend Against Terror Nonviolently," *Waging Nonviolence,* January 8, 2015, https://wagingnonviolence.org/2015/01/8-ways-defend-terror-nonviolently/. The course syllabus was published in Timothy A. McElwee, B. Welling Hall and Joseph Liechty, eds., *Peace, Justice, and Security Studies: A Curriculum Guide* (Boulder, CO: Lynne Rienner Publishers, 2009).

The problem, however, would be persuading our government to take such a bold, innovative leap. That would tread on the toes of vested interests that would veto such a radical change.

I was not surprised. This was a reprise of my previous visionary work on economic conversion: those already embedded in what President Dwight D. Eisenhower called the military-industrial complex would not give way to an alternative even if it was highly sensible. Implementing a superior means of defense, like adapting the superior economic systems the Nordics enjoy, will need to be forced, will require a power shift.

That's for people's movements to make happen, through what will amount to a nonviolent revolution. Of course, my belief is that a mass mobilization can't happen without an alternative that can be communicated in a persuasive way; therefore, we do need to do the homework on issues like jobs and national security and come up with an easy-to-communicate vision to replace what we have now. It was delightful to watch my students open as they discovered in the course how practical—and powerful—nonviolent alternatives can be.

Swarthmore College invited me back for a third year. "I didn't even know that was legal," I told the energetic Lee Smithey, who chaired the peace and conflict studies concentration at the college. He smiled, and pointed to the steadily growing interest among the students.

By popular demand, I repeated the terrorism course, and again the course filled. In addition, inspired by the students' capacity for hard work, I also started a research seminar to generate a searchable database on nonviolent action campaigns drawn from countries around the world. When we had a few hundred cases, we put the database online, with a narrative describing each case; I called it the Global Nonviolent Action Database.*

---

* https://nvdatabase.swarthmore.edu.

My research expectations were high, and the students were thrilled to get publication credit for each case I accepted. We soon found that Swarthmore was providing a resource tapped by activists, writers, and academics all over the world—who looked at the database to get ideas on what did and didn't work when campaigning on issues of social justice, human rights, democracy, environment, and war.

I remember the Romanian student who walked into the seminar with a mixed expression on her face. "Professor, I'm eager to participate, but I'm also a bit sad that there won't be cases in the database from my country's history. We don't do that kind of thing."

I smiled broadly. "We'll see."

Of course, she did discover cases in her own country's history to research and present on the database. If I weren't a Quaker, with our scruple about gambling, I'd wager that all peoples have used nonviolent struggle at times, even if their culture doesn't support or celebrate it. As my mentor Gene Sharp used to say, nonviolent struggle is deeply human: Have you never seen a small child go limp in protest?

When I ran into Eugene Lang on campus once again for his meeting with the board of trustees, I reported informally on what was happening and mentioned that this would be my last year. He objected to the idea of my leaving and arranged for me to be kept on for four more years as a research fellow with teaching privileges. I invented more new courses while continuing the research seminar that steadily added more cases to the Global Nonviolent Action Database. By the time I left, we'd published a thousand cases, drawn from the histories of almost two hundred countries, and Lee Smithey told me he'd continue the research seminar and add more cases.

ℵ ℵ ℵ

While at Swarthmore I published a book that was extra-special to me, harvesting half a century of learning how to teach and train. It was called *Facilitating Group Learning: Strategies for Success with Diverse Learners,* and it came out in 2010, the same year as the Peace and Justice Studies Association named me Peace Educator of the Year.* Swarthmore then supported me to start on my next book, *Viking Economics: How the Scandinavians Got It Right— and How We Can, Too.*** For me, the book about the Nordics was yet another expression of my visionary impulse, offering US movements for justice a tool we could use to stimulate conversation about what kind of economic institutions we want for this country.

Another source of gratitude to Swarthmore was its keeping me close to home. Christina had recently graduated from community college, with her first daughter, Crystal, graduating right beside her. Berit and I cried tears of joy throughout the ceremony. Christina's college experience was so positive that she continued on with night classes at Widener University, aiming for a bachelor's degree in social work, which she got in a rained-upon outdoor graduation ceremony in 2016. Settling into her chosen vocation, she went on to earn her master's in social work in 2019, with Berit and me cheering her on and with her now grown-up children in attendance. We added to our list of virtues "sheer grit."

A boon to our family was Janice Robinson, a Harlem nurse who'd become a leader in the national community health center movement. To her surprise, Berit fell in love with Janice, who she met at a weekend retreat center in the Poconos, just up the road from my hometown of Bangor. Janice was feeling the call to change her vocation to the ministry. By the time they mar-

---

* George Lakey, *Facilitating Group Learning: Strategies for Success with Diverse Learners,* 2nd ed. (Oakland, CA: PM Press, 2020).
** In 2021, *Forbes* magazine cited the book as one of the best five for visitors to Norway. George Lakey, *Viking Economics,* (Brooklyn and London: Melville Publishing, 2016).

ried, our whole family adored Janice, and she was already making waves in the Black caucus of the Episcopal Church's priesthood. Janice even joined Berit, another organizational consultant, and me in writing *Grassroots and Nonprofit Leadership: A Guide for Organizations in Changing Times.**

Some folks were really surprised that Berit fell in love with another woman. I'd long ago realized that the potential for same-sex attraction must be widely dispersed, although for many people hidden even from ourselves, because of the homophobes' unceasing effort for centuries to prevent people from experiencing it. Despite heterosexism's historic hold on religion, the state, and other institutions, same-sex attraction keeps breaking through everywhere for at least a small minority. What if the homophobes just gave themselves a break, so the rest of us could turn off the incessant noise of fear and, in peace, be "free to be you and me?"

Our family's happiness about Berit and Janice was reinforced when they settled in the Washington, DC area, within easy reach for family weekends and weeklong family vacations at the Jersey shore. When they told me they were planning a vacation trip to Norway for summer 2010, Johnny and I made sure our vacation overlapped with theirs in Oslo.

The consistent schedule of teaching—compared to frequent travel to deliver trainings—meant I could take more time to hang out with Christina's children: Crystal, Raquel, Chanelle, and Christopher. Great-grandchildren began to appear: another Chris, Yasin, Zaine, Anwar, Reign, and Aayah. Ingrid made her own contribution to the number of grandchildren, but Ella came late enough to fit more into the age set of my great-grands.

In 2012, Janice was stricken with cancer and, despite a valiant struggle, passed away that year. I was invited onto Janice's 24/7

---

* Berit Lakey, George Lakey, Rod Napier, and Janice Robinson: *Grassroots and Nonprofit Leadership: A Guide for Organizations in Changing Times* (Gabriola Island, BC: New Society Publishers, 1995).

care team for the last weeks of her life, a tender and very sad time working in Janice and Berit's home, side by side with others from their close women's community.

To be closer to family, Berit then moved to a Quaker retirement community just outside Philly, where she hosted larger and larger family gatherings. Berit and I have continued—without a break since 1959—to observe Christmas Eve together in the Norwegian tradition. We are grateful for the longtime specialness of our relationship, especially given the storms and tragic times our family endured—turbulence that sometimes alienates parents from each other. We tease each other that we are matriarch and patriarch of our still growing family.

※ ※ ※

During my years at Swarthmore, I noticed that there was a circle of students who took several courses with me and also went with me to Appalachia, when I filled the college van with students wanting to investigate the impact of mountaintop-removal coal mining. I seemed to be looked to for mentoring. Swatties then joined other college students in demonstrations organized by Earth Quaker Action Team, or EQAT, the new environmental group I initiated in 2009. We pronounced our group's initials as "equate," which made it fun and easy to remember. The shorthand also had a pleasant resonance for us oldsters who remembered A Quaker Action Group's acronym, AQAG (or "a quag").

History was generating increased attention to climate change, and I was eager to dance with it. So were other Quakers, who collectively sensed a calling to do more. The existing ecology of Quaker organizations working on climate had an empty niche available for a direct action-oriented, rebel-style organization— the role EQAT would fill. Even though I'd asserted, decades earlier, that environment would become a key arena for struggle for a just world, I'd focused on other issues in my activism. Now, I was ready to mentor those new to direct action in a dynamic campaign to force the seventh largest bank in the United States, PNC Bank, to give up its practice of financing mountaintop-removal coal mining in Appalachia. PNC was the largest financier of that devastating assault on the earth and the people of Appalachia. It was a long shot, but I reckoned we had a chance.

The PNC Bank near the White House was our choice for our first civil disobedience action, and two Swarthmore students joined the dozen and a half activists ready to be so bold. That bank was nicknamed "the presidents' bank" because so many White House occupants over the years did their personal banking there. The walls were covered with oil paintings of presidents and other eminent depositors of yesterday, so we went into the bank along with other tourists and looked at the paintings before gathering in the center of the lobby to form a circle. We sang movement songs and took turns praying and singing.

I was afraid the bank manager was going to have a heart attack, shrieking "Get out of here! Get out of here!" before remembering to call the police. The students looked worried, too.

The manager hustled other customers out of the bank, sent the tellers home, and locked the door. One of our EQAT members had been assigned to talk down the manager but had her hands full; none of us expected hysteria. (The manager later apologized to us.) Another EQAT member was assigned door duty, which was a good thing because when the police came, our EQAT member needed to unlock the locked door to let them in. Fortunately, before the police arrived, we had time to center ourselves, seated around a little hill of dirt we'd created from the baggies that had been concealed in our pockets. There was a little sign on the top that said "Save me." We even got to settle into some good moments of silent prayer.

The police told our person at the door that they didn't intend to arrest us because their system was clogged. This was because our action was planned to coincide with a much larger day of actions in DC by thousands of people concerned with mountaintop removal coal-mining, including many from Appalachia itself. Eager for our action to unfold with the drama we had planned, our EQAT member insisted that the police at least make some arrests. Eventually, they agreed to take three of us, and allowed us to decide who. In our circle, we quickly decided on a Swarthmore student, an activist from Chicago, and me.*

So began EQAT's rebel activity that persisted for the five years it took to win. We undertook 125 actions and inspired customers to pull their deposits of over $3.5 million. We marched two hundred miles across Pennsylvania to PNC's headquarters in Pittsburgh.** We learned to hold pray-ins and disrupt shareholders' meetings. A typical EQAT demonstration had an age range of eighteen to eighty, but sometimes we were able to include eager children.*** Haverford and Bryn Mawr students joined in to swell the college-age contingent.

We started in 2009 with a group that fit in my living room and grew steadily. By December 2014, we were able to conduct, within twenty-four hours, a total of thirty-one bank actions in twelve states and Washington, DC. It became clear to PNC that our group would keep growing and never go away until the bank changed its policy. In their announcement, they said their change

---

* A photo of the group sitting on the floor is online: George Lakey, "How a Small Quaker Group Forced PNC Bank to Stop Financing Mountaintop Removal," *Waging Nonviolence,* March 4, 2015, https://wagingnonviolence.org/2015/03/small-quaker-group-forced-pnc-bank-stop-financing-mountaintop-removal/.

** George Lakey, "How a Small Group Can Take a Long Walk–and Make a Difference," *Waging Nonviolence,* May 29, 2012, https://wagingnonviolence.org/2012/05/how-a-small-group-can-take-a-long-walk-and-make-a-difference/.

*** Lakey, "How a Small Quaker Group"; George Lakey, "Targets Matter–Why a Small Action Group Took on a Mighty Bank (and Won)," *Waging Nonviolence,* May 12, 2015, https://wagingnonviolence.org/2015/05/targets-matter-small-action-group-took-mighty-bank-won/.

was "driven by environmental and health concerns, as well as our risk appetite."*

After a growing number of Swatties cut their teeth with EQAT, they shifted to addressing Swarthmore's investment in fossil fuels. Some had taken my research seminar and understood what campaigns are made of, and they also had the model of EQAT to observe. They soon launched a nonviolent campaign for divestment, and one of my colleagues warned me that my time at Swarthmore would soon end; it would be easy for the board to blame me. Perhaps so, but I stayed on at Swarthmore for several years more.

Once the Swarthmore divestment campaign—Mountain Justice—was well underway, the students issued a national call to other students to come to Swarthmore to launch a national campus divestment movement. The business page of the *New York Times* covered the movement's rapid spread and traced its origins to my students who, in turn, said they were inspired by me.

Soon, the seniors who'd worked on those campaigns graduated, and some of them holed up in a rented house in my neighborhood in West Philly. There they studied more and planned their next big move. With others, in 2017, they ended up launching the Sunrise Movement, and I couldn't have been more proud—not only of the national media coverage they got but of their staying power in organizing young eco-activists across the nation to press in creative ways for a Green New Deal.

≈ ≈ ≈

That same year, Johnny had something additional on his mind: the gala celebration of my eightieth birthday. We were closer than ever, and he knew that every decade I had used my birthday

---

* Justine McDaniel, "PNC to Cut Back Financing of Mountaintop Removal," *Philadelphia Inquirer*, March 2, 2015, https://www.inquirer.com/philly/business/20150303_PNC_Bank_to_cut_financing_of_MTR_coal_companies.html.

celebration as a chance to bring my whole community together in support of my current project. This time it would be Earth Quaker Action Team. The party included some Broadway singing, with me at the piano, of course. A highlight for me was being serenaded by an accomplished boy soprano whose father, Jerry Hill, I'd worked with on Jobs with Peace. "My boy has serenaded the pope," Jerry said, "so I figured he was up for singing to you."

It's hard to know, when we're aging, what it is we can and can't do. In the summer of 2020, I knew something was up when I saw the images of armed federal officers intervening in Portland's Black Lives Matter protests, against the will of Oregon's governor and other local officials. President Donald Trump was running for reelection, but his favorability ratings weren't high. It seemed he might be starting to prepare a coup attempt; history was starting a new dance. I could at least beat the drum and write articles to alert social activists, helping to prepare them for the nonviolent direct action needed to defend democracy.

Almost immediately I got a call from climate justice organizer and friend Daniel Hunter. He was forming a team to help head off a coup attempt by building the supportive infrastructure that a mass resistance movement would need: training; a website with accurate, evidence-based information on resisting coups; and a pledge of resistance that people could sign and spread to others. Would I join the group, keep writing articles, and lead its training effort?

Their clarity about the task and the energizing prospect of teamwork made me say yes. I joined the small and mighty collective, which was named Choose Democracy.* My articles for *Waging Nonviolence*—an

---

* By this point, we weren't the only initiative engaging in anticoup work. A group of public policy experts in Washington, DC imagined scenarios for a possible power grab and concluded that massive nonviolent resistance would probably be needed for successful defense. Meanwhile, another team in DC formed to write the influential manual *Hold the Line*, which explained how people could organize grassroots anticoup groups: Hardy Merriman, Ankur Asthana, Marium Navid, and Kifah Shah, *Hold the Line: A Guide to Defending Democracy*, DigitalCommons@University of Nebraska-Lincoln, 2020, https://digitalcommons.unl.edu/oersocialsci/1/.

online publication read by many activists and organizers—reached more and more people as awareness of the danger grew.* National progressive mass membership organizations started to wrap their minds around the potential danger, and we began developing training formats in collaboration with my old outfit Training for Change.

While preparing for the workshops, I reviewed historical accounts of successful mass nonviolent resistance to coups in other countries; some of the key examples included France in 1961 and the Soviet Union in 1991. In both cases, the coup plotters were backed by army units, but mass nonviolent resistance was still able to uphold or restore the constitutional order.** I noticed that it was possible for people to win even when the coup plotters kept their plan a secret until the last minute—something Donald Trump wasn't doing. In fact, by tipping his hand ahead of time, he was actually helping us out!

My curiosity about my energy level at my age was soon answered: membership in a team was making a difference, as it had done repeatedly throughout my life. Within six weeks, we trained more than ten thousand people, plus trainers to train more—and I trained still others through Quaker networks.*** My most edgy

---

* George Lakey, "Understanding Trump's Game Plan in Portland Could Be the Key to Preventing a Coup in November," *Waging* Nonviolence, July 25, 2020, https://wagingnonviolence.org/2020/07/portland-trump-federal-agents-law-order-preventing-coup/; George Lakey, "We Need a Plan to Prevent a Trump Takeover—and This Anticoup Research Shows the Way," *Waging* Nonviolence, August 11, 2020, https://wagingnonviolence.org/2020/08/plan-prevent-trump-election-coup-research/; George Lakey, "Mass Direct Action Might Be the Only Way to Stop Trump from Stealing the Election," *Waging Nonviolence,* August 27, 2020, https://wagingnonviolence.org/2020/08/mass-direct-action-might-be-the-only-way-to-stop-trump-from-stealing-the-election/; George Lakey, "How to Face Right-wing Violence While Defending the Election—a Conversation with George Lakey," *Waging Nonviolence,* October 15, 2020, https://wagingnonviolence.org/2020/10/facing-right-wing-violence-while-defending-election-coup-george-lakey/.

** Stephen Zunes, *Civil Resistance Against Coups: A Comparative and Historical Perspective,* ICNC Monograph Series, (Washington, DC: International Center on Nonviolent Conflict, 2017).

*** Short film summaries of workshop content are available on the Choose Democracy website: "Videos," Choose Democracy, last accessed July 6, 2022, https://choosedemocracy.us/videos/#.YSpCqy2cZBw.

step in the trainings was to urge activists to forget about marches and rallies; in recent decades, US activists had become too fixated on those tactics. To me, relying on only two tactics suggests an appalling lack of creativity; plus, in today's highly polarized society, such visible actions are an invitation to bash-ups in the street with right-wing extremists.*

By Election Day, our Pledge for Democracy had forty thousand signers who were committed to taking heroic action if needed to stop a coup. Another article on *Waging Nonviolence*—this time by Daniel, with the catchy headline "10 Things You Need to Know to Stop a Coup"—reached nearly eight hundred thousand readers.** Along with our support for initiatives within the labor movement to prepare for a possible general strike, Choose Democracy was gaining major attention. The *New Yorker*, *The Atlantic*, the *Guardian*, the *Boston Globe*, and other media all reported on our efforts.

Fear would be a major dynamic in the struggle to come, so our Choose Democracy training offered specific ways to build a courageous movement. Our team itself demonstrated that dynamic at work; our support for one another's positivity contrasted with the experience of many activists in the stress-filled 1960s, when increased bombings, the reemergence of American Nazis, and the mushrooming of the Ku Klux Klan caused so many to burn out. It was satisfying to see Choose Democracy learning from the "dance steps" of yesterday.

In addition to rapid progress in movement building, we had another important factor on our side: Trump's incompetency. In

---

* In one of my articles for the Quaker publication *Friends Journal,* I describe the meaning of the growing political polarization in the United States: George Lakey, "The Fiery Forge of Polarization," Friends Journal, September 1, 2020, https://www.friendsjournal.org/the-fiery-forge-of-polarization/.
** Daniel Hunter, "10 Things You Need to Know to Stop a Coup," *Waging Nonviolence*, September 18, 2020, https://wagingnonviolence.org/2020/09/10-things-you-need-to-know-to-stop-a-coup/.

coup situations, I expect the leaders of mainstream institutions—when considering where to throw their weight—to gauge whether the would-be dictator has the skills to pull it off. If not, they will look to see if highly competent organizers are stepping forward to do the coup plotting on his behalf, assuming he has the self-discipline to let them. With this in mind, my strategy was to show a sufficient degree of preparedness to deter competent organizers from stepping forward. After all, able organizers don't benefit personally by staking their reputations on a losing cause. Former New York mayor Rudy Giuliani was the bumbling poster child for the inadequate organizing of the Trumpists and the limitations of a movement whose messaging depended on hate and fear. As a result, positivity and rapid mobilization linked with preparation won the day.

ᘿ ᘿ ᘿ

My life seems to be full of examples of the power of positive love, even when it's risky and breaks a norm or two to show itself. As at any college with a long history, Swarthmore's graduation ceremonies are steeped in tradition, but when the college invited me to give the baccalaureate address, I once again came to a place of innovation. When I agreed, I didn't foresee how my simple "yes" could lead to a transcendent moment affirming the life mission I'd recognized at age nineteen: to bring more justice and peace into the world.

While preparing, I was moved to share the story of Peter's death, just as I describe it in chapter twenty-seven in this memoir. I didn't want to do that. I thought it might be seen as inappropriate, and it certainly would be a stretch to be that vulnerable. During the months prior to graduation, I kept hoping that God would release me from this, but the leading was unshakeable.

I asked Ingrid to come with me for support. She sat right in the middle of the audience to be sure I could easily see her. Rain was predicted, so ushers gave out umbrellas to the attendees, as the amphitheater filled up. I felt shaky but resolute as I walked with the faculty procession down the path, then took my place on the stage.

My heart opened when I saw before me all those proud seniors and their loved ones. I first told a brief story about facing risks, largely to tune my voice and provide a context for my longer story to come. I'd resolved not to cry on this occasion; I'd previously cried when I read the story of Peter's death to my writers' group. I recalled exactly where in the story the tears came. As I neared that moment at Swarthmore, the heavens opened, and umbrellas went up. I stayed present for the audience, my voice clear and strong to the end.

Seated again, my legs began to shake. I was glad for the robes that hid the continued shaking. I started to pray for the ability to walk back up the path in the faculty recessional. The rain stopped. I knew that at the top of the hill, my job was to split off and stand in a visible spot where audience members and students could find me, as the speaker, to say whatever they wanted to say.

The recessional music began. I stumbled only once on the way up the hill. As I parted from the other faculty, Ingrid grabbed me, then planted me where I could easily be seen. She jammed her hip against mine to steady my legs.

I was grateful for her strength when people came to me to express their appreciation, one by one. A dad grabbed me hard by the shoulders, put his face an inch from mine, and said with a choked voice, "My greatest fear!" before walking quickly away. One by one, they came until finally, a student I didn't know—and who I'd noticed hanging back—came forward.

"My mother wanted nothing more than that I should attend Swarthmore," he began. "She pushed me to study hard in high school, brought me here for the interview, helped me with my application, and visited a lot once I entered. But early this year . . . early this senior year, she died. I almost didn't come to graduation. I thought I couldn't bear it, not without my mother. . . . But you made it right for me to be here. I thank you."

That student gave me a useful way to express my mission: to help make it right for everyone to be here. History happens. Everyone's invited, however they can, to join the dance.

acknowledgments

I've experienced my life as a collective enterprise, so most of all I'd like to thank the many who go unnamed in the book but who played positive roles in this story: friends and activists, students and professors, teachers and religious leaders, relatives and housemates, coworkers on projects and campaigns, neighbors and cowriters. You know who you are, and I thank you.

The actual writing was originally supported by Professor Allen Brick and his memoir writing students, followed by Viki Laura List and Antje Mattheus, who never tired of hearing me read "my latest" to them; my daughter Christina Lakey and former wife, Berit Lakey, who trusted me to write from my subjective point of view about hard family moments; my daughter Ingrid Lakey and longtime lover Johnny Lapham, who listened to me during the highs and lows of my most challenging book ever; and my granddaughter Crystal Lakey and great-grandson Yasin Ali, who as housemates respected the solitude I needed. Central Philadelphia Meeting of Friends (Quakers) has grounded my ministry for many years; this book is one more expression of that work.

Big thanks go to my book editors Bryan Farrell and Claire Kelley; both offered clarity and patience. I also want to thank Seven Stories publisher Dan Simon for his interest in going beyond an author's comfort level to find the deeper truth.

I dedicate the book to my great-grandchildren: Christopher, Yasin, Zaine, Anwar, Reign, and Aayah.

Rebel with a Mission: The George Lakey Documentary

moves back and forth in time, highlighting specific events that have shaped George's activist life including the Vietnam war, LGBTQ actions, Peace Brigades in Sri Lanka and the more recent Earth Quaker Action Team's campaign persuading PNC Bank to stop financing mountaintop removal coal mining. George presents and reflects on these events and actions to show how we can apply learnings from the past to the actions of today, even in our current polarized society. The film uses current footage, archival elements and motion graphics to tell George's compelling life story. It vividly builds a life, layer by layer, revealing his uncanny skill for serving up whatever the situation needs – fire or water, heat or cold – by asking himself, "Where can I make a contribution? Where am I led?"

Directed by Glenn Holsten, available in feature-length and shorter formats: https//:georgelakeyfilm.com

index

GEORGE LAKEY was born into a white working-class family in a small town in rural Pennsylvania and has been active in direct action campaigns for seven decades. Recently retired from Swarthmore College, where he was the Eugene M. Lang Visiting Professor for Issues of Social Change, Lakey was first arrested at a civil rights demonstration in March 1963, and his most recent arrest was in June 2021, during a climate justice march. A Quaker, he has been named Peace Educator of the Year and was given the Paul Robeson Social Justice Award and the Martin Luther King Peace Award. His previous books include *Viking Economics: How the Scandinavians Got It Right—and How We Can, Too* and *How We Win: A Guide to Nonviolent Direct Action Campaigning*. He lives in Philadelphia.

SEVEN STORIES PRESS is an independent book publisher based in New York City. We publish works of the imagination by such writers as Nelson Algren, Russell Banks, Octavia E. Butler, Ani DiFranco, Assia Djebar, Ariel Dorfman, Coco Fusco, Barry Gifford, Martha Long, Luis Negrón, Hwang Sok-yong, Lee Stringer, and Kurt Vonnegut, to name a few, together with political titles by voices of conscience, including Subhankar Banerjee, the Boston Women's Health Collective, Noam Chomsky, Angela Y. Davis, Human Rights Watch, Derrick Jensen, Ralph Nader, Loretta Napoleoni, Gary Null, Greg Palast, Project Censored, Barbara Seaman, Alice Walker, Gary Webb, and Howard Zinn, among many others. Seven Stories Press believes publishers have a special responsibility to defend free speech and human rights, and to celebrate the gifts of the human imagination, wherever we can. In 2012 we launched Triangle Square books for young readers with strong social justice and narrative components, telling personal stories of courage and commitment. For additional information, visit www.sevenstories.com.